WHY SPENCER PERCEVAL HAD TO DIE

ANDRO LINKLATER is the author of *Measuring America: How An Untamed Wilderness Shaped the United States and Fulfilled the Promise of Democracy, The Fabric of America: How Our Borders and Boundaries Shaped the Country and Forged Our National Identity,* and *An Artist in Treason: The Extraordinary Double Life of General James Wilkinson.* He lives in England.

WHY SPENCER PERCEVAL HAD TO DIE

The Assassination of a British Prime Minister

Andro Linklater

BLOOMSBURY

LONDON • NEW DELHI • NEW YORK • SYDNEY

First published in Great Britain 2012
This paperback published in 2013

Bloomsbury Publishing Plc
50 Bedford Square
London
WC1B 3DP

www.bloomsbury.com

Bloomsbury Publishing, London, New Delhi, New York and Sydney
A CIP catalogue record for this book is available from the British Library

ISBN 978 1 4088 3171 7

10 9 8 7 6 5 4 3 2 1

Typeset by Hewer Text UK Ltd, Edinburgh

Printed and bound in Great Britain by CPI (UK) Ltd, Croydon CR0 4YY

For Paul and Charlotte,
the great encouragers

Amicus certus in re incerta cernitur

Contents

I

A Horrible Event

From our report of the Parliamentary proceedings of the two Houses will an indignant and sorrowful nation learn the occurrence of one of those horrible events with which the annals of Great Britain have not often been stained – the murder of Mr Perceval the Prime Minister of these realms; a man who, in his personal intercourse gave offence to none – in his private life was an example to all; and who, however firm and unbending in his principles, yet conducted political conflicts in a way that seemed to disarm them of their characteristic bitterness.

The Times, 12 May 1812

The assassin was late. That is the loose thread in the tapestry. Pull at it, and the neat little picture of the murder that everyone knows will unravel. Behind it stands the large, ugly truth of what happened on Monday, 11 May 1812.

At half past four in the afternoon, the Prime Minister was due to appear in the House of Commons. At that moment the man who meant to kill him was a mile away in Sidney's Alley on the north side of Leicester Square. The geography of London should have saved the Prime Minister's life. By the time his murderer reached the top of Whitehall, it was already a quarter to five. Still a ten-minute walk to the Houses of

Parliament. By then anxiety must have been his killer's dominant emotion.

Murder is not entered upon lightly. The assassin had prepared himself with care for the great eventuality. His pistols had been bought three weeks earlier so that he could practise shooting with them. He had spent long evenings in the gallery of the House of Commons. He had familiarised himself with the features of the Prime Minister and checked his identity with knowledgeable journalists nearby. His chocolate-coloured coat had a secret pocket specially designed to carry the murder weapon unobtrusively. Another pistol nestled in his clay-coloured trousers. He had paced out the journey to the House of Commons. He could estimate to the minute how long it would take. But none of his rehearsals had taken into account the unfortunate circumstance that he might be delayed.

His anxiety would have triggered self-pity. That was his usual reaction to adversity. He was forty-one, and throughout his life bad luck had dogged him. However much care he took, some unforeseen circumstance would occur at the critical moment wrecking the whole enterprise. He might have grown rich in the service of the East India Company but for a shipwreck. He could have made money trading in Russian iron had it not been for the unexpected jealousy of a Dutch rival. He would have won compensation for his losses except that the British ambassador inexplicably refused to help. And now this delay in his carefully laid plan.

He should have gone straight from St James's Square to Whitehall. Instead, he had been forced to make a detour to Leicester Square, almost in the opposite direction. There had been no choice. Debt drove him there. For lack of money, he had had to walk two sides of a triangle instead of one. 'It has always been my misfortune,' he would confess to his wife Mary, 'to be thwarted, misrepresented and ill-used in life.'

But he had never given up. Some termed it obstinacy, others

madness, but he had developed a talent for endurance, for putting his head down and ploughing on until he got what he wanted. However great the obstacles, he would perform what he had undertaken to do. When he came to explain his actions, no one could miss the sense of righteousness that pervaded his thoughts. He was proposing to administer justice not commit murder, and he was doing so less for himself than for Henry, his six-month-old son. 'What man,' he would shortly demand of a group of strangers, 'would not want to make provision for his family?'

He must have tried to quicken his pace against the unforgiving clock, but May was the beginning of the summer building season, and new government offices were being constructed around Henry VIII's old palace of Whitehall. The pavements were obstructed by scaffolding and builders' rubble. The stream of traffic that came across Westminster Bridge from south of the river prevented pedestrians from overflowing into the road. To keep the weighty pistol in its special pocket from swinging against the close-packed crowd, he must have clutched his brown coat closer to him, even as he pushed forward through the press of people.

At last he entered Parliament Square, crossed to Palace Yard, and ran up the steps of St Stephen's entrance to the House of Commons. The clock in the lobby showed the time to be five minutes before five o'clock. He was more than twenty minutes late. For the moment, his anxieties and thoughts were private and of no interest to the wider world.

Conflict is inseparable from politics. Interests have to be represented by those who sit on the green leather benches of the House of Commons. Naturally interests run into each other. Noise is inevitable. Voices are raised, and tempers rise with them. In the early summer of 1812, the arguments that erupted over the government's Orders in Council reached an unprecedented pitch of fury.

The ramifications were so complex that it was difficult even for parliamentarians to understand them fully. The original purpose of the Orders issued by the Privy Council in 1807, however, was simple – to impose a naval blockade on France and its ruler, the Corsican tyrant, Napoleon Bonaparte. To this end, the Royal Navy was authorised to remove goods intended for that country from any ship flying a neutral flag on the high seas that was not sailing to or from a British port. Across the Channel, Napoleon had retaliated with his own decrees against neutral ships intending to sail to British ports. And on the other side of the Atlantic the United States, whose shippers suffered most, proceeded to enact its own embargo on trade with belligerent powers.

The consequences were momentous and unexpected. Around the world, trade slowed to a trickle as ships were searched and their cargoes impounded. By 1811, an economic recession had descended on every country from the Baltic to the Mississippi, and the value of British exports and imports had dropped by more than three-quarters. Unemployment and social distress reached such a pitch that in 1812 the House of Commons was driven to conduct an investigation into the effects of the Orders in Council.

Hearings opened on 11 May, a Monday. The lobby of the Houses of Parliament seethed with Liverpool shippers, Manchester cotton spinners, East India merchants, Yorkshire woollen weavers, Staffordshire pottery makers, and Birmingham brassmakers. All had come to plead for the continuation or abolition of the Orders in Council. Only sixty Members of Parliament were present in the chamber, but the high-ceilinged lobby rang with voices of the public raised in genuine outrage.

The rawness of their feelings must have communicated itself to the chamber. Shortly before five o'clock, Henry Brougham, leading the attack on the Orders, suddenly demanded to know why the Prime Minister was not present to defend them. It was

Mr Perceval who had persuaded the Privy Council to impose the Orders, and his authority was needed to remove them. The House had recognised the gravity of the issue, by constituting itself a committee to hear the representations of those affected. The hearings had opened promptly at half past four as advertised. Brougham had already spent more than twenty minutes examining the first witness, Robert Hamilton, a potter from Staffordshire. Hamilton was now waiting to be cross-examined by James Stephen, famous for having masterminded the successful antislave trade campaign of 1807. But the man for whom the drama was staged had not yet appeared.

The anger in the chamber was enough to convince Thomas Babington, in the chair, that the honour of the House required Mr Perceval's immediate attendance. A low-voiced consultation with the Treasury clerk resulted in a messenger being despatched to 10 Downing Street with urgent instructions to hurry the Prime Minister on. Meanwhile, Mr Stephen was permitted to begin his cross-examination. The time was almost five o'clock.

From his place just inside the pair of folding doors that led into the lobby, the man in the chocolate-coloured coat would have seen the messenger push through the groups of delegates. The large expanse of the lobby acted as the meeting place and crossroads of Parliament. To the left lay the House of Commons, to the right the House of Lords. Anyone who came in from the street, whether to badger a Member of Parliament or to enter the chambers of the Commons or Lords, would have to pass through the doors into the lobby. Once the hearings had begun, the crowd started to drift towards the Commons and the public galleries, but around thirty or forty people remained in the lobby as the messenger came through.

The sharp sense of failure must have gripped the assassin right up to that moment. But then, from the scraps of talk that eddied in the messenger's wake, he would have learned that for once in his unfortunate life fate had been on his side: the Prime Minister had not yet arrived. He still sweated and breathed heavily from his hurried walk, but all had changed. His elaborate plan was back in place. Now it was necessary to nerve himself to the great event. A supreme effort was still demanded of him, but beyond it lay a future free of debt and worry.

He had studied Mr Perceval's features often enough from the Strangers' Gallery, peering down through opera glasses at the government benches below. For reassurance, he had repeatedly asked to have the Prime Minister and other members of the cabinet identified for him. No mistakes could be allowed. Again and again he had peered at the politician's oddly childish face until he was certain that he could recognise it.

At just after five o'clock, John Norris, an employee of the House of Commons, passed through the open door of the lobby to reach the stairs leading up to the Strangers' Gallery. He passed close to the tall man in the dark brown coat who stood by the closed part of the double doors. No more than an arm's length, Norris estimated. 'I thought he appeared to be anxiously watching,' he said later. 'And as my recollection serves me, his right hand was within the breast of his coat.'

Other people would also remember exactly where they were and what they were doing in those last few minutes of normality. Henry Burgess, a well-connected Mayfair solicitor with a brief to lobby against the Orders, recalled that he was waiting close to the doorway, a convenient place to buttonhole any late-arriving MP. William Smith, anti-slave trade MP for Norwich, would later describe how he paused in the exact centre of the lobby on his way to the Commons chamber to press the case for keeping the Orders, and was speaking to another anti-slavery activist, Francis Phillips. In a members' committee room high above the lobby, General

Isaac Gascoyne, the fanatically pro-slavery MP for Liverpool, was writing a letter to the Prime Minister about the economic misery in that city, and listening through an open window to the sounds of argument below.

The normality is important. When a national leader is assassinated, normality is always the second victim, but those final moments before it is obliterated contain a clue. Stare at them long enough and you may discern the purpose of the killing.

Julius Caesar walks confidently to attend a last meeting of the senate, knowing that he dominates Rome's constitutional elite, and that when he leaves the city on the morrow it will be to take command again of his all-conquering army. But to a republican, the ease of his gait reveals the imperial nature of Caesar's command over both civil and military power. Abraham Lincoln sits in Ford's theatre at the end of his first day of happiness following the surrender of the South: the play is trashy but to a Confederate the president's delight in its mindless entertainment rubs salt in the deep humiliation of defeat. The newsreel camera captures Archduke Franz Ferdinand as he is driven slowly and amicably through the narrow streets of Sarajevo in the newly annexed province of Bosnia: but to a Serbian patriot nothing could make more patronisingly obvious the reach of Austrian power than this parade in an open, vulnerable vehicle.

Observe what the victim does in his last moments. But note too the position of those who are most outraged by his actions.

No one had ever killed a British Prime Minister. The tall man in the chocolate-coloured coat knew what he was undertaking. It was Mr Perceval who determined that Lord Wellington should fight the French in Spain; Mr Perceval who insisted that taxes be raised to new, astonishing heights to finance his army; Mr Perceval who despatched a Royal Navy squadron to enforce the ban on trading in slaves; Mr Perceval who decided that extra troops should be sent to Ireland to compel the loyalty of dissident Roman Catholics; Mr Perceval who insisted that fresh, draconian laws be imposed to execute or imprison Luddites and rioters for breaking machinery; Mr Perceval who had single-handedly brought the economy to a standstill by his support for the Orders in Council. A notoriously dissolute Prince Regent occupied the monarch's role, but in effect Mr Perceval ruled the nation.

The enormity of the act must suddenly have struck the assassin. The sweat rolled off his forehead, his pounding heart caused him to pant, and the breath rasped through his mouth as though he were a runner struggling to reach the finishing line. Very soon all these physical reactions would become public knowledge.

The messenger encountered the Prime Minister as he strolled out into Downing Street. There was a brief exchange. It was noted that Mr Spencer Perceval hurried at first then, as though remembering the dignity of his office, relapsed into a swift walk. His clothes were plain, a blue coat, white waistcoat, charcoal breeches and a short-crowned hat, and his slight boyish figure, no more than five feet four inches tall, was unimpressive. Only those familiar with political figures would have recognised him as the most powerful politician in the land, the man who combined the post of Prime Minister, or more formally First Lord of the Treasury, with that of Chancellor of the Exchequer, who dominated the House of Commons, whose irresistible energy drove the civil service to execute the policies of the most conservative government since Parliament took power in the Glorious Revolution of 1688. He was a torment to the caricaturists who could find nothing to identify him except for his small size and wide, tilted eyes. He was as anonymous as any Prime Minister could be.

To William Wilberforce, gazing out of the window of Thomas Babington's house in Downing Street, Perceval was, however,

instantly recognisable. On many political issues, they were opponents, but not on the one that was most important to Wilberforce.
Where the slave trade was concerned, he and Perceval were united
in their determination to put an end to it, and Wilberforce, scourge
of the West India lobby that represented the interests of slave
owners, was happy to call the Prime Minister 'Friend'. With
genuine affection, he watched the diminutive figure hurry out of
Downing Street. 'A man of more real sweetness of temper,' he later
declared, 'a man more highly blest by nature, was never known or
one in whom goodness of disposition was more deeply rooted.'

Spencer Perceval started up the steps to the House of Commons
shortly after five o'clock, closely following the heavily built figure
of William Jerdan, a journalist who wrote for the *British Press*. As
they were about to pass through the folding doors into the lobby,
Jerdan noticed the Prime Minister behind him, and courteously
stepped aside to let him go first. Power usually attracts attention,
but Perceval's entrance was so unobtrusive that it was scarcely
noticed in the crowded lobby. Even Jerdan did not quite see what
happened next.

The tall man beside the door pulled his right hand from the
inside breast pocket of his brown coat. The short pistol was almost
lost in his large grasp. The weapon was inaccurate over more than
five yards, but he had no intention of putting anyone else in danger
by firing from that distance. The Prime Minister was hurrying past
him. The man crossed in front to stand in his path. Perceval
stopped, and looked up at him. He was so small that the assailant
towered over him.

The Prime Minister said something – perhaps asking him to move
aside, or more probably offering an apology for pushing past – but
the words were blotted out by the cataclysm of the next moment.
Wordlessly the man stretched out his arm, pushed the wide barrel of
the gun against Perceval's chest, and pressed the trigger.

There was a flash as the powder ignited, a muffled explosion, and the force of the bullet sent the victim stumbling across the lobby. 'Murder,' he exclaimed, 'oh, murder.' Where a knife point would pierce, and a small-calibre bullet penetrate, the projectile that killed Spencer Perceval was a ball of lead almost half an inch across that pulverised the ribs, breast and heart.

The Identity of an Unfortunate Man is Revealed

John Bellingham, alias John Billingham, not having the fear of God before his Eyes but moved and seduced by the Instigation of the Devil . . . did make an Assault [with] a certain Pistol of the value of nine shillings, charged and loaded with Gunpowder and a Leaden Bullet, which he then and there had and held in his right hand to and against the Breast of him, the said Spencer Perceval and . . . then and there shot off and discharged out of the Pistol aforesaid by the force of the Gunpowder aforesaid in, upon and through the Breast of him, the said Spencer Perceval, one Mortal Wound . . .

Verdict of the Coroner's Jury – 12 May 1812

On no fewer than three occasions witnesses were called upon to describe what happened after the shot was fired. They told their first version in Parliament immediately following the murder. A day later the coroner held an inquest in a local pub and ordered three of them to tell their story again. Finally their testimony was heard for a third time in the Old Bailey when the murderer appeared in court. The sequence of events was always the same. But each time the killing was described from a new angle. Different people appeared in the foreground, while in the background there were half-obscured, tantalising hints of another, larger picture. Nothing was quite as it seemed. One witness was a government spy. Another palpably lied. They, like every other person present at the crime, had a political agenda. What follows is a composite of their testimonies, accurate as to what happened but hardly the full truth.

The most detailed testimony came from William Smith, Norwich's anti-slavery MP, given at the coroner's inquiry in the Rose & Crown tavern in Downing Street. In the moments after the shot was fired, events seemed to move with the close-up intensity of a dream. Smith said that when he heard the report of a pistol, he looked up from his conversation with Francis Phillips, and saw a crowd by the door:

> Almost at the same instant a person rushed hastily from among the crowd, and several voices cried out, 'Shut the door', and 'Let no one escape'. The person who came from among the crowd came towards me, looking first one way and then another, and, as I thought at the moment, rather like one seeking for shelter than as the person who had received the wound. But taking two or three steps towards me, as he approached he rather reeled by me, and almost instantly fell upon the floor, with his face downwards . . . When he first fell I thought he might be slightly wounded, and expected to see him make an effort to rise, but gazing at him a few moments, I observed that he did not stir at all; I therefore immediately stooped down to raise him from the ground, requesting the assistance of a gentleman who stood close by me for that purpose. As soon as we had turned his face towards us, and not till then, I perceived it was Mr. Perceval.

Phillips immediately knelt beside the fallen man and seeing the bullet hole, just above the heart and angled down, concluded that it must be fatal. There was no out-going wound. The bullet was still lodged deep in the victim's chest. Together Phillips and Smith pulled the little body upright, and each holding Perceval's arm over his shoulder carried him into the nearest room, an office used by the Speaker's clerk. In his own statement, Phillips confessed that before they could even lay Perceval down, he felt the body go limp in his arms.

With the help of some Commons officials, they gently lowered the Prime Minister onto a small table hurriedly swept clear of papers, so that he was seated upright, supported on either side with his legs resting on a chair. His face, Smith noted, 'was, by this time, perfectly pale, the blood issuing in small quantities from each corner of his mouth . . . His eyes were still open, but he did not appear to know me, nor to take any notice of any person about him, nor had he uttered the least articulate sound from the moment he fell. A few convulsive sobs which lasted, perhaps, three or four minutes, together with a scarcely perceptible pulse, were the only signs of life.'

Inside the office, the silence grew profound. Neither man dared speak aloud his thoughts. Then William Lynn, a surgeon who had been hastily summoned from his house in Great George Street, entered and having examined the body, delivered the verdict they had known but could not bring themselves to admit: 'He is dead.'

Outside in the lobby, the frozen moment of the murder had erupted into confusion. Every account refers to the shouts of 'Close the doors' to prevent the perpetrator escaping, but evidently they were not heeded. Some people ran in to investigate the shot, others raced away to inform peers and MPs of what they had seen, and soon they brought a torrent of anxious enquirers coming to check whether the Prime Minister still lived. It would have been easy, William Jerdan thought, for the assassin to get away unobserved. 'If he had risen in a minute or two afterwards,' he wrote in his autobiography, 'and walked quietly out into the street, he would have escaped, and the committer of the murder would never have been known unless he had chosen to divulge it.'

But Tom Eastaff, an official in the Vote Office, had risen from his place by the door. He had noticed the tall man approach Perceval and when voices began to call out 'Who did it?' Eastaff answered, 'That is the man,' and pointed to the figure in a deep brown coat slumped on a bench against the wall. Standing nearby, Jerdan followed the direction of Eastaff's hand and ran to catch hold of the murderer, seizing him by the collar. The man had a long face, dark hair, and when pulled to his feet appeared taller than those around him. But what Jerdan particularly noticed was the evidence of the man's distress. 'Large drops of agonizing sweat ran down his pallid face . . . [it] was of the cadaverous hue of the tomb; and from the bottom of his chest to his gorge, rose and fell a spasmodic action, as if a body as large as the hand were choking him with every breath. The miserable creature struck his chest repeatedly with his palm, as if to abate this sensation. Never on earth I believe was seen a more terrible example of over-wrought suffering.'

Henry Burgess was also nearby, and within seconds had joined Jerdan, snatching at the assassin's arms and tugging the warm pistol from his right hand. Then came a journalist, Vincent Dowling, who pulled open the chocolate-coloured coat and seized from it first a pair of opera glasses, then the second pistol out of its secret pocket. An angry scrum quickly pressed against the murderer, ripping his clothes apart. Suddenly those nearest were pushed aside as General Gascoyne drove forcefully into the crowd, and gripped the murderer's free hand so violently he cried out at the pain. In the other hand, the man held above his head a bundle of papers tied up in red tape. Gascoyne grabbed them, and tossed them over to another MP, Joseph Hume. While he was still pinioned, the man's pockets were emptied of their contents – a gold guinea, and a one-pound note, bank tokens for 8s 6d, a pocket-knife, a bunch of keys and a pencil. His captors were shouting incoherently at him when someone emerged from the Speaker's office and ran towards the murderer in a fury.

'Mr Perceval is dead,' he cried. 'Villain, how could you destroy so good a man?' The words produced a strange reaction.

'I am sorry for it,' the murderer said, and then he added something stranger still. 'I am the unfortunate man,' emphasising the word 'I'. 'I wish I were in Mr Perceval's place. My name is John Bellingham; it is a private injury – I know what I have done. It was a denial of justice.'

Although each witness remembered his words slightly differently, they all agreed on their import – the surprising claim to be a victim himself, and the implicit admission that he had killed in cold blood. What also struck them was his failure to offer any physical resistance to his arrest. 'A Mouse might have secured him with a bit of Thread,' observed Burgess.

With impressive rapidity, the forces of order started to reassert themselves. A death had been caused, and the perpetrator arrested, but to charge John Bellingham with murder, evidence that he was responsible had to be presented before magistrates.

There were enough lawyers present for this procedure to be quickly agreed and, since Parliament was technically a court of law, voices immediately called for Bellingham to be taken to the chamber of the House of Commons to be charged at the Bar of the House. He was hustled out of the crowded lobby and into the chamber. There, General Gascoyne approached the assassin again, and said with seeming surprise, 'I think I know the villain. Isn't your name Bellingham?'

Before this question could be followed up, other legal experts interrupted to point out that the proper procedure required the arrested man to be in custody before he could be charged. So, from the chamber he was hurried down long corridors and up narrow stairways into the prison-apartment of the serjeant-at-arms where he was formally arrested. Several MPs who were magistrates found seats, and in the hot, airless room the legal process began that should have revealed why John Bellingham had murdered the Right Honourable Spencer Perceval.

Among the crowd of MPs who jammed themselves into the confined space was William Jerdan of the *British Press*. He was there because no journalist would have missed the opportunity to hear the assassin explain his motives, and also because he recognised this was an historic drama. Jerdan was a failed poet, a would-be literary man. Despite his bulk, he felt himself to be an outsider perpetually under threat, 'a stricken deer' was the phrase he used to describe himself. In the committee room, he heard undercurrents that apparently escaped most others present.

The purpose of this first hearing was simply to establish that John Bellingham was indeed the man who had killed the Prime Minister. Accordingly two outside witnesses unconnected with Parliament, a journeyman printer from Lambeth and a clerk from Gower Street, were brought in to testify that they had been standing in the lobby. Each swore that he had seen the pistol fired by Bellingham at Perceval. Then Burgess and Gascoyne identified Bellingham as the man they had arrested. Another MP, Charles Burrell, produced the pistol that had fired the shot. Finally Phillips testified that Perceval had died in his arms. Having demonstrated the chain of evidence, the senior magistrate for the county of Middlesex, Harvey Combe MP, charged Bellingham with the murder.

The formalities of the law revealed less than the informalities. The most important information came from the forty-nine-year-old General Gascoyne MP, a ramrod-straight former officer in the Coldstream Guards. The general had inherited his Liverpool constituency from his elder brother, whose name, Bamber Gascoyne, represented the alliance of two of the city's leading slave-trading families. True to this double family tradition, Isaac Gascoyne made it his business to defend as forcefully as he could the trade on which Liverpool's wealth had been built. During the debates in 1807 to make it illegal to carry slaves on British ships, it was said of him that 'he considered the slave trade so great a blessing that if it were not in existence at present, he should propose to establish it'. For almost twenty years his forceful advocacy on this topic had earned him the loyalty of the city's voters, who repeatedly elected him to represent their interests in Parliament. Now, with military precision, he provided the first independent confirmation of the murderer's identity and background.

The arrested man, he informed the makeshift court, was a constituent of his from Liverpool, named John Bellingham. According to a newspaper report, the general testified that 'he had seen Bellingham often, and that he had received many petitions and memorials from him respecting some claims upon government which he ought to be allowed.' The latest interview with Bellingham had taken place barely three weeks earlier. Their discussions were always about these claims for compensation. '[They] originated in services alleged to be performed by the criminal in Russia for which he complains that he has obtained no remuneration.' The general also described how he had helped arrest Bellingham, gripping the hand that held the pistol so that he could not fire again. He gave his testimony crisply and clearly. His confidence managed to convey a sense that discipline was taking over from the chaos that had been let loose by the horrific crime.

Nevertheless, one person in the room had reservations. Although almost fainting in the airless room, William Jerdan found himself doubting the general's version of events in the lobby. Gascoyne had arrived more than a minute after the shot had been fired, after

Bellingham had been secured and after the pistol had been taken from the assassin's hand. It was possibly a mistake in the heat of the moment, Jerdan thought, and for the time being he kept his thoughts to himself.

When John Bellingham himself was questioned, he confirmed that he had indeed consulted the general on several occasions about his claim for compensation. Despite being warned to say nothing that might be incriminating at his trial, he then insisted on making known the motives for his crime: 'I have been denied the redress of my grievances by Government; I have been ill-treated . . . I was accused most wrongfully by a Governor-General in Russia in a letter from Archangel to Riga, and have sought redress in vain. I am a most unfortunate man, and feel here [putting his hand on his heart] sufficient justification for what I have done.'

Listening to what Bellingham had to say, the crowded audience in the tiny room must have felt they had missed the first half of the drama. So much appeared to have happened before the shooting, and the killer was apparently so well known to the authorities. His account suggested that he had badgered everyone possessing any influence, from the Prince Regent and the Privy Council to anonymous civil servants, with his grievances. 'They all know who I am and what I am,' he insisted. 'They knew of this fact six weeks ago through the magistrates of Bow Street.' Eventually tiring of his demands, one official had told him that nothing could be done for him, and that 'he might do his worst', but it would make no difference. 'I have obeyed them,' Bellingham concluded calmly. 'I have done my worst and I rejoice in the deed.' Incoherent though his argument was, he delivered it with a composure that shocked his audience, worse still he displayed 'not the slightest symptom of remorse'. The panting, sweating Bellingham had given way to a man at peace with his conscience.

Although fascinated by the man, and by his extraordinary

physical recovery from extreme stress, Jerdan quickly concluded that he must be mad. No sane man could be so calm after committing murder. Nevertheless, the journalist wondered whether there might be more to the tragedy than Bellingham's version of events. One piece of evidence, almost lost in the confusion of events, suggested a wider context.

Harvey Combe, in charge of the committal proceedings, was an experienced magistrate familiar with criminal investigations. He had at his disposal the services of two officers from the Bow Street magistrates' court, colloquially known as the Bow Street Runners. Their arrest records and the reports of those cases that came to the Old Bailey showed John Vickery and William Adkins to be outstandingly good detectives. Immediately before the hearing began, Combe had sent them to search Bellingham's lodgings at 9 New Millman Street. This turned out to be a quiet cul-de-sac in the almost-respectable area between Lincoln's Inn and Gray's Inn Road, where law clerks and other foot soldiers in the legal profession lived. Bellingham's room was on the first floor, and when searching it Vickery had found in the chest of drawers all the material needed by Bellingham for his crime – a powder horn, equipment for casting bullets, a pistol key for fitting an extension to the barrel, more ammunition, and a quantity of letters and papers relating to his grievances. All of these would subsequently become evidence at his trial, but only those present at the committal stage heard Vickery's account of his conversation with Bellingham's landlady, Mrs Rebecca Robarts.

When the Bow Street officer had completed his hurried search, he asked Mrs Robarts whether she could tell him anything more about her lodger. Her reply was not illuminating – simply that he was polite, regular in his habits and had been staying there for about four months – but in answer to Vickery's further enquiry, whether she had anything belonging to Bellingham in her possession, she answered that she did. As the officer related this part of the conversation, it was noted that the prisoner lost his self-possession and became visibly upset. Asked by Vickery what the object was, Mrs Robarts said it was a memorandum of twenty pounds due to Bellingham from a Mr Wilson.

Many pieces of evidence were introduced during this hurriedly cobbled-together committal hearing. Understandably it was difficult to tell which were important, and the significance of Vickery's conversation did not stand out.

Bellingham soon regained his calm, and in answer to Combe's question he confirmed that the money did belong to him, and that his landlady was holding it for him. Twenty pounds was not a small sum – in buying power today, roughly equivalent to about £8,000: Mrs Robarts' almost-respectable neighbours would have expected to work for about four months to earn £20. But at this stage the magistrate's task was simply to judge whether sufficient evidence had been presented to justify charging the prisoner. The money lay beyond Combe's immediate concerns. Nor was it relevant to question the assassin further, to ask how long he had been waiting in the lobby, what circumstances had led him there, or why he had been detained on his way to the Commons.

At approximately eight o'clock, having consulted other MPs with legal training, Combe decided they had heard enough. He formally charged John Bellingham with the murder of the Right Honourable Spencer Perceval, and informed him that he would be remanded in custody until his trial. Bellingham pulled together his dishevelled clothes and was handcuffed by Vickery and Adkins. With that, the committal proceedings and the first attempt to find out who was responsible for killing the Prime Minister ended.

Riots Break Out amid Rumours of Revolution

Bellingham was a pleasant and inoffensive companion, but when he had disputed accounts in business, which was often the case, he then shewed his obstinate and unyielding disposition.

Liverpool Mercury, 29 May 1812

Not until the shooting of President John F. Kennedy on 22 November 1963 would a catastrophe of such significance occur again – the assassination of the leader of the most powerful democracy in the world. In each event, two identical processes started immediately, the criminal investigation required by murder and, more vital for the structure of law and order, the restoration of government's authority. Only for a brief period after the crime did the discovery of guilt seem the more important. Very quickly, the second priority came to swamp the first. With the murder of Spencer Perceval, the need to restore authority became obvious when a messenger was sent to find a hackney coach to take the prisoner to Newgate prison.

About three hours had elapsed since Perceval's murder. Hidden away in the bowels of the House of Commons, neither the magistrates nor Bellingham had any idea of the impact his pistol shot had made upon the world outside. Only when the handcuffed prisoner and his escort emerged from the building into Lower Palace

Yard, between Westminster Hall and Westminster Bridge, did they realise that the murder of the Prime Minister was not just a crime.

To the crowds in Parliament Square, it was a source of jubilation. The mood spread as fast as the news. Eager to celebrate, people began to hurry north across the Thames and south from the honeycomb of slum dwellings between Soho and Drury Lane. Within an hour of the murder, they were streaming into Whitehall and packing into the streets and yards around Parliament itself. Inside the building, the law was beginning an orderly investigation into the killing. Outside a festival was taking place to mark the death of the Prime Minister.

There were loud cheers when the hackney coach that had been summoned pulled up outside the gate to Lower Palace Yard. Then, as Bellingham appeared, the mob surged forward. When he climbed into the coach, the nearest celebrators swarmed over the vehicle, and tried to get in at the other door. 'By main force only could they be prevented from mounting the coach-box, clinging to the wheels, and even entering the coach to shake hands with and congratulate the murderer on his deed,' reported one eyewitness, the diplomat Sir George Jackson. 'They were whipped off, beaten off – there was no other course left – amid the execrations of the mob on the police, and the vociferated applause and hurrahs for Bellingham.' In alarm, Vickery pulled his prisoner out of the coach, and hurried him back into the building.

There was no mistaking what London's mob felt about the assassination of Spencer Perceval. For them, it represented a liberation from tyranny, a cause for unrestrained rejoicing. Within two hours, flyers and news-sheets were being sold on the streets with news of the murder. Emerging from the Commons, Samuel Romilly, an MP and Perceval's political opponent, was alarmed to hear 'the most savage expressions of joy and exultation' in the streets around Parliament. And the extraordinary demonstration carried an even more sinister undertone.

What sent shivers of alarm through the nerves of those who exercised power in Westminster was the smell of revolution in the air. Bellingham had become the people's hero. 'Oh I will fire my gun tomorrow,' shouted one demonstrator enthusiastically. 'I did not think there was an Englishman left that had such a heart. He could not have shot a greater rascal!' A constable brought his outburst to a halt by arresting him, but most of the crowd shared the demonstrator's feelings. From the heaving bodies around Parliament emerged chants, 'Perceval is down, the Prince Regent must be down next.' Take out the Prime Minister, followed by the acting monarch, and what was left of government?

All across London, the forces of law and order were called out to contain the wild demonstrations erupting in the streets. On behalf of the Home Secretary, John Beckett, permanent under-secretary in the Home Office, authorised the regular troops responsible for the safety of the capital, the Foot Guards and Horse Guards, to be ordered from their barracks to preserve the peace. Members of Volunteer regiments reported to their quarters. In the City of London, the mayor called out the militia. Elsewhere, justices of the peace commanded the watch to be reinforced, and instructed parish beadles to enrol special constables, known as 'bludgeon men', to patrol with them.

By nightfall, repeated charges by the Horse Guards had at last cleared the crowds from around Parliament, and the frenzy began to die down. At about midnight, the streets were quiet enough for the magistrates in the Commons to make a second attempt to send Bellingham to prison in Newgate. Instead of a hired coach, Lord Clive, the well-heeled, twenty-seven-year-old grandson of the nabob, Robert Clive of India, offered them the use of his six-seater chariot in which he had raced across London to give assistance. With an escort of Life Guards clattering on either side, a pair of policemen acting as coachmen, and a party that included a magistrate, the two Bow Street officers and Lord Clive inside, the Prime Minister's murderer was taken up Whitehall and along the Strand. Despite the late hour, a crowd was waiting to cheer Bellingham's arrival at Newgate prison on the edge of Smithfield meat market, although the horsemen kept them at a distance as he was hurried into the great stone fortress.

Once the door of Newgate thudded shut, responsibility for Bellingham's security rested with John Newman, the chief keeper. The City of London's sheriffs ordered him to take every precaution to prevent the prisoner committing suicide or being poisoned. The legal machinery had reached the discovery stage. So Bellingham had to be kept alive until the law could find out why he had killed Perceval, and who else was involved.

The keeper loaded the prisoner's arms and legs with a double set of irons, and posted two keepers in his cell to watch him through the night so that he could not harm himself. But the precautions were unnecessary. Bellingham showed no signs of anguish or of wanting to escape. Even weighed down by two sets of manacles around his wrists, and two around his ankles, he eagerly consumed a light meal. Then, as though exhausted by the great challenge he had overcome, he fell into a deep, untroubled sleep.

By contrast, the members of Perceval's decapitated cabinet sat up late into the night. Eleven ministers were present, including the most senior, the Lord Chancellor, Lord Eldon, normally forthright in defence of conservative values, and Richard Ryder, the Home Secretary and Perceval's closest friend. But Eldon seemed momentarily too shocked to give a lead, while Ryder, responsible for internal security, was prostrated by grief and barely able to speak. Lord Castlereagh, the secretive Ulsterman newly appointed as Foreign Secretary, would soon emerge as a political force, but he was still feeling his way. In these first hours on their own, the ministers still seemed stunned by what had happened. A single bullet had deprived them of four officers in one person: Prime Minister, Chancellor of the Exchequer, leader of the House of Commons, and Chancellor of the Duchy of Lancaster. Such was Perceval's dominance, a colleague had termed him 'the Supreme Commander'.

Yet every minister was acutely aware that, even before the murder, rioting and violence were widespread in the Midlands and north of England. Weapons had been stolen, buildings torched and factory owners murdered. To many it seemed the country was lurching towards revolution. Luddites opposed to industrial modernisation provided the armed edge, but in the cities the chief threat came from the mischief stirred up in the teeming slums by democratic firebrands still inspired by the ideals of the French Revolution. Already stringent precautions had been taken to monitor these dangers.

Barely two months earlier, the House of Commons had voted to re-establish a Committee of Secrecy to coordinate information-gathering on political radicals. The Aliens Office was mandated to collate rumours of insurrection issuing from Ireland. The private office of the Post Office was authorised to open the letters of suspected troublemakers. The centre of intelligence relating to security, however, was the Home Office. A stream of reports arrived there from paid spies as well as unpaid sources such as magistrates, justices of the peace, and clergymen, supplemented by intelligence from the self-appointed Association for the Preservation of Liberty and Property against Republicans and Levellers.

Next to grief, the strongest emotion driving the cabinet was fear – that John Bellingham might be part of some wider circle, that the murder might be a signal, the opening shot in a plot to create a nationwide rebellion, that the riot in Parliament Square was a rehearsal for the violence that would engulf them all. Ministers who were peers had just come from the House of Lords where they had voted to send a message to the Prince Regent expressing their horror at the crime, and their hope that the prince would take 'the speediest and most effectual measures for bringing the *perpetrators* of the crime to justice'. The plural revealed what they, and everyone who heard the news of Spencer Perceval's murder, feared most – a conspiracy.

The first decision of the cabinet was to order the guards to be doubled at the Tower of London and the Bank of England. Then messengers were sent to warn the lord lieutenant of each county of what had happened. Most of these were peers, already assembled in the House of Lords, and they soon left the capital in a string of private carriages carrying them out into the dark countryside. Back at home, they would instruct the justices of the peace to arrest radicals, troublemakers and insurrectionists, and to have the yeomanry and volunteers ready for action against the mob. At about eight o'clock, another edict was issued forbidding mail coaches to leave London in order to delay news of the assassination getting out.

After that the ministers stalled. There was discussion about imposing martial law, and sending the Prince Regent away from London. But no decision was taken. The gap left by Spencer Perceval was too big to be filled. A messenger was sent to Viscount Sidmouth, a former Prime Minister, to help them in their deliberations. Eventually the cabinet turned to the easier questions of funeral arrangements and the provision of financial support for the Prime Minister's family.

Shortly after midnight, the ministers ended their meeting in order to join the Speaker, Charles Abbott, as he accompanied the body of Spencer Perceval back to Downing Street. Even at that hour, onlookers still clustered in Whitehall. They jeered derisively when the coffin and the procession of political leaders went by. Soldiers on the street prevented any more active demonstration, but the hatred felt for Perceval's ministry could not be doubted.

The body in its open coffin was placed in the drawing room of

10 Downing Street surrounded by tall candles. The Prime Minister's brother, Lord Arden, sat next to it crying without restraint, but his widow, Jane Perceval, could not bring herself to look at the body. At six o'clock that evening, she had been visiting her closest friend, Frederica Ryder, wife of the Home Secretary, when the news was brought to her that her husband had been shot. Neither then, nor in the hours since, had she wept. Now she lay on her bed upstairs, dry-eyed, too shocked to move.

While 10 Downing Street remained frozen in grief, the printing-rooms of London's daily newspapers were a frenzy of noise and activity. To the rapidly developing trade of journalism, the murder presented a challenge. In twenty years, the number of papers and magazines had doubled to more than 240 in Britain, with fifty-two in London alone, about a dozen of them dailies. But all were still hand-printed on iron-framed presses – the steam-driven, rotary presses that *The Times* was planning to install were still two years away. Given the need to compose lines of new type by hand, to ink the frame that held the lead letters, and to pull each four-page sheet individually from the press, workers were restricted to printing about 250 impressions an hour from each press. Such an important, late-breaking story strained the primitive technology to its limits.

By six o'clock, when news of the murder became public, the country editions had already been printed and bundled for the mail coach. The London editions were set up, even at *The Times* which boasted that the last edition did not go to the printing-bed before five minutes past six. But on that evening all the London dailies held the presses.

The majority took time only to insert a few paragraphs into the already closely packed columns of print. With a print run lasting most of the night, any longer delay threatened to deprive readers of their morning paper. *The Globe* managed to get an extra edition away on the last mail coach before the ban was announced with three stark lines of print, 'Mr Perceval was SHOT DEAD this evening in the House of Commons. It is said that the Assassin was a Liverpool Merchant. His name was John James Bellingham.' But at *The Times*, the editor John Stoddard pulled out three columns of type to make way for a detailed report that began with an emotional tribute to the victim, 'a man whose personal qualities gave offence to no one – whose private life was an example to all – and who, however firm and unbending in his principles, yet conducted political conflicts in a way that robbed them of their characteristic bitterness'.

Then Stoddard voiced the only question that needed to be answered, 'What could have excited the wretched assassin to the commission of so diabolical an act?' He did not speculate further about Bellingham's motives, but even in this warmly felt tribute, Stoddard felt bound to refer to the widespread conviction that Perceval's 'firm and unbending' principles were 'narrow and bigotted [*sic*]', and liable to be replaced by 'a more enlightened policy or more beneficial maxims'. Like the cabinet, *The Times* implicitly assumed that Perceval's murder must be connected to the policies his ministry had followed.

Stoddard's editorial was pushed in among reports of the war in Spain against the occupying French forces, and a worrying account of violent disturbances in the north of England. Two nights earlier, several gangs of Luddites, twenty or thirty strong, had raided scores of private houses around Huddersfield and demanded that the owners hand over any weapons they had. 'By this means they have obtained possession of upwards of 100 stand of arms, and not one night has passed without some arms having been so taken.'

It was not difficult to see a connection between the assassination of the Prime Minister in the House of Commons and the organisation of these sinister events. Across London, the talk at fashionable parties was of impending revolution. The Prince Regent was rumoured to have fled to the safety of Brighton. 'Nobody knows at present whether it was the sole act of this man, or whether it is a plot,' the Irish society hostess, the Honourable Frances Calvert, wrote nervously in her journal. 'At all events, independent of the horrible thing it is, it is very alarming, the guards were all out for fear of any tumult.'

Until the cabinet could reassemble its collective will, the immediate priority for everyone with influence, politician, journalist and metropolitan hostess, was the discovery of Bellingham's motives. Everything hinged on his sanity. *The Times* editorial referred to the widespread rumours that his behaviour showed 'proofs of temporary derangement'. That was the good outcome. A mad gunman could have acted alone. But if John Bellingham proved to be sane, then it seemed likely that he was part of a wider conspiracy among Spencer Perceval's many enemies to overthrow the government.

Long before the assassin woke from his tranquil sleep the following day, journalists had begun to congregate round the door to the evil-smelling fortress of Newgate prison.

4

A Free and Easy Conspiracy?

Welcome Ned Ludd, your case is good,
Make Perceval your aim;
For by this Bill, 'tis understood
It's death to break a Frame.

> Luddite poem pinned up in Nottingham, February 1812

The assassin awoke on Tuesday morning, 12 May, with an over-whelming sense of relief. He had been daunted by the difficulty of killing the Prime Minister. The prospect of it had oppressed him for weeks, and he had repeatedly put it off, been 'dilatory' as he himself put it. But Spencer Perceval had had to be killed. It was not something that could be avoided. Now he had done the deed a great weight of anxiety had slipped from his shoulders. News of the assassin's satisfied state of mind was passed on to waiting reporters by John Newman, the chief keeper at Newgate prison, and a constant source of information about John Bellingham's behaviour while in custody. Having slept soundly, Bellingham had risen on the morning following the murder, Newman revealed, and breakfasted with a good appetite off buttered rolls and a large basin of sweetened tea prepared by the keeper himself. The image the keeper conveyed to reporters was of someone sane and at ease with the world.

Nothing in his appearance suggested that he was mad. John Bellingham stood about five feet ten inches tall, with dark, curly hair, and deep blue eyes. He had a long, saturnine face which bore a surprising resemblance, as everyone who saw him remarked, to that of the aristocratic, aquiline-nosed, radical MP, Sir Francis Burdett. His clothes were good but not foppish – a dark brown coat, now torn by rough handling, a striped toilinet waistcoat, dusty yellow nankeen trousers, and Hessian boots. These, as it happened, were almost exactly what the fashion magazine, *Le Beau Monde*, advised for a gentleman's morning wear. The brown coat, calf-length Hessian boots and waistcoat made of toilinet, a woven mixture of silk, cotton and wool, were particularly specified by the *Monde*, although it permitted bottle-green as an alternative for the coat. Kerseymere, or twilled cotton, was what the magazine recommended for trousers, but nankeen, a hard-wearing cotton akin to denim, though a little coarser, did not destroy the overall effect.

The impression of respectability was underlined by the apparently reasonable letter that Bellingham wrote to his landlady, Rebecca Robarts, later that morning after breakfast:

Dear Madam, Yesterday midnight I was escorted to this neighbourhood by a noble troop of light horse, and delivered into the care of Mr Newman as a State Prisoner of the first class. For eight years I have never found my mind so tranquil as since this melancholy but necessary catastrophe. As the merits or demerits of my peculiar case must be regularly unfolded in a Criminal Court of Justice to ascertain the guilty party, by a jury of my countrymen, I have to request the favour of you to send me three or four shirts, some cravats, handkerchiefs, night-caps, stockings &c out of my drawers, together with comb, soap, toothbrush, with any other trifle that presents itself which you think I may have occasion for, and inclose them in my leather trunk. And the key please to send sealed, per bearer; also my great coat, flannel gown, and black waistcoat, which will much oblige, Dear Madam, your very obedient servant,

John Bellingham

To the above, please to add the prayer book.

His handwriting was as neat and composed as the tone of the letter. The meaning was lucid, and the phrasing regular. And the desire to appear smart in court was understandable. Only the context made the message bizarre. The 'neighbourhood' was Newgate prison where he was confined, the 'noble troop' of cavalry had been guards posted to prevent his escape, Newman was his jailer, the 'melancholy but necessary catastrophe' was murder, and the country was in uproar. To be tranquil in such circumstances suggested that either he suffered from an impaired sense of reality or he was a genuinely wicked character. As Tuesday wore on the newspapers grew more inclined to believe the latter.

The reporter on the Whig paper, the *Morning Chronicle*, clearly had a source among the MPs who were present when John Bellingham was charged. As a result, the paper was able to add some detail to the prisoner's motives for killing the Prime Minister. They concerned 'a dispute which he had with the Consul in Archangel by which he incurred a loss of seven or £8,000, but in which the British Government had nothing to do'. Bellingham, a Liverpool merchant, had been imprisoned in Russia following the dispute, the newspaper explained, and since his arrival back in Britain had sought compensation from 'the public offices', but had been told the government could not interfere in 'private affairs'. 'He says that he was driven to despair; that three weeks ago he bought the pistols for the horrid deed, which he has at last perpetrated.'

A FREE AND EASY CONSPIRACY?

Throughout Tuesday, reporters questioned their political and social contacts, and especially keeper Newman, for any additional information they could offer about the murderer. All those who had encountered Bellingham in the hours since he pulled the trigger remarked upon his peace of mind, and most newspapers followed the keeper's line about his mental state.

'At first it was impossible to believe that such an act could be committed by any but an insane man,' *The Courier* declared, 'but it would be difficult to come to this conclusion from the manner and demeanour of the prisoner . . . nothing appeared in his conduct to induce a suspicion of his labouring under insanity. He has since been very much employed in writing, and there is nothing of that hurry in his action, or want of method in his style, to induce us to believe that he does now or has ever laboured under mental derangement.'

This was the crux of the problem facing the legal investigation. Was Bellingham sane, and if so was his crime committed with the help of others? These were the questions that the two Middlesex magistrates, Harvey Combe and Michael Angelo Taylor, posed when they arrived to question him at about nine o'clock that morning.

They too noted that Bellingham appeared calm, self-possessed and respectful. He was no longer burdened by chains. His room next to the chapel, reserved for distinguished prisoners awaiting trial, was large and well-lit. It overlooked the chapel yard, and was almost free from the rank odour of sewage and despair that visitors associated with Newgate. In answer to their questions, Bellingham firmly assured the magistrates that he had acted alone, without any accomplices. Furthermore, he had intended to kill no one but the Prime Minister. Other members of the cabinet, he made clear, were not his targets. Probing his behaviour, the magistrates suggested, because of the sharp downward trajectory of the bullet, that he might have leaned over someone else to shoot. Bellingham indignantly rejected the suggestion, and for the only time in the interview showed signs of being upset. He would never have dreamed of putting anyone at risk except for the Prime Minister. It was a matter of justice, he insisted, brought about by the business in Russia.

Unlike Newman, who thought there was nothing wrong in Bellingham's mind, the magistrates went away uncertain about his sanity. That doubt overshadowed everything they had learned from him. However reasonable his manner, his motive for murder made no sense. Until they could be sure about his state of mind, the magistrates could not decide how much weight to attach to his declaration of having acted alone. It became supremely important to find out the murderer's background, and what he had been doing in the days before he killed Spencer Perceval.

This was the focus of the investigation directed by Harvey Combe, a former lord mayor of London notable for his staunchly Whig politics. So long as the legal process continued to dominate, the inquiry into Bellingham's character and contacts would remain the top priority. The groundwork was handled by the Bow Street Runners, William Adkins and his brother Richard, led by the talented John Vickery. The wealth of information they discovered about the killer in a very short time testified to their energy and detective skills. But Combe had two other sources of information: the surprising number of people who actually knew Bellingham and the indefatigable journalists on the London papers.

The first information came from a visitor to Newgate prison known only as Hokkirk, who claimed to be a friend of the Bellingham family. Although forbidden to see the prisoner, he and Newman obviously talked because reporters soon learned that when Bellingham was a child, his father, a painter, had gone mad and been confined in St Luke's mental asylum in London. The place of confinement was significant. Unlike the better-known and older asylum of Bethlem, or Bedlam, St Luke's did not allow visitors to come round and gawp at its inmates, and for a good reason. It gave priority to violent lunatics who were, under the definition of the 1744 Vagrancy Act, 'furiously mad, or so far disordered in their Senses that [it] may be dangerous [for them] to be permitted to go Abroad'. Most of its 260 patients had to be physically restrained in some way.

The news gave ammunition to those, like Jerdan, who were convinced of the murderer's insanity. Madness obviously ran in the family. Bellingham's studiously calm behaviour now took on a different complexion. It could have been a mask to conceal the mental chaos within. The father's descent into furious madness had been more clear-cut, but at least he had not killed anyone. The son's derangement was undoubtedly more severe.

Then two other items of information emerged that appeared to tip the balance the other way. The first came from Bellingham himself. He revealed that he had been brought up in St Neots, a small market town in Huntingdonshire about sixty miles north of London where the surroundings could not have been more secure. As was soon confirmed, his mother came from a long-established, prosperous family in the area, and after his father's death he had grown up surrounded by loving and supportive relatives. A second pointer towards his stability was the discovery that he was married and the father of three children, all living in Liverpool.

The most revealing clue found on Tuesday, however, was more ambiguous. This was the discovery of a pamphlet that Bellingham had written in March, eight weeks earlier. It described his experiences in Russia from 1804 to 1809, and he had had it printed at a cost of £9 15s 0d shillings for distribution to every Member of Parliament. The pamphlet had made no impact at the time, but by Tuesday afternoon typesetters on every London daily were setting chunks of its text on their formes. The writing was clear, but it did not explain why misfortunes that took place in Russia in 1805 should have led to murder seven years later.

What the pamphlet did make obvious was how well known Bellingham was to the authorities. It revealed that he had taken his complaints to senior civil servants, like John Beckett, under-secretary at the Home Office, and Michael Herries, permanent secretary at the Treasury, and that while he was in Russia he had even tried to claim asylum in the home of Lord Granville Leveson-Gower, the wonderfully handsome, impossibly vain, former ambassador to Russia. To the well-connected Combe, it would have been obvious that one or more of these encounters might have offered some warning of Bellingham's intentions. In the structure of law enforcement, magistrates responsible for policing London occupied a pivotal position. Like all magistrates, they took charge of both the investigation of crime and the maintenance of order within their county. But the law officers of the capital carried an extra burden: to prevent any kind of subversive activity that might endanger the government of the land. This added responsibility brought them into frequent contact with the Home Office and its unrivalled resources for gathering intelligence. When Combe met Beckett, he must have expected the under-secretary to be able to supply him with background reports on the assassin.

The industrious, efficient Beckett had access to information from across Britain and Ireland. In those turbulent days, so much flowed in that it was impossible for him to see it all. Reports of arson and rioting came from the textile counties of Lancashire and Yorkshire as well as from the manufacturing hotbed of the Midlands. There were waves of rick-burning in the south, and industrial sabotage in Wales. The Napoleonic Wars had introduced large numbers of men to weapons and disciplined organisation, and what especially frightened local informants was the potential alliance between military experience and social insurrection. The most urgent reports always concerned the groups of men who arrived at night to smash up stocking-machines or mechanical threshers, declaring themselves to be under the command of 'Captain Ludd' or 'Captain Edward Ludd'.

One note recently forwarded to Beckett had linked threats of destruction to a wider plan to overthrow the government and 'that damned set of Rogues, Perceval & Co to whom we attribute all the miseries of our country . . . we hope for assistance from the French Emperor in shaking off the Yoke of the Rottenest, wickedest and most Tyrannical Government that ever existed'. It was signed 'General of the Army of Redeemers Ned Ludd'. In Yorkshire alone, if one frightened informant were to be believed, eight thousand men were already under arms, including many militia soldiers, whose plan for 'bringing about a revolution, would be to send parties to the different houses of the members of both Houses of Parliament, and destroy them'. Nor did it escape the attention of magistrates that such reports very often mentioned the muskets and pistols carried by the mob. 'What the danger of assassination is,' Earl Fitzwilliam, lord lieutenant of Yorkshire's West Riding, reported to a fellow peer, 'your Lordship will readily collect from the readiness with which this abominable *banditti* fires on every occasion.'

Guns had never been so plentifully available to anyone intent on resisting authority. During two decades of war with France, the army had trained thousands of men to use muskets and supplied them by the ton to both regular soldiers and the part-time militia. Most householders owned at least a blunderbuss, to protect their property, and a variety of more portable, sophisticated weapons were available to those who needed them. The popularity of duelling, hunting and travelling – especially on roads frequented by highwaymen and *banditti* – had created a demand for small arms that made their manufacture a thriving industry. For the

magistrates, their production simply increased the danger in a time
of turmoil, but for later generations this was the classic era made
famous by firearms artists such as Durs Egg and Joseph Manton
who produced beautiful, lethal flintlock pistols for duelling; by
James Purdey who manufactured sporting shotguns for wildfowl-
ers; and by William Beckwith of Snow Hill in London who, as the
Bow Street Runner John Vickery would shortly discover, made
squat, half-inch calibre, steel pistols for sale at the price of four
guineas a pair.

Yet where revolution was concerned, it was urban rather than
rural violence that caused the government the greatest anxiety.
Every large town was growing fast as manufacturing and commercial work lured people from the country. The population of
Glasgow had tripled since 1750 to 100,000 people, the thriving
port of Liverpool had quadrupled to almost 80,000 inhabitants
in barely forty years, Manchester and Birmingham were only a
little smaller at 70,000. None, however, came close in size to
London where the population had exploded to almost one
million, forcing thousands of families to live crammed into 'rook-
eries', made up of hovels piled one on another, where a dozen or
more people might share a single squalid room. Such conditions
incubated sickness, drunkenness, crime and, the Home Office's
many spies reported, insurrection.

When the poet Samuel Taylor Coleridge visited a London pub
on the morning after Perceval's murder to investigate public reaction, he was horrified by the sheer bitterness expressed by ordinary
people. No regret for Spencer Perceval's death. No anger at the
murderer. Just a savage pleasure in what had been done. 'These
were the very words,' Coleridge reported for the *Morning Post*.
' "This is but the beginning" – "More of these damned Scoundrels
must go the same way & then poor people may live." '

Influenced by the French Revolution and the writings of Tom

Paine, the poor saw a direct connection between their misery and political corruption. 'Every man might maintain his family decent & comfortable,' one person asserted in Coleridge's hearing, 'if the money were not picked out of our pockets by them damned Placemen.'

Those were the sentiments of the Corresponding Societies, set up in 1789 to share the ideas of the French Revolution, but supposedly suppressed in the 1790s by laws against political dissent and unauthorised meetings. As a Whig, and a declared supporter of Charles James Fox's liberal policies, Harvey Combe had opposed this draconian legislation, but he knew that the societies' former members had found ways of getting round the bans. They now assembled informally in pubs, ostensibly for 'free and easy evenings' of singing and drinking, but in reality to keep alive dreams of replacing a corrupt society by one based on liberty and equality. 'Yes we must lay on a general plan of Insurrection,' one of these radicals declared, according to a government spy, 'which must be agreed to be acted upon, and not debated afterwards.' Fear of what might happen when guns and urban revolutionaries came together led the Home Office and London magistrates to flood the revolutionary underworld with paid informers. Their reports were filled with wild talk and plans to storm Parliament and kill all the cabinet, or to take over the Bank of England, or to invade Carlton House where the Prince Regent lived, hang him and set up a republican government that would serve the people. Anger at a government that oppressed the poor and rewarded its friends with pensions and well-paid jobs appeared in the extravagant toasts the radicals offered as they downed their porter and ale: 'May the guillotine be as common as a pawnbroker's shop and every tyrant's head a pledge', 'Let the barren land of our country be manured with the blood of our Tyranny', and, most popular of all, 'To the last king, strangled by the guts of the last priest'. It was apparent too in their songs, one of the most popular being sung to the tune of 'Sweet Lass on Richmond Hill':

> Tis in Pall Mall there lives a Pig [the Prince Regent]
> That doth this Mall adorn.
> So fat, so plump, so monstrous Big,
> A finer ne'er was born.
> This Pig so sweet, so full of Meat,
> He's one I wish to kill.
> I'll fowls resign on thee to dine,
> Sweet Pig of fine Pall Mall.

Among the violent graffiti scrawled on the walls along Whitehall was one at least that came from the free and easy clubs, 'Perceval's ribs are only fit to broil the Prince Regent's heart on'. Revolutionary words might quickly lead to revolution itself. A London magistrate had to know whether Bellingham's bullet could be the signal the revolutionaries were waiting for. In his meetings with Beckett, Combe would therefore have asked whether the assassin's name had been mentioned by any of the under-secretary's spies in the underworld. Almost inevitably, given their number, one of the government's spies had met the murderer in the weeks before the killing.

Sitting up in the narrow press gallery that overlooked the chamber of the House of Commons, Vincent Dowling, parliamentary reporter for *The Day*, had been joined by Bellingham who carried with him the same opera glasses that were seized from him in the lobby. At the committal hearing in the Commons, the reporter testified that the stranger had come there more than once, and had asked him to identify the different members of the cabinet sitting on the government benches below. Dowling particularly remembered pointing out Richard Ryder, the Home Secretary. As a reporter, he declared that he only appreciated the significance of these encounters in retrospect.

Dowling, however, had a secret that never emerged in his testimony. He was also paid by the Home Office to infiltrate the groups of political extremists who met in drinking clubs to talk and sing and plot ways of creating a new, radical society. He was sufficiently conscientious to pass on several long accounts of treasonable meetings to the Home Office. A stranger with an interest as persistent as Bellingham's in identifying senior ministers, including the spy's employer, should have aroused his suspicions, and Dowling admitted that on the second or third meeting he had had a long conversation with Bellingham. He must have asked the stranger his name and business. It is possible that Dowling filed no report of his encounter, certainly none exists today. But the presumption must be that he did provide some note of the meeting, because the Home Office continued to pay him for information after Perceval's murder, indicating that no blame had been attached to his conduct regarding the murderer. Perhaps Beckett missed the significance of the warning, but it is equally probable that he had passed the information on to the Home Secretary, and in that case Combe would have understood immediately why no further action had been taken. The inadequacies of the Home Secretary and the paperwork that accumulated on his desk were notorious in government circles.

Richard Ryder had been Perceval's friend since their days at university. He had been appointed Home Secretary because the Prime Minister wanted the post to be held by someone whose loyalty was beyond question. But, physically delicate and crippled by lack of confidence, Ryder was ill-suited to the demands of a brutal portfolio that placed him in charge of the internal security of the kingdom. The Home Secretary was widely rumoured to retire to bed with a headache rather than take a difficult decision to deploy troops on the streets or to order the round-up of suspected troublemakers. To keep the department functioning, much of the minister's work had in practice been shouldered by the Prime Minister. Amidst Spencer Perceval's many other duties, sifting significant information from the dross did not rank high. The possibility existed, nevertheless, that Perceval himself might have been ultimately responsible for failing to prevent his own murder.

Whatever the failures of the Home Office, Combe would have learned much about the case from his meetings with Beckett. The murder did not come out of the blue: Bellingham had approached many people and his demands were well-known to every area of government. His crime was not spontaneous, and his preparations had none of the disorder that would indicate madness. And all of his actions indicated that he had acted alone.

On the afternoon of Tuesday, 12 May, less than twenty-four hours after the murder, members of the House of Commons met to pay tribute to their murdered colleague. The most eloquent expression of their feelings came not in words but in uncontrollable weeping. It was an emotional society, the last before the responsibility of running an empire made it desirable for men to stiffen the upper lip and keep their feelings under control in public. But even so their demonstration of grief was remarkable. The Speaker, Charles Abbott, noted that Richard Ryder could not even speak for crying, and that 'in most faces there was an agony of tears; and neither Lord Castlereagh [Foreign Secretary], Ponsonby [leader of the Whig opposition], Whitbread [a radical Whig], nor Canning [Perceval's Tory rival] could give a dry utterance to their sentiments.'

Shock at the violence of the Prime Minister's death, and that it should have taken place within the palace of Westminster, contributed to the depth of emotion, but their tears sprang also from genuine affection. The Whig leader, George Ponsonby, declared in a choking voice that while he had opposed Perceval bitterly on political matters, there was no one 'of whose sense of honour he had a higher opinion, or for whom he had a greater personal affection', at which point according to the *Parliamentary Register*, 'the emotions of the right honourable gentleman were such as for a few moments to deprive him of the power of utterance'.

In the House of Lords, the Lord Chancellor, Lord Eldon, was so convulsed by tears that he had to let Lord Ellenborough, the Lord Chief Justice, take his place on the woolsack as Speaker. Even after his return, Eldon was, in the words of the *Register*, 'so overpowered by his feelings that he could not read the message [of condolence from the Prince Regent] audibly and it was with great difficulty his lordship got through it'.

Their anguish provided a sharp contrast to the scenes of riotous celebration that were already rippling outwards from London. From towns in Hertfordshire and Essex, reports came in of the joy and often of the wild gunfire that broke out as people learned of Spencer Perceval's death. In the days to come the Midlands, Yorkshire, Lancashire and the Lowlands of Scotland would be convulsed by a wave of outrageous delight at the Prime Minister's murder. The forces of law and order in the country seemed as powerless to contain it as those in London.

On Tuesday evening, according to the *Nottingham Journal*, a mob 'proceeded with a band of music all through the principal streets. They were soon joined by a numerous rabble who, in the most indecent and reprehensible manner, testified their joy at the horrid catastrophe by repeated shouts, the firing of guns and every species of exultation.' Similar demonstrations were reported in Birmingham as people heard what Bellingham had done, and crowds 'stood huzzaing and expressing their savage joy'. Bellingham's health was drunk in Glasgow, Liverpool and Manchester. In the Lake District, a shocked

William Wordsworth warned his sister, Dorothy, 'The country is no doubt in a most alarming situation; and if much firmness be not displayed by the Government, confusion & havoc & murder will break out and spread terribly.' From Cambridge, another poet, the Irishman Tom Moore, reported apprehensively that 'all the common people's heads are full of revolution'.

It was still possible that Perceval's murder might have been designed to detonate the bomb of revolution, but in London the first fears were receding. Combe's initial conclusion that Bellingham was a lone eccentric would have been reported to Beckett and others responsible for law and order. And the political forces in Westminster were already beginning to regroup. With each new report of riot and disorder, ministers like Castlereagh, Eldon and Ellenborough grew increasingly determined to demonstrate the might of government forcefully and without delay.

When the cabinet assembled late on Tuesday night, their uncontrollable grief gave way to anger, and a savage desire to wipe out the affront done both to Parliament and to them personally. Bellingham had to be executed as quickly as possible. In the Commons, Castlereagh, who had taken over leadership from the paralysed Ryder, made it plain that in his opinion the murder 'was confined to the individual who had perpetrated the act'. Time spent searching for accomplices would be wasted.

Eldon went further. In the Lords, he had been braced by a conversation with Ellenborough, a legal neanderthal notorious for being the last judge to sentence a man to be hanged, drawn and quartered. The Lord Chief Justice was convinced that Bellingham should not only be executed without delay, but that in order to demonstrate the power of government as dramatically as possible to the rioters who had dared celebrate his atrocious crime, he should be hanged publicly in Palace Yard before the House of Commons.

Not every minister sympathised with this suggestion, but there was no dispute within the cabinet that public policy and personal feeling demanded the death of the murderer. The case would be handled by the Attorney General, Sir Vicary Gibbs. The Lord Chief Justice would be told to set the earliest possible date for the trial. The political machine was about to swamp the criminal investigation.

Examining the Enigma of the Assassin's Sanity

I must begin to explain the origin of this unhappy affair, which took place in 1804. I was a merchant at Liverpool, in that year I went to Russia on some mercantile business of importance to myself, and having finished that business I was about to take my departure from Archangel for England.

John Bellingham, 15 May 1812

Once it was decided to bring John Bellingham to trial, a solicitor had to be appointed to act for his defence. The choice was easily made. Most defence solicitors had a reputation for being as ignorant and disreputable as their criminal clients. But in London, there was one notable exception.

When James Harmer, the son of a Spitalfields weaver, apprenticed himself to a firm of lawyers in the early 1790s, he discovered that the defence of clients usually depended on invented alibis or suborned witnesses. From the moment he set up on his own, however, he built a reputation for knowing the law, and for the care he took in briefing barristers. By the early 1800s, his offices in Hatton Garden, within shouting distance of the law courts, had become the first place to go for anyone, as a contemporary put it, 'whose natural destination was the Old Bailey'. Portly and successful, Harmer was destined to become a pillar of the legal profession, and an alderman of the City of London, yet he never lost an edgy loyalty to the underdog. By the time he retired, his commitment to the overhaul of his seedy end of the law had transformed court-room practice in criminal trials. In the judgement of Charles Phillips, the outstanding attorney of the early Victorian law courts, Bellingham's solicitor was both 'a worthy and a clever man'.

With characteristic energy, Harmer read all the material available about his client, and late on Wednesday morning interviewed him at length. He found the prisoner in triumphant mood. That morning the newspapers had printed large portions of Bellingham's pamphlet containing the petition that he had sent out to MPs in March. 'The people will now be able to judge my case,' he declared, 'and do me the justice to say, I have only done my duty.' This remained Bellingham's unshakable conviction, that once it was known how unjustly he had been treated, everyone would understand why he had been forced to kill the Prime Minister. When that was understood, no jury could possibly convict him of murder. With difficulty Harmer persuaded him that he still needed to mount a defence in court. Eventually, he got from Bellingham the names of several people who knew him and might be able to give evidence on his behalf.

Having promised to read the pamphlet himself, Harmer returned to his office, then sent a series of urgent messages by the evening mail coaches to Liverpool and Southampton. The former were directed to John Bourne, mayor of Liverpool, and to Bellingham's business partner in the city, John Parton; the latter was addressed to Bellingham's cousin, Mrs Ann Billett. All of them asked for evidence of John Bellingham's insanity.

Harmer had reasonable grounds for believing that his client could be defended on the grounds of insanity. That Bellingham was obsessive could hardly be doubted. A strong case could be made that he was also delusional. And with the right witnesses, it might be convincingly argued that he was indeed mad, at least so far as the law understood the word.

Until 1800, the definition had been unambiguous. At the trial of Lord Ferrers in 1760, it was held that his lordship, having killed an employee while in a state of paranoia, must be found guilty because only a 'total, permanent or temporary want of reason would acquit a prisoner'. To be judged insane, the criminal's mental state had to be akin to that of 'a wild beast', unable to distinguish between good and evil. But in 1800, James Hadfield, a veteran severely wounded in battle by sabre cuts to his head, stood up in a theatre and fired a pistol at King George III in the belief that his death would bring about the new millennium. In court, his lawyer, the brilliant Thomas Erskine, successfully pleaded that Hadfield was suffering from so profound a delusion that he was incapable of telling right from wrong simply at the moment of firing.

The Hadfield judgment was suspect, partly because of the sympathy aroused by his terrible wounds, and partly because the judge had stopped the trial rather than letting the jury decide. Nevertheless, it was enough to give a solicitor hope that Bellingham could mount a successful defence on the same grounds. Harmer next wrote to two of London's most eminent experts on mental health, Dr Thomas Munro, who had given testimony on behalf of Hadfield, and Dr Samuel Simmons, who had attended George III during the king's madness, asking them both to testify to his client's insanity. He then instructed the flamboyant Irish attorney, Peter Alley, to defend John Bellingham on the grounds that at the time of the murder he was out of his mind.

On the very day that Harmer's letters went out, however, two witnesses tracked down by the Bow Street Runners, John Vickery and the Adkins brothers, cast severe doubts on the line of defence he proposed to adopt. The first was the gun-maker, William Beckwith, who testified that he had sold the murder weapon to Bellingham on about 20 April, three weeks before it was used.

The type of pistol showed that it had been chosen specifically to be concealed. It was equipped with a detachable barrel so that if necessary the firing mechanism could be carried unobtrusively in one pocket and the barrel in another. Beckwith had advised his customer to get accustomed to how the weapon behaved when fired, and he also informed the officers that Bellingham had then gone to a park to practise shooting with the pistol.

The second witness found by Vickery and his colleagues added to the impression that the crime had been carefully premeditated. Evidently Bellingham had tried screwing the barrel into place – a special key was provided for the purpose – and found the process too complicated. William Taylor, suitably enough a tailor by trade, told the Runners that he had been asked by Bellingham on about 23 April to alter his brown coat so that he could carry a concealed weapon that was exactly the size of Beckwith's pistol with the barrel already attached.

The testimony of these two witnesses not only illustrated the murderer's unmistakably rational state of mind but the carefully thought-out steps he had taken in preparation for his deed. It confirmed the impression given by Rebecca Robarts, his landlady. Vickery, who had briefly questioned her, went back to New Millman Street for a more extensive interview. Her evidence showed that Bellingham had stayed in her lodging-house from the beginning of January 1812, and that throughout that time he had behaved quite normally, indeed had been a model tenant.

Potentially, Rebecca Robarts was the most damaging witness of them all. For more than four months, she had seen John Bellingham almost every day. On Sundays, she and her son would go with him to the fashionable church in the Foundlings' Hospital in Guilford Street. Often she and Bellingham would also visit exhibitions and museums together. They went out so frequently that Vickery must have guessed that the young widow had developed a certain tenderness for her tall, well-dressed lodger. On one occasion, she recalled, her son had gone missing. She had immediately run to Bellingham for help, and he had searched through the streets until he found the boy and brought him back to his mother. No jury who heard Mrs Robarts's testimony was likely to suppose that Bellingham was mad.

Yet Harmer's reading of the pamphlet revealed a man acting so obsessively in one particular circumstance that it did create a clear impression of madness. Where righting a personal wrong was concerned, Bellingham did not behave rationally. In pursuit of justice for himself, he knew no limits.

Bellingham's troubles had begun in the summer of 1804 when he chartered a ship to sail from Hull to Archangel in northern Russia. From there he intended to bring back a cargo of timber and iron but, in the words of his pamphlet, 'was illegally prevented from returning to England by the said ship, as was my intention, and also was so much injured as to be deprived of the opportunity of loading my own goods on board of her'. As a result he had 'suffered very serious losses'. What he sought was compensation from the government because the British ambassador to St Petersburg had failed to support his efforts to obtain justice in Russia.

In the context of conducting trade during a time of war, the detail of his business dealings contained a powerful logic. Bellingham was obeying the same rationale of taking risks to make a profit that had also created the gigantic edifice of Britain's world-encircling trade. From the top of Ludgate Hill, a short walk from Hatton Garden, Harmer could see a forest of masts and spars rising above the Pool of London where vessels waited to load cargoes for Russia, India, the United States and the West Indies. What drove their owners had also driven Bellingham. And like them he had expected the laws of international trade to protect him from wrongdoing.

Trade with Russia always carried risk, but it promised huge profits, because the country's main exports – timber, iron, hemp and tallow – were strategic materials needed for shipbuilding and lighting, and demand for them was always strong. The usual route in peacetime was through the narrow Skagerrak strait between Denmark and Sweden, and across the Baltic Sea to St Petersburg. But in wartime, French and Dutch privateers – privately owned ships authorised by their governments to attack enemy shipping for their own profit – preyed upon British-flagged vessels near the coasts of Europe, and once Denmark fell within Napoleon's empire in 1800, the Skagerrak route became exceptionally hazardous. Consequently, many 'charter-parties', the contracts made between cargo-owners and shipowners, specified that the vessels were to sail around the northernmost point of Scandinavia to the port of Archangel in northern Russia, far away from the dangers of privateers and Danish guns.

Despite these dangers, the Baltic trade as it was known had become the fastest-growing financial sector in the City of London. A new dock dedicated to Russia's four main exports had just been opened on the south bank of the Thames, and the dealers, brokers and shippers in the Royal Exchange who specialised in these commodities had set up an unofficial exchange in the Baltic Coffee House. But every profitable deal came with stories of St Petersburg's intolerable weather, its stultifying bureaucracy and its backward conditions. And the memoirs of diplomats posted to Russia suggested that everything was even worse in Archangel. Surrounded by dark forest and impenetrable swampland, its winter temperatures dropped far below freezing, and the brief summer boiled with black swarms of mosquitoes from the stagnant pools that bordered the slowly oozing River Dvina. To administer this remote corner of the empire, the tsars appointed not one but two governors, one civil the other military, each equipped with a retinue of officials to enforce a different set of regulations.

Nevertheless Archangel had been a considerable trading centre for more than two centuries, and Bellingham's pamphlet pointed to the reason why. The port gave access to a region with seemingly inexhaustible reserves of timber and iron ore, and its trade, though dominated by a few, long-established Dutch companies, was well-regulated. Several British companies kept permanent agents there.

Bellingham had sailed for Archangel in June 1804, taking with him his young wife Mary, and their six-month-old son, James. Open water at the port was guaranteed for only five months during the year. Since the Russian port was less than twenty days' sailing from Hull, Bellingham should easily have been able to return with his cargo before the autumn. But, as the pamphlet suggested, something went wrong in the negotiations, and he was prevented from loading his cargo of timber and iron. He was still there in November long after ice had closed the port. That month he decided to leave Archangel and travel to the Russian capital of St Petersburg. For this he needed a *petrovnik*, or pass, but as he prepared for his departure, 'the said *petrovnik* was forcibly taken from me by the police Master without any cause whatever, and soldiers and police officers were placed on [my] person day and night to prevent [my] quitting the place'.

For Harmer, trawling the pages for evidence of his client's mental unsoundness, there were two unmistakable conclusions to be drawn from Bellingham's story: the first was the author's conviction that he had been the victim of commercial blackmail, and the second was that the author possessed an almost infantile refusal to accept the reality of events outside his control.

Bellingham's arrest was brought about by an influential Dutch merchant, Solomon van Brienen, who was a friend of the mayor of Archangel, Vasiliy Popov. The ostensible cause was to recover a debt of 4,890 roubles, approximately £500. Another Dutch merchant, Conrad Dorbecker, had bought a consignment of iron on behalf of

Bellingham from van Brienen, but had gone bankrupt before paying for the goods. Because Dorbecker and Bellingham were business partners, the Englishman was deemed to have become liable for the debt.

The pamphlet made it plain, however, that van Brienen's real purpose was revenge. He and Popov had been partners in the *Soyuz*, a vessel insured with Lloyd's of London for £3,800. When it sank in 1804 their insurance claim was refused by Lloyd's, on grounds of fraud. According to information passed secretly to the insurers, the ship was still afloat under another name. Unfortunately for Bellingham, the ship's owners decided that he must have been the Lloyd's informant. And so for good measure, van Brienen and Popov also brought a second, criminal suit against the Englishman for illegally depriving them of the money for the *Soyuz*.

According to Bellingham, no documentary evidence was ever produced to show that he had ordered the iron. If the supposed contract was concocted, and Dorbecker had indeed acted in collusion with his fellow Dutchman, Bellingham's anger was understandable, but the injury so overwhelmed him that he could see nothing else. Throughout his time in Archangel, Bellingham never looked for any settlement, or compromise. He simply demanded justice.

At first his persistence was rewarded. In response to his barrage of complaints, officials agreed that Popov and van Brienen 'had all along acted beyond the Law' as the pamphlet put it; in March 1805, he was released and actually on the road for St Petersburg before being stopped and brought back after the influential Popov persuaded the military governor, General Furster, to issue new orders for his arrest. On that occasion, Bellingham lost his self-control, creating a scene that the governor called 'highly indecorous'. The victim himself only admitted to having been 'a little vociferous'. Nevertheless, his case was then submitted to a court of commercial arbitration made up of two British merchants and two

Russians. As a compromise – and it signified the weakness of van Brienen's suit – they decided that Bellingham should pay just 2,000 roubles, approximately £200, to van Brienen for the non-existent iron purchase. This proposal was indignantly spurned.

Until then, his quarrel was confined to Russia, but in his fury Bellingham next appealed for help to the British ambassador in St Petersburg, Lord Granville Leveson-Gower. Unfortunately for Bellingham, the ambassador was about to take an eighteen-month holiday, and his appeal was passed on to the consul, Stephen Shairpe. A long-time resident of St Petersburg, and leader of the British expatriate community there, Shairpe quickly established that the dispute concerned a civil debt, and concluded that neither he nor the ambassador could intervene. With that refusal to help, Shairpe had apparently set in motion the convoluted sequence of steps that led Bellingham to the lobby of the House of Commons seven years later. To Bellingham, the logic was compelling – he had been denied help by the British government in his hour of need, and was thus entitled to seek redress later – but to Harmer, scouring the pamphlet for symptoms of lunacy, it must have offered the first faint hopes of showing that his client was indeed deranged.

In October 1805 a new civil governor arrived in Archangel, to be greeted by a letter from Bellingham not only demanding his release from confinement but also payment of compensation for unlawful imprisonment. Surprisingly, the governor promised to take another look at his case. A fresh hearing in court was ordered where, as Bellingham reported triumphantly, 'I obtained judgment against the whole party, including the Military Governor who had injured me.' However, as Harmer could easily discover, this was not the entire truth. The criminal suit was thrown out, but the judgment for debt still stood. Nevertheless, Bellingham's *petrovnik* allowing him to leave Archangel was at last restored. It was too late in the season to sail back to Britain, so in November 1805, eighteen disastrous months after he had arrived, Bellingham departed for St Petersburg.

Waiting for him in the capital were his twenty-three-year-old wife Mary and his son James. They had been with him when he was stopped on the road to St Petersburg earlier in the year, but unlike him they had been allowed to travel on to their destination. During the summer, Mary might have returned to Britain, but she had refused to leave without her husband. As she later explained, she supported herself and James by making hats and dresses for the families of the Factory, the powerful, well-entrenched association of British merchants in St Petersburg.

To Harmer, it was obvious that the reunited family could then have obtained permission to leave for home. The Factory carried influence with the Russian government, and both British and Russians were only too anxious to be rid of an embarrassment to the trading community. Had he followed this rational course, Bellingham would have shown himself to be sane. Instead he took the mad option of issuing a *ukase*, or writ, in St Petersburg demanding compensation from the tsar and the impeachment of General Furster, the military governor of Archangel, for his illegal detention. It was such an extraordinary demand that he could not get his writ printed until he had indemnified the printer against the risk of being sent to Siberia. Outraged that a foreigner should impugn the integrity of the tsar's government, the *duma*, or Parliament, in St Petersburg ordered him back to jail.

By now Leveson-Gower had returned from his extended holiday. Occasionally, as Bellingham was moved from one prison to another, he passed along a route in front of the residence of the ambassador 'who might view from his window this degrading severity towards a British subject'. Increasingly embittered, Bellingham began to blame Leveson-Gower for all his woes. Finally he made a desperate attempt to escape his guards and ran to claim asylum in the ambassador's house. To Bellingham's utter despair, Leveson-Gower refused to allow him to stay. 'I must therefore request you to give yourself up again into custody,' he wrote to the fugitive, 'but shall think it my Duty to make representations to the Government upon your affair, & shall be happy to use any means in my Power towards forwarding an arrangement of the Business in which you are involved.'

But no arrangement was possible. In July 1807 Bellingham's case had become ensnared in international politics, when Tsar Alexander I signed the Treaty of Tilsit with Napoleon, thereby altering the balance of power in Europe. From being a neutral country, Russia was transformed into an ally of France and an enemy of Britain. Caught in these great events, Bellingham's appeals for justice became still more hopeless. He endured another year of confinement in the city prison before being released in October 1808. Even then he remained under house arrest. In December he desperately appealed to the tsar for permission to leave – and, characteristically, to be paid compensation – but another eleven months passed before the necessary permit was issued. Early in December 1809 John Bellingham finally returned to London, financially ruined.

For a lawyer searching for signs of insanity, the pamphlet demonstrated an unmistakable loss of any sense of proportion, and arguably a breakdown of reason in the face of intolerable misfortune. Bellingham's conclusion that he deserved compensation because the ambassador was responsible for his ill-treatment was utterly illogical, and his recourse to the same argument more than two years later showed that he was still in the grip of the same obsession. As a defence, it only offered a slim chance of success. Backed by affidavits from those who knew him personally and professionally, however, and buttressed by Alley's combative advocacy, Harmer could only be sure that the strongest possible case would be presented that his client was unable to tell right from wrong. Why so much time should have elapsed before Bellingham determined to exact retribution, and why his target should have been Spencer Perceval rather than Granville Leveson-Gower, was not the concern of a defence solicitor.

By Wednesday evening the Attorney General, Sir Vicary Gibbs, had heard enough from Combe and the Bow Street officers to become as convinced of Bellingham's sanity as Harmer was of his madness. Where the two sides did agree, however, was in the belief that he had acted alone. From the prosecution's point of view, the criminal investigation had done its work. The political priority was now to have Bellingham hanged as an example to others, and any consideration of an accomplice could only delay proceedings. Harmer was equally averse to the idea of a conspiracy. To convince a court that a solitary murderer was mad would be hard enough. It would become impossible if Bellingham had been acting in concert with others.

Neither side had any interest in extending the scope of their inquiries. There was no need to discover why Bellingham had suddenly decided to kill Spencer Perceval, no need to enquire how he had maintained himself while in London, and above all no need to learn whether anyone else had been involved in the murder.

The Victim is Seen as a Fond Father
and Attentive Husband

I was born of Parents, powerful, honourable and happy till a cruel
blow deprived my mother of a husband, and her family of a father.
John Perceval, *Narrative of the Treatment experienced by a
Gentleman, during a state of mental derangement*, 1838

On the same Wednesday afternoon that James Harmer set in
motion his plan to save the murderer's life, the House of Commons
took steps to look after the victim's family. Spencer Perceval had left
a widow and no fewer than eleven children, most of whom had still
to be educated. In an age when politicians were expected to make
money from their time in office, the Prime Minister was virtually
unique, as more than one speaker pointed out, in leaving his family
poorer at his death than when he first entered the cabinet. It was
fitting therefore, Lord Castlereagh told the Commons, that some
financial compensation should be offered for the terrible tragedy
they had suffered. He suggested a grant of £50,000 for the upkeep
of the late Prime Minister's family, together with an annuity of
£2,000 for his widow, Jane.

It was a phenomenal sum, the price of six warships, and yet to
many MPs it was not enough. There were calls to allocate £60,000,
even £100,000 for the benefit of the Percevals. Compared to the

undiluted hatred that was the Prime Minister's legacy in the street, the affection he aroused among his colleagues was truly astonishing. So far as Spencer Perceval as a private individual was concerned, all who knew him agreed on his virtues, from the admiring George III who labelled him 'the most straightforward man I have ever known', to the opposition MP, Samuel Romilly, who wrote, 'No man could be more generous, more kind or more friendly than he was. No man ever in private life had a nicer sense of honour. Never was there, I believe, a more affectionate husband or a more tender parent.' The Percevals were indeed the antithesis of Regency London, where young bucks gambled away their inheritance at Crockfords and Whites, and fashionable ladies spent fortunes in order to secure an invitation from the social arbiters who controlled entry to the dances held at Almack's Assembly Rooms.

As though the Victorian age had arrived a generation early, Spencer and Jane were earnest, ambitious and devoted to family values. They adored gardening, bought toys for the children, played practical jokes on one another, went to church, and put money aside for a rainy day. Defending the pleasure he took in his family, Perceval told a friend, 'I assure you that it is as great as anything in this world can produce.' Exasperated by his attachment to domestic life, the Princess of Wales once loftily declared that 'Perceval is entirely governed by that silly woman, his wife.' The truth, however, was that his priorities grew out of the kind of enduring love that always escaped the unfortunate princess.

Perceval's domestic happiness was famous, and to his admirers, such as the earnest essayist and politician, Robert Plumer Ward, it made him exceptional. He was, wrote Ward, 'so perfect in private life that to name him seemed to be to name virtue'. The sheer romance of how his happiness began ensured that the story was widely known.

In 1786, at the age of twenty-four, he and his elder brother Charles, Lord Arden, were invited to stay at Charlton House, on the south bank of the Thames. As boys, they had grown up in the house, a magnificent Jacobean mansion and the grandest building in the neighbourhood. Since then it had been sold, and now belonged to Sir Thomas Wilson, an old soldier who had been lucky enough to marry an exceptionally wealthy heiress. The Perceval brothers were attracted back to their former home, not simply by nostalgia but by the presence of the Wilsons' two high-spirited daughters, Margaretta and Jane. In due course, the two brothers fell in love with the two sisters but, as readers of Jane Austen's novels were constantly reminded, romance was inseparable from finance. As the younger son of an earl, Spencer Perceval had the right connections but, alas, the wrong income.

Older readers who preferred the previous fashion for the Gothic novel, with its hauntings and echoes of a mildewed past, were better able to understand Perceval's background. He had been born in 1762 the second son of the second marriage of the second Earl of Egmont, a peer whose outlook was so rooted in the past as to be generally termed medieval. The Percevals had originally been impoverished Irish landowners, but political connections gained the first earl his title, and inspired him to compile an imaginative genealogy showing the family to be descended from Norman aristocrats. This spurious background helped the second Lord Egmont to marry two wealthy wives in succession, and acquire an English title together with a valuable government sinecure, registrar of the high court of the admiralty, worth £12,000 a year. But his money and the sinecure had all gone to the eldest son of his second marriage, Lord Arden.

Consequently, Sir Thomas Wilson had no qualms about giving his elder daughter, Margaretta, immediate permission to marry her wealthy and titled suitor. In 1787 she became Lady Arden and scandalised her antediluvian in-laws by espousing the radical politics of William Cobbett. But Jane, then only eighteen, was forbidden to see the impoverished Spencer who was struggling to earn a living as a barrister. A miniature of her at that age reveals a proper Jane Austen heroine – all curls and muslin, wilful expression, large dark eyes and amused mouth – and on her twenty-first birthday she eloped through a drawing-room window dressed in riding clothes, and hurried with Spencer to East Grinstead where they were married.

That was the story they both delighted in telling. Nor was Spencer Perceval shy about confessing that their first home was in rented lodgings above a carpet shop in London's Bedford Row. According to his own account, after a wedding celebration at which £21-worth of port and sherry was consumed, they could afford to drink nothing more expensive than beer. Fortunately, Jane's father soon forgave his errant daughter and, as Perceval joyfully informed his friend Dudley Ryder, elder brother of Richard, 'He has also told me that he will make up her fortune to just what it would have been had she married with his consent. In short, everything that I could have wished and much more than I could have expected has concurred to make the step I have just taken the happiest and most prosperous event of my life.' But wine did not return to their table for several years.

In his early days as a lawyer, Samuel Romilly met Perceval frequently as they both ground out cases on the Midlands circuit between Nottingham and Birmingham. Charm and obstinacy were the qualities he remembered best. Perceval, he said, had been a high-spirited, half-educated young man 'with very little reading, of a conversation barren of instruction [and] with strong and invincible prejudices on many subjects . . . [Yet] by his excellent temper, his engaging manners, and his sprightly conversation, he was the delight of all that knew him.'

That blinkered vision of the world was derived from his father. The second Lord Egmont held strong views that ran clean contrary to the prevailing appetite for rationalism and enlightenment. What he wanted was the restoration of the absolute authority of monarch and Church together with the return of feudal society. It was said that when he built himself a mansion in the country, he designed it so that it could be defended by bow and arrow 'against the time in which the manufacture and use of gunpowder shall be forgotten'. Egmont died when his fifth child was only eight years old, an age when a boy is ready to take his father's beliefs as the bedrock of reality.

In the Whiggish opinion of Henry Brougham, Perceval's politics never really developed beyond that stage. His education at Harrow school left him with 'no information beyond what a classical education gives the common run of English youths'. His intellectual background was not materially altered by two years at Trinity College, Cambridge. And since the legal system was a conservative bastion, he found no reason to expand his views after he became a barrister. Any change from the status quo was, in his opinion, always for the worst.

'I am sorry to say,' Perceval declared to a lawyers' debating club in 1783, 'that we live at a time . . . when men adopt opinions as they choose their dresses, according to the mode of the hour, when nothing is followed but what is fashionable, and nothing esteemed fashionable but what is new'. Anyone who felt that it was 'desirable to preserve anything of our ancient and venerable establishments', he argued, had no choice but to resist 'every fresh attempt at innovation'. He was not expressing a mere point of view that might eventually be modified. It was a conviction that guided his life. To modify the social order was to tamper with God's estate.

Still in his twenties, he established his anti-liberal credentials beyond doubt by writing a pamphlet calling on magistrates to crack down on 'violations of the public peace', and by his own successful prosecution of the publisher of Tom Paine's *Rights of Man*, in the course of which he damned its democratic author as 'wicked, malicious, and ill-disposed'.

His income rapidly increased, partly from the law, partly from the interest on Jane's dowry, and partly from government sinecures that came his way such as the post of Clerk of the Irons and Surveyor of the Meltings in the Mint, which brought in £100 a year. Each time he returned home, however, Jane's passion and his excitement had their inevitable consequence. In the first fourteen years of their marriage, she gave birth to twelve children, eleven of whom survived, and the money went out almost as fast as it came in.

They had to rely on help from Perceval's brother to buy their next home, a semi-detached house in desirable Lincoln's Inn Fields, acquired in 1792. Eight years later, Perceval was wealthy enough to purchase the other half of it for his enormous family. In 1802, at the age of forty, he transferred from the criminal law to the more lucrative area of chancery law, dealing with property and commerce, and soon earned up to £10,000 a year. It allowed him to employ a coachman and liverymen clad in 'scarlet plush breeches'. He bought toys for the children, including a doll 'to dress and undress complete', from George Grosvenor's fashionable cosmetics and fashion shop in Chancery Lane. In search of fresh air for them, he and Jane first rented Belsize House and its park on the edge of Hampstead, at the time virtually in open country, then in 1807 bought a substantial manor in thirty-six acres of fields and parkland, Elm Grove in Ealing. By that date, he had become Chancellor of the Exchequer, and their town address was 10 Downing Street.

That Spencer Perceval would follow a political career was almost inevitable. Powerful families, like the Percevals, liked to have one of their kind in government to protect their interests, and from university onwards Perceval had gravitated naturally towards friends and colleagues, such as the Ryders, Charles Abbott and Samuel Romilly, who were parliamentarians in the making. And as would quickly become apparent, a rare combination of political and spiritual conviction gave him an almost limitless desire for power.

In 1796 his cousin, the earl of Northampton, found him a constituency in Northampton, conveniently within the Midlands law circuit. Although he had to fight an election, the earl's influence made victory certain. In the House of Commons, Perceval identified himself with the party of the Prime Minister, William Pitt the younger, out of which the modern Tory party was to grow.

From the moment he took his seat in the Commons among the followers of William Pitt, it is clear that Spencer Perceval fused the moral certainties of his faith with the expediencies of conservative politics as seamlessly as the Moral Majority in the United States wove its fundamentalism into the Republican programme almost two centuries later. But he did so at the very moment when steam was transforming Britain from an eighteenth-century rural society into a nineteenth-century industrial power.

Compared to the energy of wind or water, the power of the new machines was astonishing. Even a hostile observer like the American republican Thomas Jefferson, who visited Britain in 1784, was impressed. 'The most striking thing I saw there, new, was the application of the principle of the steam-engine to grist mills', he wrote in his journal. 'I saw 8 pair of [grinding-]stones which are worked by steam, and they are to set up 30 pair in the same house.'

What Jefferson did not mention was that each set of steam-driven grinding-stones put a traditional miller out of work. When the power of steam was applied to spinning, weaving and knitting, with enormous mechanical jennies, looms and stocking frames replacing hand-worked models, great numbers of skilled spinners, weavers and knitters found themselves deprived of a livelihood. Many left the countryside to find employment in the towns, others enlisted in the battalions of Captain Ned Ludd, but most went to work for a new, increasingly wealthy class, known generically as 'the manufacturers', who built and bought the great machines.

To be opposed to social change in such turbulent times was not a rare ambition. William Pitt himself had abandoned most of the liberal agenda of political reform and religious toleration he espoused in his early years. Alarmed by the democratic ideology spawned by the French Revolution in 1789, conservatives became convinced that any reform would constitute the first step on a road to mob rule. When war was declared against France in 1793, French ideas were seen to pose a greater, more insidious threat than French attack. To contain them, Pitt's government undertook a punitive programme curtailing civil liberties, including the suspension of habeas corpus, the censorship of printed material, and the severe restriction of public meetings.

Perceval committed himself to these measures with a passion that was evident in his first speech in the House of Commons. The country needed to be saved, he insisted, 'from the delusions of popular opinion, from the plausible fallacies of democratic theories . . . [and] from the spirit of democracy'. In 1798 he made a withering attack on the most effective of Pitt's opponents, the liberal Charles James Fox, who had called for 'a total and radical and fundamental reform of our late system'. Either Fox meant what he said, Perceval asserted, in which case he was encouraging 'revolutionary violence', or he meant tinkering with 'some parts of the system', thus showing himself to be a rhetorical windbag.

His attack was aimed at the man as much as the matter under discussion – a quality that became the hallmark of a Perceval speech – and its effectiveness marked him out. From the House of Lords,

Leveson-Gower deemed it 'incomparable', while William Pitt, a consummate debater himself, termed his speech 'in all respects one of the best I ever heard', and soon afterwards paid him an even greater tribute. Challenged to a duel in May that year by the Whig MP, George Tierney, for having accused him of 'a desire to obstruct the defence of this country', Pitt was asked who he felt should succeed him if he failed to survive Tierney's shot. 'He thought,' his second recorded solemnly, 'Mr Perceval was the most competent, and that he appeared the most equal to Mr. Fox.' Since both duellists missed their targets – Pitt intentionally firing his second shot in the air – the recommendation remained theoretical, but Perceval was on his way.

In public life, Perceval's adamant hostility to progress involved him in repeated confrontations. Within the walls of his house, on the other hand, his refusal to change anything and his unalloyed affection for his family promoted both harmony and happiness. His fourth son, John, carried into old age joyful memories of an untroubled childhood in Hampstead when he would dance with his mother and sisters in the dusty roadway to the tune of a barrel organ. As the childen grew older and more numerous they behaved increasingly like a tribe whose behaviour was ruled by unchanging rituals and precedents. Thus the entire family was united in the desire to keep everything the same.

The three eldest children were daughters, Jane, Frances (known as Fanny) and Maria, who operated as a trio, whether swooning over the same handsome man or skewering their father's political opponents with barbs of fizzing outrage. In 1809, at the height of a political scandal orchestrated by Gwillym Wardle, MP, over the sale of army commissions by the duke of York's mistress, Mrs Mary Clarke, eighteen-year-old Maria wrote to her brother, Spencer Perceval junior, then aged fifteen: 'Do not think by my silence on the subject that I am an unconcerned spectator of what is passing in the House of Commons. I assure you I am not but I have no remarks on it at present except that it is evidently false, that I hate and detest Mrs Clarke, a noisy toad, and that I am not over-partial to the Hon. Gentleman, Mr Wardle.' Her sisters were in total agreement. 'I think it was as clear as possible from the beginning that the Duke knew nothing about it,' Fanny, aged seventeen, told her brother, 'and that it was all an invention of that nasty wretch Clarke to get some money. Don't you hate her?'

They were in unison too about men. 'Fanny and I have found a most excellent, ridiculous and striking likeness,' Maria wrote excitedly after one of their father's uglier supporters had come to dinner with them in Downing Street, 'Mr Oldham in side-face to a fish. Any fish will do, but a cod particularly. He dined here the other day, and it was then we saw it. He opens and shuts his mouth just as fish do when they breathe.' And over an anonymous Greek god of a man known only as 'Him', all three were in a state of weak-kneed unanimity. At dances and visits to the ballet and theatre, they scanned the crowds for a glimpse of Him, and the then fifteen-year-old Maria was mortified when her two elder sisters met Him at a ball to which she had not been invited. Trying to divert her daughters from their endless discussion of His good looks, their mother invited an alternative attraction to dinner, the famously handsome Lord Granville Leveson-Gower, when he came back to London in 1805 from his duties as ambassador in St Petersburg.

'I never was so much disappointed except with Sir Arthur Wellesley,' Maria wrote scornfully. 'He is a tolerably good height, but he slouches horribly, and can that be compared to Him! His face is handsome enough, but his features are too pretty for a man and he is rather silly looking – and how can that possibly be compared to Him! Instead of His beautiful, exactly wellproportioned figure, he is too slim, and instead of

His lovely, divine, sensible, expressive face, he has a rather silly look.' In the face of her daughters' withering disdain, Jane threw in the towel, admitting that 'she never really thought him handsomer than Him'.

By comparison, the boys were duller and lazier, but on them too, Perceval lavished a warmth quite unlike the stereotypes of the remote Georgian father or the stern Victorian paterfamilias. Not even his incorrigibly idle, and unappreciative, eldest son, Spencer junior, could make him irritable. When George Butler, Harrow's new, reforming headmaster, complained that he could not get the boy out of bed in time for his classes, Perceval wrote back good-humouredly, 'Do not let that make you uneasy, for I can promise you that he is far more advanced than I was at his age.' He paid the boy's debts without quibble, and could hardly have chosen a more delicate way of reminding him to acknowledge the gift. 'Papa desired me to tell you,' Maria wrote in 1811 to her brother, then approaching his last year at Harrow, 'that, without goading your tender conscience too much, he thinks he might expect when he sends you money to pay your debts, and only desires you to send him a receipt, that you should do so. So pray send it.'

Even when he had become both Prime Minister and Chancellor of the Exchequer, and shouldered the burden of running a wartime government with a wafer-thin, occasionally non-existent majority, Perceval still found time in 1811 to buy his son an anthology of poetry and send it with a letter giving him the gentlest of nudges about the need to work harder: 'Remember this is the last year of your schooling, and I have always told you more may be done in the last year than in any of the five years which have preceded it.' It was written more in hope than in confidence. 'From your mother's account of the heat in which she has twice found you,' he ended sadly, 'I fear that football is upon the whole a more favourite pursuit with you than your books.'

The private side of his life proved impossible to separate from the political. Physically, there were Perceval children scattered through almost every room in the sprawling, knocked-together double house that existed behind the door of 10 Downing Street. Apart from the housemaids, kitchenmaids and footmen who lived under the rafters, the family occupied not only all of the modern top-floor flat but today's staterooms on the first floor as well. Spencer Perceval worked on the ground floor, but when Spencer junior at last came home with some worthwhile school exercises, his gratified father was promptly summoned upstairs and 'seemed very much pleased at seeing so many, and said they were worth coming up for'.

At home Jane and Spencer said prayers every day, and lived simply. In an era when fashionable society left London to take the waters expensively at Bath and other spas, and the Prince Regent's friends journeyed from the opulence of Carlton House to the gilded dome of the Royal Pavilion in Brighton, the Percevals preferred to spend their free time together, either in Downing Street or at weekends in Elm Grove in Ealing. He gave generously and privately to charity, supporting the poor through donations to individuals and to organisations like the Shoreditch Refuge for the Destitute. When his friend, Dudley Ryder, later Lord Harrowby, lost £800 gambling at faro, Perceval wrote reprovingly to him, 'Only suppose that instead of having flung these £800 into the sink of a Pharaoh-bank, you had distributed them in equal shares to 80 poor housekeepers . . . How many units go to make that sum, 80 families with suppose only 4 to a family – 320 fellow creatures – think of it a little in its detail, of widows, orphans etc. raised from a pinching state of penury to a comfortable existence.'

His personal behaviour was all the more admirable when contrasted with that of other politicians. The haughty Marquess of Wellesley, for example, was so notorious for neglecting his business as foreign secretary in favour of his mistresses that even Wellington, his own brother, exclaimed, 'I wish that Wellesley was castrated or that he would, like other people, attend to his business and perform too.' For Perceval, the idea of 'performing' outside the marriage bed would have been unthinkable. 'Tricking in love and tricking the public are both unquestionably immoral,' he told the opposition MP, George Tierney, making a connection between private and public integrity that few in his time took seriously.

Yet, even at that period, the Prime Minister's obviously happy family produced an undeniable political advantage. Everyone recognised that he was, in the words of *The Courier*, 'at once an attentive husband, a fond and instructive father, an affectionate friend and an active servant of the public'. And Perceval had no compunction about using his private image to sway public opinion in favour of his policies. It was a tactic that infuriated his political opponents.

'You spend a great deal of ink about the character of the present Prime Minister,' the progressive-minded clergyman, Sydney Smith, wrote in his satire, *Peter Plymley's Letters*, addressed supposedly to a Perceval supporter. 'Grant you all that you write – I say, I fear he will pursue a line of policy destructive to the true interest of his country: and then you tell me, he is faithful to Mrs. Perceval, and kind to the Master Percevals! These are, undoubtedly, the first qualifications to be looked to in a time of the most serious public danger; but somehow or another (if public and private virtues must always be incompatible), I should prefer that he . . . whipped his boys, and saved his country.'

Sydney Smith's Whig readers laughed, and quoted his clever phrase as a criticism. They failed to appreciate the political calculation in Perceval's widely publicised domesticity. More astutely William Cobbett commented on the Prime Minister's shrewdness in building a reputation on 'the fact that he was wont to go to church, every Sunday, with a large quarto gilt prayer-book under one arm, his wife hanging on the other, and followed by a long brood of children'. However much he disliked innovation, Perceval became the first British politician to demonstrate how to exploit a happy family in the race for political power. To that extent, the principles that guided his private life are inseparable from his assassination.

A Prime Minister Put There by Providence

Most people believe that the danger to the constitution of this country arises from the spirit of democracy.

Spencer Perceval to the Benchers of Lincoln's Inn, 1802

At 7 a.m. on Thursday, 14 May, John Bellingham awoke 'obviously refreshed and,' according to Newman's report, 'apparently unaffected by the unfortunate circumstances of his situation'. He washed, shaved, and had his usual breakfast of sweet tea and bread. Later in the day, he would lunch heartily on minced veal, boiled potatoes and a pint of porter. Soon afterwards he was visited by Charles Litchfield, the Treasury solicitor, who informed him that he would be tried for the murder of Spencer Perceval the following day.

This extraordinary rush to judgement, allowing the lapse of just three days from the charge of murder, and less than forty-eight hours from the appointment of a lawyer to represent him, represented the triumph of the political agenda over the criminal investigation. It also made a travesty of the trial. Since Bellingham's solicitor needed to summon witnesses from Liverpool, and to call on expert testimony on the matter of insanity, the government's timetable prevented the preparation of any adequate defence. Harmer's legal colleagues reminded him sympathetically that had his client been charged with treason, the law would have required a minimum of fifteen days between the charge and the trial in order to give both prosecution and defence time to assemble their evidence.

The legal profession was not alone in being outraged. Those most frustrated by the government's indecent haste to kill the murderer were the late Prime Minister's closest companions. They more than anyone else needed to understand why Spencer Perceval had been murdered. To Robert Plumer Ward, it was a catastrophe beyond reason, so profound that it challenged the very idea of a benign God. In his novel, *Tremaine*, he put his doubts into the mouth of the main protagonist: 'that such a man, the delight of his friends, the adoration of his family, the admiration of his opponents; that one so mild, yet so brave; so single-hearted, yet so keen, should be cut off by murder . . . that such a thing should be, leads for ever to despair of that protection from Heaven, which . . . is afforded to mankind'. The Prime Minister's assassination had to have a meaning or serve a purpose, otherwise everything became meaningless and purposeless.

What gave Spencer Perceval's killing this resonance was his faith. Writing to George Butler, the headmaster of Harrow, the Prime Minister once said that his ambition for his eldest son was that he should be 'a champion of true religion in a careless world'. By this, he meant something quite specific. The true religion was that of the Evangelical Anglicans who in the 1780s had begun to shake an almost moribund Church of England into new life. Although divided in their methods – the brothers John and Charles Wesley preached to thousands in the open air, whereas the father and son pairing of Henry and John Venn restricted their message to middle-class church congregations – the founding Evangelicals were united in holding that true belief came from an immediate, personal experience of God, to be found in the Bible and expressed through action. It was a physical rather than an intellectual faith

– 'Experience,' declared Henry Venn, 'is a living proof, stronger than a thousand arguments' – and, unlike the careless world that agreed with Lord Melbourne's clever dictum that 'Things are coming to a pretty pass when religion is allowed to invade private life', Evangelicals believed that the whole point of religion was to transform both private and public life.

The word they used to describe God working in the world was 'Providence', and any action that made the world a better place was therefore termed providential. The spread of civilisation itself and the general improvement of mankind through laws and moral education could therefore be taken as evidence of a divinely ordered creation. 'God has so assigned to things their general tendencies,' declared William Wilberforce, a standard-bearer for the faith, 'and established such an order of causes and effects, as . . . loudly proclaim the principles of his moral government, and strongly suggest that vice and imprudence will finally terminate in misery'.

Thus to be good was not enough. In order to help the work of Providence, it was necessary to do good. 'Action is the life of virtue,' wrote Hannah More, the Evangelical poet and friend of Wilberforce, 'and the world is the theatre of action.' It was not just the Church of England that needed to be actively reformed, but society itself had to be cleaned up. Consequently, some Evangelicals, and especially the followers of the Wesleys who broke with the Church of England to form the Methodist Union, became radicals devoting their lives to the poorest in society.

At first glance, Perceval seemed an unlikely adherent to such a faith. Like so many other guiding principles in his life, however, his Evangelical beliefs originated with his father's example. The second Lord Egmont favoured the spread of Bible-based religion, not least because it would counter any desire among the lower classes for material progress. Other Evangelicals, including Wilberforce, took a similarly conservative view. Although they attacked slavery, few criticised the horrific conditions of factory-workers or the squalid housing of the poor. Political radicals jibed, not altogether fairly, that Evangelicals preferred 'to look abroad for examples of cruelty and oppression' in order to avoid tackling social injustice at home.

The faith that he had inherited moved to the centre of Perceval's life in 1796 soon after the birth of his eldest son, Spencer junior. The baby fell seriously ill, and seemed likely to die until, in despair, both Spencer and Jane knelt to pray for his recovery. Almost at once the child started to improve and, as Perceval reported to Dudley Ryder, 'by the blessing of God our boy was restored to us'. After that he never doubted. When he entered Parliament later that year in the September election, he did so in the assurance that he was to be an agent of Providence.

Perceval's political ascent was rapid, and he owed it not just to his speeches against change but to an unremitting hostility to Catholics, another symptom of his Evangelical beliefs. It led directly to his first promotion to be Solicitor General in 1801. Pitt had brought Ireland into the United Kingdom in order to prevent it becoming the backdoor for a French invasion. But when he attempted to repeal the anti-Catholic legislation that banned 80 per cent of Ireland's population from holding office as magistrates, army officers and MPs, Pitt ran into George III's adamant opposition. Forced to resign, Pitt handed over to his picked successor, the anti-Catholic, Henry Addington, who did not hesitate to appoint Perceval to the second most important law office in the cabinet.

As a minister Perceval won the approval of both Addington and the king. In 1802 he successfully prosecuted the Irish-born Colonel Edward Despard for treason, despite clear evidence that the colonel had been entrapped by government informers. Ignoring the jury's strong recommendation for mercy, the judge, Lord Ellenborough, then sentenced Despard and a confederate 'to be hanged by the neck, but not until you are dead; for while you are still living your bodies are to be taken down, your bowels torn out and burned before your faces, your heads then cut off, and your bodies divided each into four quarters, and your heads and quarters to be then at the King's disposal; and may the Almighty God have mercy on your souls!' The hangman proved more merciful, and allowed Despard to swing for twelve and a half minutes, long enough to ensure he was utterly dead, before cutting him down and chopping off his head. The disembowelling was dispensed with.

Having demonstrated his anti-Irish credentials, Perceval reinforced his anti-liberal reputation by prosecuting William Cobbett for an article he published in the *Political Register* criticising the government's Irish policy. As was his habit, Perceval attacked the person rather than the principle. 'Gentlemen,' he demanded of the jury with an arrogance that only a peer's son would attempt, 'who is Mr. Cobbett? Is he a man writing purely from motives of patriotism? *Quis homo hic est? Quo patre natus?* [Who is this man? Who's his father?].' Before being found guilty by a sycophantic jury, Cobbett had enough time to study his prosecutor, and retorted with a disparaging comment of his own, describing Perceval as 'a sort of understrapper to the Attorney-General . . . a short, spare, pale-faced, hard, keen, sour-looking man with a voice well-suited to the rest'.

When William Pitt returned to office in May 1804 after the collapse of Addington's administration, Perceval had his reward, promotion from understrapper to Attorney General. He was now back in the cabinet, but with too little influence to be more than a small fish in the parliamentary pond. Yet when his Evangelical friends looked at his career, this was the point where they recognised it to be unmistakably providential, a 'blessing' as Wilberforce put it, in the sense of being divinely shaped to achieve good.

Regardless of their class or politics, Evangelicals were united in their desire to achieve one good in particular. Their commitment to it was both humanitarian and the inevitable outgrowth of their belief that to find God was, in Charles Wesley's phrase, to be 'a slave redeemed from death and hell'. As a group they were unique in mainstream Christianity in finding slavery so morally abhorrent that destruction of the trade in humans had come to be of paramount importance.

The greatest demand for captured Africans came from plantations in the Americas and the Caribbean: in the southern states of the United States, the crop was cotton, and the work planting and picking, but elsewhere, in Brazil, Cuba and Europe's colonies in the West Indies, it was the near-factory requirements of sugar growing, cutting and refining that created the need for slave labour. In 1790 a total of almost 1.5 million slaves were held west of the Atlantic, but to meet the growing demand for the raw products of the plantations, and to make good the deaths that resulted from the cruelties practised especially by sugar growers, about 70,000 more were shipped across the ocean every year.

Slavery had existed since the earliest records were made, and however deplorable it was as a practice, to condemn it appeared to fly in the face of history. Tactically, therefore, its opponents sidestepped the institution and focused on the transport as the most vulnerable link in the system. The shipping was supplied by some six hundred vessels, especially adapted to carry cargoes of around 250 slaves lying prone and chained side by side. Their hulls were designed for maximum speed to reduce the extravagant death toll from disease and despair. Almost half of these specialised ships were registered in Britain, and about two hundred sailed out of Liverpool.

The Evangelicals' attack on the trade was carried out on many levels, through leaflets, public meetings, sugar boycotts and preaching, but its cutting edge was the political campaign. Its roots were in Clapham, where Henry and John Venn preached, and where many of the politicians most fervently committed to the cause lived. With unwavering persistence William Wilberforce, as leader of the Clapham Sect, or the Saints, had introduced a bill in Parliament almost every year from 1790 to abolish the trade, and on every occasion it failed. The fault lay not just with the lack of support in the Commons, but with the reluctance of the Prime Minister to give it his backing.

William Pitt had repeatedly expressed his sympathy for Wilberforce's attempts to ban the slave trade, but in practice would never confront the West India lobby, the powerful group representing the shippers who carried slaves from Africa, and the sugar planters in the Caribbean who bought them. Nor was anyone in cabinet sufficiently committed to the cause to push it forward. A note that Wilberforce made in his diary in 1805 was therefore of considerable significance: 'I have hopes Perceval will still prove a blessing in a high station.'

Perceval's hostility to slavery and its trade was of no conceivable interest to the millions who hated him and rejoiced at his murder. Nevertheless it was as integral to his beliefs as his die-hard opposition to change. From his first involvement as Attorney General he brought to it the same combination of moral passion and political cunning that infuriated Catholics and reformers, and by the time of his murder his efforts had saved as many as forty thousand Africans from shipment across the ocean into slavery. There was sound reason for Evangelicals to feel that his career must be providential, and for the question that occurred so urgently to them – How could Providence allow such a force for good to be eliminated?

In the summer of 1805 the Attorney General justified Wilberforce's optimism by finding a typically roundabout means of achieving a good end. As the government's law officer, Perceval pointed out that it would be possible to restrict the trade without recourse to new legislation. Instead of aiming at a complete ban on the trade, as Wilberforce had done in thirteen earlier bills, Perceval concentrated only on the new colony of Guiana, modern-day Guyana, recently captured in the course of the war. After a policy meeting with supporters in June 1805, Wilberforce made another note in his diary: 'Guiana slave-trade, Attorney-General Perceval honest, warm, steady and intelligent on the subject.'

Formerly a Dutch possession, Guiana had been taken because the Netherlands were allied to France. It was chosen as a target because up to fifteen thousand slaves were expected to be brought in to work the virgin, sugar-bearing soil. Pitt was too sick and physically worn out to conduct a bruising battle in Parliament, but Wilberforce's next diary entry indicated the tactic Perceval intended to employ: 'Busy with [James] Stephen and Attorney-General on Order in Council.'

An Order in the Privy Council allowed the government to adjust existing policy without the need for parliamentary approval. Unlike an Act, it was open to legal challenge and in the long term usually had to be backed by legislation, but as a temporary measure it took immediate effect. Perceval convinced the Prime Minister that such an Order could be used to ban the trade to Guiana on the grounds that it merely modified the regulations for the island's government. In August 1805, relieved of the need to introduce new legislation, Pitt finally committed his government to the abolitionist cause by issuing an Order in Council banning the import of slaves to Guiana. At a stroke, a trade that had already carried six thousand slaves in its first year was made illegal. But six months later William Pitt died and his Tory government collapsed.

The election that followed in 1806 was dominated by the single issue of the slave trade. It returned a majority of Members of Parliament committed to its abolition, and the one notable achievement of the Whig ministry formed under Lord Grenville was to pass the legislation in 1807 that finally banned British involvement in the slave trade. On the opposition benches, Perceval showed that he could still be a blessing to the cause. With the Grenville ministry on the verge of collapse, and the bill not yet passed by the House of Lords, Perceval intervened with the Tory peers and persuaded them individually not to block the legislation.

By then, it was clear how formidable Perceval had become as a politician. What made him uniquely effective, in a way that Wilberforce could never be, was his ruthlessness. To achieve ends he decided were right, he would adopt whatever means were at hand, regardless of the consequences. That there really were no limits he had demonstrated in his defence of the Princess of Wales, Caroline of Brunswick.

In 1806 the princess, who had separated from her husband, the future George IV, was alleged by close friends to have given birth to a son by an unknown lover. The allegations would have been explosive enough in her role as wife to the future king, but the unpopularity of the Prince of Wales and her own good looks, especially her 'quick, glancing, penetrating eyes . . . and a remarkably delicately formed mouth', gave Caroline a popular celebrity that made her the people's princess. The alleged affair not only became the subject of intense political argument but inflamed the public's contempt for the Prince of Wales. In an attempt to limit the damage, the new Prime Minister, Lord Grenville, who also happened to be a friend of the prince, immediately launched a high-powered investigation into the alleged affair.

The findings of the inquiry were politically convenient for Grenville and the Whigs. It decided that the princess was guilty of unbecoming conduct, especially in her flirtatious behaviour with unmarried men, but cleared her of bearing a child. Perceval, however, decided that the libertine prince was really to blame for having sent her away from court. In a moral crusade that had the added political convenience of embarrassing the government, he took up Caroline's cause.

First he compiled a minority report that exonerated the princess, and implicitly blamed the prince, then he had five thousand copies printed as pamphlets and held ready for distribution. At that point, Perceval let it be known that he intended to put them on sale unless the princess was publicly received back in court as an innocent woman. The Prince of Wales was said to have responded by swearing 'with most offensive personal abuse, and an oath which cannot be recited, that he felt he could jump on [Perceval], and stamp out his life with his feet'. Nevertheless, the blackmail was effective. Early in 1807 the princess was allowed back in court, and Perceval set a match to a bonfire of his pamphlets in Lincoln's Inn Fields.

In March Grenville's brief government collapsed, and in recognition of the influence he now commanded Perceval was appointed Chancellor of the Exchequer in the new Tory administration under the duke of Portland, and its leader in the House of Commons. In this position, Perceval suddenly became of supreme importance to the abolition campaign.

Even Wilberforce understood that making the slave trade illegal was only the first step. Unless the traders were physically stopped from reaching the coast of Africa, they would continue to buy humans as commodities. To enforce the law, a police force was needed on the high seas, incentives had to be offered for the arrest of law-breakers, a court was required in west Africa to try those charged with breaking the law, and an identification system for existing slaves had to be set up to prevent new ones being smuggled in. Each of these measures was expensive, none was popular, and so all required political clout to push them through. Whatever his gratitude to Grenville's ministry for passing the Abolition Act,

Wilberforce had no hesitation in pledging his loyalty to the new government. 'My principles would govern my vote,' he confessed to his diary, 'even if I did not think so favourably of . . . Perceval as I do.'

His good opinion was justified. Within the cabinet, the Chancellor of the Exchequer would become the scourge of the flourishing though now illegal slave trade. Indeed for the next five years, until the day he was shot, no one did more to give teeth to the Abolition Act than Spencer Perceval.

To the Evangelical mind, Perceval's final promotion to Prime Minister raised the extraordinary possibility that Providence intended to use him to end not just the trade but slavery itself. At least three of his colleagues in Portland's cabinet were not only younger, but more talented and experienced: Viscount Castlereagh, Lord Hawkesbury, shortly to become the second earl of Liverpool, and George Canning. The last two were both to become Prime Minister, but Perceval reached the top of the greasy pole ahead of them. Although not obvious, his personal abilities were effective. The ruthlessness that he demonstrated in defence of the princess was well disguised by his personal charm. He had neither intelligence nor depth, but his absence of doubt won him political battles that a cleverer man might have lost. And, as Charles Arbuthnot, the veteran Treasury secretary, remarked when Perceval finally manoeuvred his way into the premiership, 'He has the best regulated ambition I ever witnessed.'

He possessed, however, another, greater advantage. During the confusing cavalcade that saw five different administrations hold office in the seven years after 1801, the king became increasingly aware of Perceval's entrenched attitudes and happy domestic life. They reflected almost exactly the priorities that George III looked for in a minister and a man. When Castlereagh and Canning took themselves out of the running for the leadership by fighting a duel in the summer of 1809, the king no longer hesitated.

In October 1809, with Portland only three weeks from death, George III wrote to the one politician who shared all his views about the various dangers presented by Napoleon, Catholics and reform: 'Mr Perceval's conduct has so fully confirmed the impression which the King had early received of his zeal and abilities, of the honourable principles by which he is invariably activated, that His Majesty cannot pause in the choice of the person he should intrust a situation at all times most important, but particularly so under the present arduous circumstances.'

That Providence should have promoted Spencer Perceval to become Prime Minister at the age of forty-seven only to allow him to be shot less than three years later challenged the deepest beliefs of the Saints. 'Of all the cases in which man seems to have been abandoned by Heaven, and which leave the upholder of Providence without hope,' Ward wrote in *Tremaine*, 'I have always thought this the clearest.' His bewilderment is forgivable. Unless John Bellingham was so mad as to make his actions entirely unpredictable, there had to be an explanation. One answer lay in the very ascendancy that appeared so providential to the Evangelicals.

The Pervasive Power of Little P

If, therefore, we can accomplish our purposes, it will come to this, that either those countries will have no trade, or they must be content to accept it through us.

Spencer Perceval explaining the goal
of the Orders in Council, 1807

The choice of Spencer Perceval in 1809 as Prime Minister, so obvious to George III, came as a surprise to almost everyone else. The radical MP, Henry Hunt, only slightly exaggerated when he recorded in his memoirs, 'Mr. Perceval, an insignificant lawyer, now suddenly became First Lord of the Treasury, and Chancellor of the Exchequer, to the astonishment of the whole nation.' Tory peers, familiar with the difficulties faced by the duke of Portland, had advised the king to select the new Prime Minister from the Commons, and the clear favourite was the clever, ambitious George Canning, who had a personal following of about twenty MPs. By the most generous count, Perceval appeared able to rely on just five votes.

Behind his back, cabinet colleagues referred to him as 'little Perceval', while the Lord Chancellor, Lord Eldon, diminished him further by calling him 'little P'. His lack of influence was reflected in the reluctance of former ministers to serve in his cabinet. Not only did Canning prefer to sit on the backbenches, he was followed there by William Huskisson, the financial genius who had guided Perceval's policy as Chancellor of the Exchequer under the duke of Portland. Acknowledging the significance of losing him, Perceval exclaimed, 'This is the worst and most unexpected stroke of all.'

The absence of any other candidate willing to take on the job left Perceval with no option but to double up the chancellor's portfolio with the Prime Minister's. Four times in the first months after taking office, his makeshift government was defeated in the House of Commons, and there was a general expectation that one of his rivals, Canning or Liverpool, or even his predecessor Lord Grenville, must shortly take over.

The king refused to have second thoughts, however, telling Perceval that he had 'drawn his line, and no prospect of harrassment or opposition shall induce him to stray from it'. This was, as Perceval remarked, 'very fine, firm and noble – but not very helpful'. Yet, as awareness of the King's unwavering commitment to his new Prime Minister filtered through Parliament, it produced an effect that virtually made up for Perceval's own lack of a personal following.

Royal approval was the invisible glue that held a parliamentary majority together. Its adhesive effect was felt most strongly by the heart of the Commons, the roughly one hundred and twenty 'country gentlemen' with independent incomes who spent most of the year on their estates. When they came to Westminster, it was to represent the patriotic instincts of their patrons and fellow property-owners where important legislation was concerned. With the additional support of about eighty government office-holders, and a shifting number of MPs anxious to secure a government job for themselves or their family, Perceval could eventually count on a majority for the most crucial measures. But for day-to-day votes, it was his personal reputation that came to weigh most heavily.

Parliament usually only sat from January to June or July. Even in session, its business began in late afternoon when the working day was almost over, and continued if necessary into the early morning. Most of its deliberations took place in a building lit by huge banks of candles, hanging in candelabra from the dark, vaulted ceilings, or standing in tall sticks above the green benches of the chamber, or arranged in sconces along its shadowy corridors. The windows often had to be kept shut, for, with the regularity of the rising and falling tide, the Thames carried the sewage of almost one million Londoners up and down outside its walls. Trapped in the fetid, oxygen-starved atmosphere of the chamber, MPs listened to the rhetoric of the front benches emerging from circles of golden candlelight amid the gloom. In such surroundings, finely honed arguments rarely carried as much weight as the character of the speaker and the interests he represented.

Thus Perceval's irreproachable personal behaviour, well publicised by his friends, was crucial to his success. In 1810 the independent newspaper, *The Day*, decided that 'in these times of imputed corruption when everything is supposed to be vendible' they would rate leading politicians on a trustworthiness table measuring them against the value of a pound. Canning was judged to be 'worth a song', Castlereagh 'a bad shilling', and Tierney's price was 'known only to his political friends', but Perceval was valued at 25s, a premium of 20 per cent above par, making him the most trustworthy commoner in Parliament.

In the jaundiced view of Henry Hunt, the moral ascendancy that Spencer Perceval came to exercise over the country gentlemen and the government's placemen led directly to his assassination. 'It was the protection that he was sure of receiving, from a corrupt majority of a corrupt and packed House of Commons,' Hunt declared, 'that induced him to persevere in denying justice to Mr. Bellingham; and if ever a man received the reward of his own injustice, it was Mr. Perceval.' Hunt was a far from disinterested spectator, but his suggestion that outright control of the Commons corrupted Perceval's judgement is worth picking out. Writing to Wellington in Spain in the summer of 1811, Lord Liverpool declared the Prime Minister's command to be 'completely established in the House of Commons; he has acquired an authority there beyond any minister in my recollection, except Mr Pitt.' Not by chance was Wellington the person told, because one vital element that underpinned Perceval's authority was his unquestionable effectiveness as a war leader.

Viewed down the long avenue of two centuries of history, the significance of his premiership has diminished to near-invisibility. But in the judgement of the *Dictionary of National Biography*, by the day of his death Perceval had 'carried on the government single-handed, prosecuted the war, defeated his opponents and disarmed his critics'. That is a notable record, achieved during the most dangerous days of the Napoleonic war. Not until the summer of 1940, when Winston Churchill's government confronted a Nazi government in full control of Western Europe, would a British Prime Minister have to deal with a power comparable to that facing Spencer Perceval in 1809. Having defeated the Prussians at Jena in 1806, the Austrians at Wagram three years later, and then occupied Vienna, Napoleon's armies bestrode the continent from Spain to the borders of the Russian empire, and from Sicily to Sweden. And just as Britain's capitulation seemed the most probable outcome in 1940 following the failure of the campaign in Norway, so did the expulsion of British forces from Corunna and their defeat in the Walcheren expedition in 1809 appear to extinguish its last military opposition to Napoleon.

Unfortunately for his reputation in history, Perceval's leadership lacked both Churchill's flair and his rhetoric. But to his parliamentary colleagues, his command seemed peerless.

Efficiency was what Perceval prized. In 1809 he had no hesitation in sacking Lord Chatham, the ineffective general of the forty thousand troops despatched to Walcheren island in the Netherlands, who had achieved nothing but the loss of half his force to malaria. The Prime Minister battled equally hard in 1810 to keep in office the duke of York, the army's commander-in-chief and its most energetic and effective organiser, after he was found to have sold military commissions through his mistress, the 'noisy toad', Mary Ann Clarke. Despite the scandal, and his own disapproval of 'tricking in marriage', Perceval restored the duke as soon as possible, an event triumphantly announced in 1811 by Fanny Perceval – 'the dear duke of York has at last had justice done to him and he is what (in my opinion) he ought always to have been, Commander-in-Chief'.

His greatest achievement, and one that ultimately proved decisive in swinging the military balance against Napoleon, was to keep Sir Arthur Wellesley and a British army in the Iberian Peninsula when every financial and military expert pressed for their recall. That Perceval never received credit for this success was because it grew out of a cheese-paring approach to the dreary business of public finance. Neither a reformer nor an innovator, he was dogged, industrious, and above all committed to making the existing system work. Indeed nothing demonstrated better the single-minded, blinkered drive that encouraged people to contemplate murdering him than his success as Chancellor of the Exchequer.

The nature of the challenge he faced was obvious to both supporters and opponents. From 1807 to 1812 Perceval had to find enough money to cover the costs of the Royal Navy at £19 million a year and the army at £17 million, as well as paying annual subsidies averaging £3 million to keep Portugal, Prussia, Saxony and Austria in the war against France. Since this wartime annual expenditure of almost £40 million represented about three-quarters of the total national budget, it strained the financial resources of the country to breaking point.

Even under William Pitt, the great financial reformer, who

introduced income tax and levies on items like houses, windows and hats, it had not been possible to squeeze much more than £23 million from personal taxation. Another £24 million came from permanent taxes such as customs and excise duties. But the 1806 budget, the first after Pitt's death, projected an estimated expenditure of £68 million, leaving an enormous gap of £20 million that had to be filled by borrowing.

Where Perceval excelled was in squeezing. As Chancellor of the Exchequer in Portland's ministry, he pressed the Bank of England and City financiers to reduce their gouging fees for handling government finance, and forced the Bank to make an interest-free loan of £3 million repayable only after peace was restored as compensation for past profiteering. With the help of William Huskisson, the financial wizard who as Treasury secretary was responsible for war finance, Perceval tightened the Treasury's auditing system, clearing up a backlog of accounts reaching back to 1776; slashed wastage from the notoriously inefficient military bureaucracy, including an inflated barracks building programme; appointed his own private secretary, Michael Herries, to cut through the mass of corruption that bloated the army's commissariat; and sent teams of auditors to flush out unpaid arrears of revenue from the ports, bringing in £100,000 from Ipswich alone and another £30,000 from Bristol.

Under his relentless prodding, Treasury auditors generated a torrent of reports written in a clerkly sloping hand, most of which Perceval insisted on checking himself. He presided over twice-weekly Board of Treasury conferences, as well as daily cabinet meetings, and constantly urged his colleagues to behave less extravagantly. The nagging insistence on efficiency had its effect. Expenditure came down to nearly £54 million a year in 1807, and remained near that level throughout his lifetime, and annual borrowing was reduced to around £11 million.

The military importance of Perceval's parsimonious accountancy while Chancellor of the Exchequer was revealed in 1809 when he became Prime Minister, and virtually every economic expert warned him that the country could no longer afford to fund Sir Arthur Wellesley's small army in Portugal, the sole remaining British force on the continent. It cost £2.5 million a year to finance his operations, and the absence of banking facilities in Portugal meant that most of it had to be paid in silver dollars which could only be bought in sufficient numbers in South America and China. Not only did the added cost and complexity threaten to break Britain's tightly stretched economy, critics pointed out that despite the expense Wellesley remained pinned in a remote southwest corner of the Iberian peninsula.

'To carry on the war on the present scale of expense with the ordinary means of the country, or anything approaching to it,' the knowledge-able George Rose wrote with italicised urgency in November 1809 'is *utterly impossible*'. Military expenditure had to be cut by one-third, he warned, or the whole economy would begin to collapse. In effect, the Peninsula campaign must be ended. Rose's call was supported by the entire Whig opposition, as well as many Tory supporters on the back-benches. Even Richard Wellesley, Arthur's elder brother and Perceval's Foreign Secretary, privately condemned 'the impolicy of sending a regular English army to act permanently in Spain'.

Impervious to this mounting barrage of criticism, both military and financial, Perceval insisted that the Peninsula force remain in the field, whatever the cost, and he signalled his approval by persuading the king to make Sir Arthur Wellesley a viscount, taking the name of Wellington. But by the spring of 1810, Rose's dire fore-cast seemed to be justified. The exchange rate plummeted, the price of gold rose, and the value of a pound note fell – the classic signs of inflation running out of control.

A parliamentary inquiry, the Bullion committee, blamed the Bank of England for printing too many notes in order to cover the excess in government expenditure. The cure that it recommended was convertibility, keeping the value of a pound note equal to the value of a gold sovereign so that paper could always be converted to metal. Crudely speaking, this would require the government to reduce the number of notes sharply and to cut its own spending drastically. It was a recommendation supported by, among others, David Ricardo, the outstanding economist of the day, the doyen of City banking, Sir Francis Baring, and the fiscal wizard, William Huskisson, Perceval's former colleague.

Although admitting 'he was aware that he was not as well informed on the question as he hoped yet to be', Perceval was quite clear about the implication of the Bullion committee's proposed remedy: not only did it mean the end of Wellington's expensive campaign, but an acceptance that the country could not afford to wage war in Europe. It was, he said, 'tantamount to a Parliamentary declaration that we must submit to any terms of peace rather than continue the war'. Grimly declaring that 'I retain all the ignorance and [remain] under all the prejudice which influenced me', he flatly rejected its recommendation. Wellington's men would stay in the field. Yet no sooner had Perceval stated his position than the stakes were raised higher still.

In the summer of 1810, Wellington abruptly announced that the cost of the Peninsular army had doubled to £5 million. Even he, normally unconcerned about the storm of criticism at home, felt compelled to promise his supportive Prime Minister that he was doing his best not to overspend. Unperturbed, Perceval replied that he was sure Wellington must already have made all possible economies, knowing 'that the failure of our pecuniary means is one of the most probable causes of our being compelled to discontinue our assistance to the Peninsula'. Consequently, he could assure Wellington of his 'perfect and unaffected reliance upon you'.

That September, however, the Bullion committee published its report, and the stark warning of economic collapse produced a panic in the City. The value of a basket of blue-chip stocks dropped 10 per cent in two days. Abraham Goldsmid, the government's senior broker, who was holding £2 million worth of stocks, found himself facing bankruptcy. On 28 September he committed suicide by cutting his throat. The next day the stock exchange was in melt-down. 'We think this,' *The Day* reported with some restraint, 'one of the most trying circumstances in which the Government of this country was ever placed.'

At that point a more rational Prime Minister might have thrown in the towel. On the continent, Napoleon had destroyed Britain's coalition with Austria, so expensively put together the year before. Two of its former members, Sweden and Russia, had actually declared war on Britain, and Austria's place in the French camp was confirmed by Napoleon's marriage to the Archduchess Marie-Louise. Worst of all, Wellington's latest attempt to break out from his corner in Portugal had failed.

In the autumn of 1810, he again retreated with his ruinously expensive army behind the Torres Vedras, the line of fortifications he had built along a range of hills outside Lisbon. Territorially, he had gained nothing. London gossip was dominated by the defeatist opinions of 'croakers' – serving officers who had returned from the Peninsula convinced that Wellington could achieve nothing. And the markets had lost all confidence in a government committed to keeping such an ineffective force in the field at the expense of the nation's economy. Commonsense dictated that the Prime Minister should restore confidence at a stroke by announcing his intention to bring Wellington home.

Among the threads leading to the Prime Minister's murder, one

of the most notable was the motive that made Perceval so determined to defy the best financial advice and every logical argument,
and insist on keeping an army in Portugal.

The absence of reason from the Prime Minister's calculations has
encouraged historians to write his contribution out of the narrative
of Wellington's military triumph. But without Perceval's irrational
conviction that he was right, Wellington's victorious Peninsula
campaign would not have happened.

The whole of Spencer Perceval's political life was spent in the
shadow of the French Revolution, and he responded to it in a quite
specific way. The conventional Tory response was expressed by
Edmund Burke who condemned the revolution for attempting to
replace a flawed system with an experiment in democracy, which
was bound to lead to mob tyranny. 'Of this I am certain,' Burke
asserted, 'in a democracy the majority of the citizens is capable of
exercising the most cruel oppressions upon the minority . . . and
that oppression of the minority will extend to far greater numbers
and will be carried on with much greater fury than can almost ever
be apprehended from the dominion of a single scepter'. For him as
for most Tories, the French Revolution was a political failure. For
Perceval it was quite simply a manifestation of evil.

Since even evil was part of God's plan, the temporary success of
French armies against the Catholic powers of Spain, Austria and
Italy must serve a divine purpose – 'they [the French] have been
raised up by Providence for the overthrow of popish superstitions,'
the Prime Minister confided to a friend, 'for, with some few excep-
tions which may have been permitted to prevent this object of
God's Providence from being too strikingly apparent, you will find
their progress most destructive where the popish superstitions most
prevailed'. In the long run, however, Providence always worked to
improve the world, and so the French in turn would inevitably be

defeated. Perceval's confidence in this outcome sprang from an unexpected source. It was prophesied in the Book of Daniel, as he explained in a pamphlet published in 1800, *Observations intended to put the Application of a Prophecy in the eleventh Chapter of the Book of Daniel to the French Power*.

The particular part of chapter eleven that interested him was Daniel's vision of an epic war between 'the king of the north', easily identified with Britain, and 'the king of the south', clearly meaning France. What made it especially attractive was that it predicted victory for the king of the north. His trust in Daniel's prophecies was shared with his brother-in-law, Thomas Walpole, and together they regularly consulted the Bible for prophecies that would throw light on difficult policy decisions. He and Walpole were in complete agreement, for example, that the passage in the Book of Revelation about 'the woman who rides upon the beast, who is drunk with the blood of the saints, the mother of harlots', could only refer to their enemies on the other side of the Channel. The major difference between them was that Perceval felt sure she was Napoleon, whereas Walpole, who must have been something of a literalist, argued that being female she was probably France. On a lesser point, Walpole was convinced that the Pope was the entire beast with all its seven heads, whereas Perceval thought it obvious he could only be one of the heads. Neither doubted, however, that the Book of Revelation provided a reliable pointer to the overall shape of international politics.

'I have been so forcibly impressed with the advantages to be derived to the world from making that study a more general pursuit,' Perceval told the *Orthodox Churchman's Magazine* in a letter praising the values of Bible prophecy, 'that, if any observations of mine can have that effect, I am persuaded I cannot perform a more useful work for mankind.'

The sensible Victorians always deplored this habit of divination, exercised while Perceval occupied the supreme elected office. Most later commentators have followed their lead, adding it to the list of disreputable traits that have condemned him to historical oblivion. But the charge misses the point. Certainty is vital to leadership, and few politicians achieve power without learning to follow their convictions, however illogical. Biblical prophecy merely added to Perceval's unwavering purpose at a moment of crisis. What was reprehensible was that he never followed anything but his convictions. Yet that very fault paved the way for Wellington's glittering victories. In Perceval's favourite eleventh chapter in the Book of Daniel, the critical moment in the war between the king of the north and the king of the south was described in verse fifteen: 'So the king of the north shall come, and cast up a mount, and take the most fenced cities: and the arms of the south shall not withstand, neither his chosen people, neither shall there be any strength to withstand.'

It needed no great insight to see that the decision to cast up a mount could only refer to the fortifications that Wellington had cast up along the hills of the Torres Vedras line. Nor could Perceval doubt Daniel's revelation that it would prove to be the decisive move in winning the war. Thus, however powerful the logical arguments against the deployment of Wellington's Peninsular army, nothing could persuade the prime minister to summon the commander back home.

His solution to the 1810 financial crisis triggered by Abraham Goldsmid's suicide was less esoteric but equally effective. He persuaded the City's leading financiers to take over Goldsmid's affairs, and in return promised that the government would not sue his estate for the money that he owed the exchequer. In the short term, City confidence was swiftly restored by the knowledge that its own bankers were in charge. But in the longer term, it became clear that Perceval's lean budgeting was holding down government expenditure. There was inflation, but it was not uncontrolled. This meant that Wellington's costly force could continue to be financed.

When Perceval returned to borrow more money for his 1811 budget, the City demonstrated its trust in his economic management by lending him a larger sum than the year before, slightly more than £11 million, but at a lower rate of interest.

In January 1812, the Peninsular army finally left for good the mount it had cast up, and advanced into French-held territory. As one enemy fortress after another fell before it, praise replaced the criticism. The confidence of the country gentlemen in their Prime Minister became set in stone. The cabinet publicly declared they would resign en masse if he stepped down. 'People,' Wellington announced with satisfaction that summer 'are in great good humour with the affairs in Portugal.'

But by then Spencer Perceval had been killed.

The Beauty of Double Bookkeeping

Do you suppose me the man to go with a deliberate design without cause or provocation with a pistol to put an end to the life of Mr Perceval? No, gentlemen! Far otherwise. I have strong reasons for my conduct, however extraordinary, reasons which when I have concluded, you will acknowledge to have fully justified me in this fatal act.

John Bellingham addressing the jury, 15 May 1812

On Thursday, 14 May, James Harmer had a break in his search for a defence for his client. Into his Hatton Garden office stepped a well-dressed, briskly competent lady in her mid-forties. Her name was Mrs Ann Billett. She was a property-owner in Southampton and, that rarity in the early 1800s, a woman accustomed to running her own affairs. More importantly from Harmer's point of view, she had been born Ann Scarbrow, first cousin to John Bellingham, and had grown up with him in St Neots, Huntingdonshire. Most importantly of all, Mrs Billett was adamant that her cousin was mad. The specific word she used was 'deranged'.

Of the women who found themselves alternately loving Bellingham and being driven to distraction by him, Ann Billett had the widest and longest experience of his different states of mind. She had known his family and played with him as a child, and remembered him with affection. She had seen him as a young man at the beginning of his career. And he had stayed with her immediately after his return from Russia. From her account of John Bellingham's emotional life, a pattern emerged of repeated, dizzying swings from security to anxiety. Time after time, he appeared to have reached a place of comfort only to slip back into penury and distress. From cousin Ann's point of view, Bellingham's grasp of reality was shot through with a sense of fragility.

Comfort came first from his mother, Elizabeth Scarbrow, who belonged to a solid, well-to-do family in St Neots. In the church records her father was described as a 'gentleman', and her elder brother was so notable a benefactor that on his death he was buried within the church itself. Elizabeth must have had an adventurous streak because in 1767 she escaped the provincial limitations of St Neots, and went to live amid the clamorous excitement of London's Fleet Street. There she married an artist, John Bellingham senior, who was then at the height of his small success as a painter of miniature portraits. His work was on show at the annual exhibition of the Society of Artists of Great Britain, and his patrons included Caleb Whitefoord, a friend of Benjamin Franklin and Samuel Johnson. Their son, John, was born, according to the Evangelical bishop, Daniel Wilson, 'in London about 1771'.

Bellingham's anxieties began simply as a consequence of his father's uncertain profession. To be an artist of any kind at that time was to be involved in the great battle of the day between defenders of the beautiful and advocates of the sublime. It was a conflict that convulsed music and literature as well as painting. Neutrality was impossible. On the one side was beauty, well-proportioned, pleasing and regular; on the other, the sublime – romantic, turbulent and awe-inspiring.

In his *Philosophical Enquiry into the Origin of Our Ideas of the Sublime and the Beautiful*, Edmund Burke offered an almost Freudian explanation of the battle. Our love of beauty has 'its origin in gratifications and pleasures,' he argued, specifically in sexual desire or 'the purposes of propagation', so that when we see people or places that we desire, they 'give us a sense of joy and pleasure in beholding them'. The sense of the sublime, by contrast, is grounded in the instinct for self-preservation. 'The passions belonging to the preservation of the individual turn wholly on pain and danger,' he insisted. Thus whatever tends 'to excite the ideas of pain and danger, that is to say, whatever is in any sort terrible, or is conversant about terrible objects, or operates in a manner analogous to terror, is a source of the sublime'. Such terror, created by threats of violence and death, was 'the strongest emotion which the mind is capable of feeling'.

In a strikingly modern way, which anticipated both Freud's theory about the conflict between the desires of sex and death, and the rival attractions of romantic and horror films, Burke compared the contrary appeals of beauty and the sublime. The latter, he concluded, created a sense of danger that gave rise to a pleasure more wild and powerful than that of beauty.

This struggle between the classical sense of beauty and the romantic sense of the sublime was fundamental to late eighteenth-century thought. And it offers a key to understanding the swings of John Bellingham's mental state. However much his fragile mind strove for the comfort of order and beauty, it would always be tempted by the all-consuming savagery of chaos.

As a miniaturist, Bellingham senior was enlisted on the side of beauty – small art was automatically debarred from being terrifying – but during the early 1770s he gradually slipped from the intensely controlled concentration that miniature painting required into the chaos of mental illness. The Bellinghams moved back to St Neots, presumably to receive support from Elizabeth's family, and there the anxious little boy became friends with his elder cousin, Ann Scarbrow, who all her life would maintain a protective affection for him. As the painter's behaviour grew wilder, he must have required some care or restraint, but no parish wanted the expense of maintaining a madman from outside its boundaries. In 1780 Bellingham senior was shuttled back to London to be confined as a pauper lunatic in St Luke's charitable asylum for the violently insane.

The effect on the young John Bellingham of his father's lunacy and increasingly violent behaviour can only be guessed, though his self-contained manners and his neat, abnormally regular handwriting offer an indication of the rigid control he felt necessary to impose upon himself. Even Daniel Wilson, who saw Bellingham as an unregenerate sinner, felt bound to admit that despite everything, 'his manner was mild, not at all resembling the coarseness of the ruffian'. He was not clever but, to judge by his literate, highly formalised letters, he must have been a diligent schoolboy. Eventually John Bellingham's father was discharged as incurable, and died in lodgings in Titchfield Street, behind the thoroughfare of Oxford Street, in 1781.

Security returned in the person of William Daw, who had married Elizabeth's sister, and was not only a barrister but held a handsome sinecure as Clerk of the King's Silver. Elderly, childless and wealthy, he found the fifteen-year-old Bellingham an opening as an apprentice goldsmith, a trade that conventionally led on to a financial career. Daw had to lay out a large sum of money to secure such a promising place, but it went for nothing because the boy ran away within a few weeks. When the sententious Wilson came to write up an account of his interview with Bellingham, he ascribed this rebellion to the murderer's 'very perverse and troublesome' character, and to 'that dreadful obstinacy which hurried him on at last to the foulest of all crimes'.

More charitably it might also be called the behaviour of a troubled teenager, and uncle William evidently sympathised, because less than a year later he bought the boy a cadetship in the East India

Company. But this still more promising route to riches was cut off when the ship carrying him out to India, the 900-ton *Hartwell*, was wrecked on rocks in the Azores. Despite the cost, wealthy William Daw apparently stepped in a third time by helping him set up in Oxford Street as 'a tin-plate worker', that is, supplying the thin, glossy metal that artists, jewellers and others used for etching, ornaments and decorations.

Its outcome too followed a familiar pattern. In 1794 the tin-plate retail business failed when the premises burned down in a fire, and the twenty-three-year-old Bellingham went bankrupt. Records suggest that he or his uncle soon paid off his debts, but this latest disaster marked a turning point. Evidently deciding that he had no future in art or retailing, and with no further backing from his uncle, Bellingham chose the safest profession open to an impoverished young man, and became an accountant.

The evidence of his neat handwriting and the meticulous itemisation of his sufferings suggest that Bellingham was well-suited to the profession. But his absolute insistence on justice, his determination to be compensated for his wrongful arrest, indicates that the match went deeper. A loss had to be balanced out by a gain. Accounts needed to be evened. It was the opposite of his father's chaos. And his career proved that he did indeed make an excellent accountant.

Having apprenticed himself long enough to learn the skill of double-entry bookkeeping, he found work in the counting-room – the accounts department – of a commercial firm trading with Russia. It promised lifelong security. A growing army of dealers, brokers, insurers and shippers were engaged in the business of importing Baltic iron, hemp and tallow, and exporting textiles, pottery, glass and metal. But Russian merchants required credit to be extended up to twelve months, payment to be made with bills of exchange that might fluctuate by as much as 20 per cent, and cargoes of cloth to be bartered in one year for the delivery of timber in the next. To keep the records of these complex financial transactions, the rapidly developing Baltic trade desperately needed reliable counting clerks.

In terms of order, regularity and smallness, the business of the countinghouse was beautiful. That was precisely what Goethe meant in *Wilhem Meister*, when he put into the mouth of Werner, his prototypical businessman, the assertion that 'Double-entry bookkeeping is one of the most beautiful discoveries of the human spirit'. It was beautiful because it introduced order and regularity to the chaotic forces of fear and greed. 'What a thing it is to see the order which prevails throughout [the merchant's] business,' Werner asserted. 'What advantages does he derive from the system of bookkeeping by double-entry!' Not only could he see the column of his assets balanced against those of his debits, Werner insisted, 'it organises perceptions into a system'.

The Russian business was particularly suited to Bellingham's orderly temperament because it dealt with items in constant demand. Timber, iron and hemp were essential to the fleets of great commercial enterpises like the East India Company and to those engaged in the West India sugar and slaving trades, and they were absolutely vital to the Royal Navy with its incessant hunger for ships and cannon and rigging. Tallow was even more valuable because everyone was in need of candles and artificial light. Wholesalers came to meet the brokers in London who had suppliers in St Petersburg and Archangel. Once the deal was made, a shipbroker would produce a vessel, an insurer would cover the risk of loss, and a financier would advance credit. In normal times, the deals were standard, and competition kept prices reasonable. It was only in war when the rapacity of privateers increased and the deals grew riskier, and prices soared, that a beautiful business became sublime.

As early as 1796, the French port of St Malo alone sent out twenty-nine privateers that captured thirty-eight British cargo ships. Once Napoleon's power spread across the continent, they were joined by Dutch and Danish raiders. The value of the losses could be measured in the insurance rates at Lloyd's of London, which doubled in ten years. In 1800 the trade faced a still greater threat when the Russian tsar, Paul I, created a league of armed neutrality that included Denmark, aimed at giving peaceful aid to France.

To safeguard their interests, several Baltic firms sent out representatives to St Petersburg and Archangel. Such was Bellingham's reputation for reliability, his London employers selected him to represent them in Archangel during this anxious period. Given the possibility that trade with Britain might be stopped altogether, he would not have been expected to do more than supervise the execution of existing contracts. When the armed neutrality league ended in 1801 with the tsar's assassination, and the destruction of the Danish fleet by Admiral Horatio Nelson, Bellingham was summoned back to London. He had been in Archangel less than a year, but the experience had given him a first taste of how business operated in the port.

For some reason, perhaps because his old job had become less attractive after working on his own in Archangel, he left London. With fateful consequences, he chose to move to Liverpool, a city that, in the boast of one of its two Members of Parliament, General Banastre Tarleton, had risen 'to become the second place in wealth and population in the British Empire'.

In his meticulously detailed petitions, John Bellingham always described himself as a 'Merchant of Liverpool'. Neither term was entirely accurate. When he first set foot there in 1801, he was still an accountant, and he lived in the city for less than five years. Yet from the moment he arrived, it was certainly his ambition to become a Liverpool merchant.

Within the memory of many people still living then, Liverpool had possessed only a single small dock on the River Mersey, and the streets were still 'tortuous and narrow, with pavements in the middle, skirted by mud or dirt as the season happened. The sidewalks [were] rough with sharp-pointed stones that made it misery to walk upon them.' By 1800 the port had expanded to include five docks capable of handling 20,000 tons of shipping at once. The port's tough, marine character still remained, especially down by the river, where taverns, brothels, pawnbrokers, and low-beamed, small-windowed houses were jammed into narrow lanes and round the dank backyards that hid behind chandlers' stores and tall warehouses. 'Scarcely a town by the margin of the ocean could be more salt in its people than the men of Liverpool of the last century;' wrote a nineteenth-century Liverpudlian, 'so barbarous were they in their amusements, bull-baitings and cock and dog-fightings, and pugilistic encounters.'

Yet already the city's phenomenal growth had tilted the balance decisively towards commercial grandeur. Away from the docks, magnificent public buildings had been constructed, such as the Exchange where commodity traders, brokers and their agents met, the Athenaeum with its superb library where financiers congregated, and the Lyceum for important shippers and merchants, their interests catered for by a weather-vane let through the ceiling that told them when the wind was set fair to take their vessels down the Mersey. Substantial houses with tall windows were being built at the top end of Hanover Strret, the wide, paved thoroughfare that climbed up the slope from the docks towards Mount Pleasant overlooking the Mersey. The population was less than a tenth of London's, but growing fast at 77,000, and per head the town's inhabitants were more prosperous by far than Londoners. Almost all of them depended for their earnings on the port – skippers, tide-waiters, customs officers and harbour masters; shipowners, bankers, insurers and brokers; riggers, carpenters, porters and dockers, even house-builders, shopkeepers and brickmakers.

Bellingham put his accounting skills to work for a company that specialised in trade with Ireland, importing linen, bacon and cattle, and exporting Lancashire cloth, Birmingham brass and Staffordshire pottery. The Irish trade had been a small, reliable, coastal business, until in 1801 Ireland was incorporated within the United Kingdom. Once customs duties were abolished, imports of wheat, linen and cattle jumped by 25 per cent. However, it never generated the sort of profits that came from the blue-water trade that made Liverpool merchants wealthy – raw sugar from the West Indies; Cheshire salt to Newfoundland; tobacco, cotton and wheat from the United States in exchange for machinery, glass, china and textiles; beads, iron and bolts of vividly dyed cotton for Africa to be traded for ivory, wax, spices and, the most profitable commodity of all, humans.

In the slave trade, Liverpool had long swamped rivals like London and Bristol. It sent out more than 120 slave ships a year from the Mersey, accounting for two-thirds of Britain's traffic in people, and nearly half of Europe's, and the city's dominance was becoming more marked. Not only had the number of ships increased by a fifth since the 1780s, their average size had grown from around 280 tons to close to 350 tons, each one representing an investment of up to £8,500. Strong demand from new markets such as Brazil and Cuba as well as from established buyers in the West Indies and the United States was driving up the sale price of each slave from around £40 in the early 1790s to £60 in the new century. It was the jewel in Liverpool's trading crown.

The town owed its success in the trade partly to its infrastructure. As its leading merchants explained in a 1788 petition to Parliament, they had invested heavily in 'the constructing of proper and convenient wet docks for shipping . . . [and] the numerous canals and other communications from the interior parts of this kingdom'. But the critical ingredient was Liverpool's unique network of shippers, bankers and insurers, who spread the risks of each twelve-month voyage so that none was wiped out by disaster, and all profited from success.

John Norris, a successful trader himself, estimated that altogether the town invested about £1 million annually in the slave trade. On average, investors could expect a healthy if not spectacular 10 per cent return, but with insurers taking another 6 per cent, and suppliers between 5 and 7 per cent, the overall return to Liverpool from the trade was around £220,000 a year. For someone like Thomas Leyland, one of Liverpool's richest men, worth almost £740,000 at his death, the rewards were so great that he gradually moved from being a shipper, personally responsible for transporting nearly 3,500 Africans across the Atlantic in twenty-five years, to advancing credit to other slavers, and eventually ended as the founder of one of Liverpool's largest banks.

Without capital or credit, it was impossible for Bellingham to earn money on so large a scale. No more than a week was required for a voyage to and from Dublin or Belfast, so any profits were made quickly and with little risk, but intense competition kept margins thin. The high returns from slaving reflected the dangers and length of time between investment and pay-off. Even in the United States trade, the fastest growing business sector in Liverpool, a round trip across the Atlantic taking four to six months meant a long delay before any return was seen.

Bellingham soon moved from the counting-room to become a trader on his own account, making a slim though predictable, and therefore beautiful, profit from dealing in livestock and cloth in one direction, and metal and pottery in the other. But it took money to make real money.

His reward came in a different fashion. One of his Irish business associates was an unsuccessful but histrionic shipbroker in Newry named John Nevill, who had been bankrupted once and was on the verge of going under a second time. He could hardly have made a congenial companion to the fastidious Bellingham, but he had a nineteen-year-old daughter, Mary, 'a very pleasant, affable woman' according to a later description, 'genteel in her manners: rather short, and inclined to be lusty [plump]'. Bellingham was almost fifteen years older, and five or six inches taller. He may have thought her youth and size would make her biddable, or he may simply have fallen in love. Her motives may have concerned nothing more than escape from Newry and a hopeless father, but her personality suggests a stronger drive. Mary Nevill would surely have responded to the attractions of John Bellingham's dark face, precise mind and elegant taste in clothes. She may even have fallen in love with him. Whatever the impulse, in 1803 they were married, and set up house together in Liverpool.

All of the few facts known about Mary, and each of her surviving letters, show her to have been feisty, jealous, energetic and enterprising. However disturbing her character may have been to her highly controlled husband, he obviously found her physically exciting and within months of the wedding Mary was pregnant. But in that summer of 1803, at the age of thirty-two, he took what turned out to be a life-changing choice in his career. He gave up the Irish business, and returned to Archangel, acting for a group of Liverpool traders. His presence there was proof of the flexibility and enterprise of Liverpool's trading culture.

In 1802 the Peace of Amiens had brought a brief halt to the war with France. Yet even in a year of peace when commodity prices and shipping rates had slumped, the value of timber, tallow, and iron that passed through Archangel reached five million roubles, approximately £500,000. More than three-quarters of this trade was destined for Britain, where its value would be doubled. In 1803 war with France broke out again, offering irresistible prospects for business. The price of Russian timber, cut by serf labour from virgin forests owned by the tsar or his nobles, could not have been cheaper, and the demand could not have been more urgent. It was too good an opportunity to leave to London traders. As they were accustomed to do in the slave trade, the group of Liverpool investors and bankers for whom Bellingham acted as agent would have put up the money to charter a ship, approximately £4,000. Although based on the wrong side of England, they intended to ship the timber to Hull on the east coast, the nearest convenient port to Archangel, involving a round trip of no more than forty days. Since Bellingham's experience of conditions in Archangel and his accountant's knowledge of the Russian trade were essential – indeed he may have suggested the enterprise – he would have been offered a share in the profits.

Despite his experience, everything in Bellingham was psychologically attuned to the order and neatness of the counting clerk rather than to the chaotic switches of fortune that a born trader could exploit to make money. What he possessed was dogged determination and an attention to detail. He could read accounts, find a broker to charter the cargo vessel, and arrange the insurance with Lloyd's of London, but to negotiate the purchase of timber, assess its quality, make a deal, and arrange delivery and finance required other skills. Anyone trading in Archangel needed local contacts, but Bellingham needed them more than most. From his earlier visit there, he would have known most of the Dutch traders. The contact he chose turned out to be the man who would become his nemesis, Conrad Dorbecker.

Not only was Dorbecker highly experienced in the intricacies of Russian business, as a Dutchman he was deeply integrated into the expatriate community of Archangel with its unrivalled access to information and resources. It appears that his initial partnership in 1803 with Bellingham and the Liverpool backers was successful. The timber, bought in Archangel, was landed in Hull and sold at a profit.

Had Bellingham taken his earnings and returned home to Liverpool, the tranquillity of mind that he so valued might have remained intact. But that was not how a Liverpool merchant behaved. Risk, enterprise and the chance to become a second Thomas Leyland drove Liverpool traders on. And so, fatally misjudging his own capacities, Bellingham decided to undertake a second expedition, again in partnership with Dorbecker, but this time he himself would be in charge of the English side, organising the investment and trading on his own account.

While he had been in Archangel, his aunt, the widow of his wealthy uncle, William Daw, had died leaving £400 to Bellingham's mother. Since Elizabeth Bellingham was already dead, the money had come to him. He invested the inheritance and his earnings from the earlier voyage in chartering a vessel and, since it was a matter with which he was familiar, he presumably took personal charge of arranging insurance with Lloyd's of London. If he did alert the insurers to the *Soyuz* scam, as his Archangel enemies alleged, he certainly had the opportunity, and the information would have earned him a reward. But thousands more were needed to finance the purchase of iron and timber. Following the Liverpool model, he evidently raised the money by persuading a group of Hull merchants to invest in his project. Then, as befitted a potentially wealthy merchant, just before embarking, he made a generous contribution to charity. 'The debtors of Hull gaol,' the *Hull Advertiser* announced in May 1804, 'return thanks to Mr Billingham [*sic*] of Archangel for his kind donation of one guinea.'

When he set sail for Russia on this occasion, his young wife
Mary accompanied him together with their new-born son, James.
Her presence was living proof of her support and encouragement
of his ambition to make his forturne.

Bellingham himself had no doubt about the profitable outcome of
this venture. According to a confused account cobbled together by a
pamphlet-writer in a hurry, he had in fact 'entered into engagements
with the merchants of Hull for the delivery of deals to the amount of
£12,000', implying that he intended to organise not one but several
voyages. Thinking big was the mark of a Liverpool merchant.

The story that Ann Billett told James Harmer on the day before the
trial mostly concerned Bellingham's behaviour after he was finally
released from his St Petersburg prison in December 1809. On the
day before Christmas, when he had at last set foot in London again,
he appeared on her doorstep at 104 Sloane Street in a state of such
anxiety that, despite the impropriety of a married man living under
the same roof as an unmarried woman, she immediately took him
in and insisted he spend Christmas with her.

While her cousin was lurching between triumph and disaster,
Ann Scarbrow's life had followed a more conventional and less
fraught pattern. After their childhood together, she had gone to
live in London where she met and married Edward Billett, a property-owner originally from Hampshire. Although she had been
widowed and left to bring up two young daughters alone, she
possessed enough energy and intelligence to take over her late
husband's large property near Southampton as well as the house in
the newly fashionable west end of London, and run his estate
herself. Her evidence was the more convincing because she was so
obviously someone accustomed to taking charge of her life.

While Bellingham was still in Sloane Street, Ann insisted that
he write home to his wife, now back in Liverpool, to tell her of

his release. Then after Christmas she moved him into lodgings nearby in order to preserve the proprieties. Nevertheless, she continued to see him frequently for the next four months. The Bellingham she described was in an almost manic state. He blamed all his troubles and financial losses on the failure of the British ambassador, Lord Leveson-Gower, to intervene on his behalf. During the first months of 1810, he hurled himself into a furious round of petitions and visits to government offices in an attempt to gain compensation for his losses in Russia. Ann Billett remembered especially his wild talk of the great schemes he would undertake when the money was paid.

'He said he had realized more than an hundred thousand pounds with which he intended to buy an estate in the west of England, and to take a house in London,' she told Harmer. 'I asked him where the money was. He said he had not got the money, but it was the same as if he had, for that he had gained his cause in Russia [referring to the trial in Archangel that led to the return of his passport], and our government must make it good to him.' Ann Billett summoned her friend Mary Clarke to help reason with him. Both women came to the blunt conclusion that he was, as they later put it, 'in a state of perfect derangement'.

In February 1810 Mary Bellingham came down to London from Liverpool in response to her husband's letter. It was two years since she had last seen him in detention in St Petersburg. Heavily pregnant with their second child, she had been allowed to leave Russia with the young James, her voyage home being paid for by the expatriate British community in St Petersburg. As the newspaper reports all recognised, she had displayed extraordinary resilience in bringing up a child in a foreign land where she did not speak the language and her husband was in prison. While John Bellingham grappled hopelessly with the enemies who denied him justice, she had held the small family together through her work as a dressmaker.

Once back in England, she had gone to stay with her uncle, James Nevill, a Quaker who worked as a heel-maker for the shoe industry in Wigan, about twenty miles from Liverpool. There she met Mary Stevens, a young, unmarried friend of Mrs Nevill, and together they set up in business in Liverpool as dressmaker and milliner.

Ann Billett had been to visit them and could testify that the two Marys made a successful team, designing, making and selling clothes and hats. The Mrs Bellingham who came to join her husband in London in 1810, having left her two young children with Mary Stevens, was a woman of both courage and resource. She and Ann Billett accompanied Bellingham in his restless visits to government offices demanding redress for his wrongs, but they retained their own judgement about his chances of success.

Each quickly came to the conclusion it was a lost cause. That much was clear from the moment when the Foreign Office spokesman replied that 'his Majesty's government is precluded from interfering in the support of your case'. Not only were Britain and Russia nominally at war, but his imprisonment had been for debt, a civil matter between two businessmen, and thus not of government concern. Bellingham might have been blind to the difficulties, but both his wife and Ann Billett realised that his plan to get compensation was doomed. 'Neither she nor I gave any credit to it,' Ann commented briskly to Harmer.

In their exasperation, both women must have told Bellingham that they thought he was mad, because in a bizarre episode he took them back to the Foreign Office to ask the under-secretary for an opinion on his sanity. 'Sir, my friends say that I am out of my senses,' Bellingham said bluntly, 'is it your opinion, Mr Smith, that I am so?' With a nice display of Foreign Office tact, Mr Smith replied, 'It is a very delicate question for me to answer. I only know you upon this business, and I can assure you that you will never have what you are pursuing after.'

His negative should have been clear enough, but Bellingham appeared to be delighted by it. To Ann's incredulity, as she told Harmer, he turned to his wife as they were driving home in the coach, and patted her hand saying, 'Now I hope, my dear, you are well convinced all will happen well, and as I wished.'

For Mary Bellingham, it was the last straw. Ann Billett told Harmer that Mary had returned to Liverpool, determined to leave her husband, but the matter became less clear when she discussed it with her uncle and aunt, and Mary Stevens. All of them felt she should give the marriage another chance. Her uncle James admitted that 'I was one that advised her to live with him "as she had taken him for better or for worse".' In the end Mary let herself be talked into keeping the marriage alive. But even so she was determined that, as the newspapers reported, 'she would not live with him until he made a Solemn promise to give up wrong thoughts of his wild goose schemes & expectations'.

Her husband delayed his answer while he applied unsuccessfully twice more for compensation, first to the Treasury, then the Privy Council.

In May 1810 Bellingham made one last, desperate effort, going in person to 10 Downing Street where he gave Michael Herries, private secretary to Spencer Perceval, a document for the Prime Minister. Herries asked him to return later when he had read its contents. The author described himself as a frustrated petitioner who, 'having suffered a long and improper detention in Russia, has applied to His Majesty's Privy Council for redress, and it appears by their lordships' answer to be of a nature not their power to grant'. Consequently he wished the Prime Minister to allow him to present the same petition to Parliament. Still docketed with the paper is the brief reply that Herries gave Bellingham when he returned: 'Answered him verbally the 22nd May that Mr Perceval could not give permission for the introduction of his petition.'

Rebuffed by the Prime Minister himself, Bellingham at last accepted defeat. He returned to Liverpool, and agreed to his wife's condition that he must abandon his plans for compensation. 'This he did most solemnly promise,' James Nevill explained, 'and even burnt a parcell of papers which he stated was those relating to the affair.' Trustingly Mary welcomed him back, and was soon pregnant with baby Henry.

Even in his most deranged ravings in 1810, John Bellingham never hinted at any thought of taking violent retribution. Two years later, he returned to London with the calm intention of executing Spencer Perceval as a matter of justice. During that time, something evidently happened to change his mind. If any rational motive did exist for the killing, it had to be found in Liverpool. As part of his investigations, John Vickery, the Bow Street Runner, would routinely have asked for further information from the magistrate's officer responsible for carrying out investigations in Liverpool. But time ran out before any reply arrived. On Friday, 15 May 1812, Bellingham stood trial at the Old Bailey for the murder of the Prime Minister.

The Prosecution Presents its Case

The only question you have to try, is, whether the prisoner did wilfully and maliciously murder Mr. Spencer Perceval or not.

Lord Chief Justice Mansfield's instruction to the jury, 15 May 1812

In the four days since the murder, John Bellingham had emerged from anonymity to become a celebrity. From daybreak on the day of his trial, crowds thronged into the streets around the Old Bailey. Windows in the houses overlooking Newgate Prison and the court-house filled with spectators, many of them women, and it was noted that fashionably dressed ladies were conspicuous amongst those attempting to gain entry to the Old Bailey itself. Ever since the initial reports of his resemblance to the radical MP Sir Francis Burdett, whose saturnine good looks were well-known, rumours had spread about Bellingham's dark complexion and tall frame. 'Women were struck by his fine and manly person,' ran the gossip. 'Strange tales of his amorous complexion, whispered abroad, did not weaken that favourable impression.'

Admission was supposed to be by ticket only, but bribery proved just as effective, although the price quickly rose from one to three guineas before the trial opened. 'So great was the press,' a horrified *Courier* reported, 'that a great number of eminent persons of both Houses of Parliament were compelled to intermix indiscriminately with the multitude in the body of the Court.' The sweaty odour of rarely washed bodies must have mingled with the scent of herbs and flowers that were placed along the window ledges, in the dock and in front of the judges' bench to counteract the muddy, sewage-flavoured air that floated up from the underground passageways connecting the court to Newgate prison. No one, however, appears to have left.

At ten o'clock, the trial began with the arrival of the seventy-nine-year-old judge, the Lord Chief Justice of the Common Pleas, Sir James Mansfield. The Lord Mayor of London, two other judges, and various peers of the realm, including the royal duke of Clarence, packed on to the bench on either side of him. John Bellingham, standing alone at the bar of the court, was almost the only person not rubbing elbows with his neighbours. He was wearing the same clothes as in the House of Commons, though the brown coat, torn in the struggle, and the waspish yellow and black-striped waistcoat were now the worse for wear. A sketch of him in profile showed a long face, whose pronounced nose and slightly undershot jaw were striking although too stretched to be handsome. With his dark hair cut short by a prison barber, he appeared respectable but, as events were to show, he would have done better to appear in rags, unshaven and gibbering nonsense.

There could be no doubt that he had killed Perceval. He had admitted it at the committal proceedings, and many times subsequently, and eyewitnesses had sworn to it at the coroner's inquest. From the legal point of view, the only question was whether he had committed the murder while mad. Bellingham's fate depended upon Harmer's ability to assemble convincing evidence of insanity.

The previous night the solicitor had taken a long affidavit from Ann Billett testifying to his derangement. At her suggestion, Harmer had then taken a shorter statement from her friend, Mary Clarke, who had also witnessed Bellingham's behaviour in 1810 after his return from Russia. But in a setting that placed the greatest reliance on 'the masculine intelligence', they needed reinforcement from male witnesses. These were conspicuously lacking. The mail coach took twenty-two hours to reach Liverpool, so there had been no chance to get anyone from Bellingham's home city to give testimony, although Harmer had hopes that witnesses might arrive before the end of the day. Of the two experts on insanity he had asked to testify, only Samuel Simmons had replied, excusing himself on the grounds that he was seriously ill – and indeed he died a few months later. No word had come from Thomas Munro, the man who had helped secure Hadfield's acquittal. As the trial opened, Harmer's greatest need was for time. A postponement until after the weekend would be enough.

The calibre of the defence team he had assembled offered at least a glimmer of hope. Peter Alley, later famous for his eloquent defence of the Manchester demonstrators caught up in the Peterloo massacre of 1819, already had a reputation as an abrasive cross-examiner. Charles Phillips, the ultimate authority on his fellow attorneys, judged him to be 'zealous, industrious, bold and impassioned', but if anything, Alley was too volatile, too liable to anger at judicial interference, for such a political trial. His junior, Henry Revell Reynolds, who would epitomise the new breed of careful, professional Victorian lawyers, might have been better suited to the circumstances. But he too could barely contain his contempt for the lynch mentality that gripped both prosecution and bench. The conduct of the trial was, he said later, 'the greatest disgrace to English justice'.

Until 1836, legal procedure did not permit professional counsel to plead on behalf of murderers, only to cross-examine witnesses and to offer advice. Within those limits, Alley fully intended to test the sanity argument in court. When Mansfield asked how the prisoner pleaded to the charge of murder, Alley promptly stood up and asked for a postponement 'to shew that the prisoner could be proved to be insane'. He must have guessed he would get nowhere. The Old Bailey sat for eight sessions a year, each lasting about ten days. The trial had been rushed into the first days of the May session, forcing already scheduled cases to be postponed until the next session in July. The judge was not likely to let the case drag on.

Stonily, Mansfield swept away Alley's interruption, repeating that the accused must first plead guilty or not guilty before evidence of insanity could be addressed. At that, Bellingham himself protested that he could not plead until he had the papers that had been taken from him in the struggle after he had shot Perceval. His objection received the same treatment. For the third time the accused was asked how he pleaded. 'Not guilty,' Bellingham replied at last. 'I place myself upon God and my country.'

Alley returned to the attack, asking how he could defend the prisoner without his papers and without witnesses. He cited the affidavits given by Ann Billett and Mary Clarke stating that John Bellingham had been deranged since his return from Russia. Their important evidence could be corroborated by his friends in Liverpool. But the government had allowed no time for these witnesses to be presented. As a matter not simply of justice but of humanity, a postponement was essential.

'It was only on Monday that the alleged act was said to have been perpetrated,' Alley declared, working up his temper. 'A letter could not have been sent until the next day. It is impossible that any answer could have been received by today. Even where a person is tried in the town in which he resides,' he ended in exasperation, 'some time must be necessary to enable him to provide evidence for his trial.'

The Attorney General, Sir Vicary Gibbs, who was leading the prosecution, dismissed Alley's plea contemptuously. It was, he declared, nothing more than 'a contrivance to delay the administration of justice'. Whatever the women's affidavits maintained about the past, the fact was that while Bellingham was in London, he had been leading a perfectly normal life. There was no need to wait for Liverpool witnesses. The Attorney General had an acid manner that earned him the nickname of Vinegar Gibbs. 'Where has the Prisoner been for these four months?' he demanded. 'He has been resident in this town, in the midst of a family in this town, known to multitudes of persons in this town, transacting business in this town, and with as much sagacity and as perfect and masculine an understanding as any man who now hears me.'

Rubbing salt in the wound, he blamed the defence for not securing evidence from experts 'whose statement your Lordship would have regarded as of deep importance'. Angrily Alley corrected him, but the Lord Chief Justice was as anxious to hurry on as the prosecution, and he brushed the objection aside. The defence application for a postponement had to be dismissed, Mansfield announced, because the affidavits of the two women were not enough to suggest he was insane. Carefully misreading their import, he said the testimony related to his behaviour in Russia. 'Now could it be supposed,' he asked, 'that [Bellingham] went, or would be permitted to go, to Russia if he were in a disordered state of mind?' There were, therefore, no grounds for postponement, and the trial could continue.

The jury was sworn and Gibbs began to set out the case against John Bellingham in all its stark detail. The victim, he reminded the jury, was the sort of man who, given the chance, would have used his last conscious moments praying for forgiveness for his murderer. But Bellingham had denied him that Christian consolation. He had prepared carefully for the crime, planning and practising for weeks beforehand. He had waited by the door of the lobby until the prime minister appeared, then coldly murdered him.

There could be no question of insanity. Even someone incapable of looking after his own affairs would be 'criminally liable', the

Attorney General insisted, 'provided he had a mind capable of distinguishing between right and wrong'. Bellingham not only managed his own affairs in London, but his wife's as well. Finally, Gibbs pointed out, it was beyond question that this sane, strong-minded man had acted alone. Having outlined the prosecution case, the Attorney General then began to call witnesses to the murder itself and to the prisoner's meticulous planning.

To spectators in the courtroom, Bellingham remained an object of fascination. Whatever James Harmer believed, it was apparent to them that the prisoner himself agreed completely with both the judge and prosecution about his own sanity. What struck everyone was his composure. Undisturbed by their gaze, he himself 'frequently looked round and appeared to contemplate the crowd with a curious eye'. At one point, he refreshed himself by eating an orange taken from his pocket, then he asked for a chair and sat down 'very much at his ease', according to *The Globe*. While witnesses were being questioned, he distracted himself by rubbing in his hand the herbs that were scattered around the dock, and smelling their scent on his fingers.

The evidence should have concerned him more. Its purpose was to convince the jury not only of his sanity, but of his premedita-tion. Like a film run backwards, it began with the pistol shot, the dying prime minister falling to the ground, and the arrest of his murderer. The witnesses who had given evidence at the committal proceedings described the scene once more, and the only new detail came from the enigmatic General Isaac Gascoyne. He revealed that when the murder took place he had been writing in a committee room upstairs whose door opened onto a balcony overlooking the lobby. 'It was nearly the same thing, as to hearing, as to being in the lobby of the House,' he testified. 'I heard the loud report of a pistol shot, and almost instantaneously the cry of "Close the doors." I rushed downstairs, through the House, and into the lobby.'

Having established that Bellingham was in the general's grasp, the Attorney General called John Norris, the House of Commons servant, as a witness. He pushed the clock back to about five minutes past five o'clock, the last moments before the living prime minister arrived in the House of Commons. As Norris passed through the door on his way to walk upstairs from the lobby to the passage to the Strangers' Gallery, he noticed the tall man in the dark coat by the door. 'I observed him, as if watching for somebody that was coming,' he said, adding that the man seemed anxious and had his hand inside his coat. 'Perhaps the impression is stronger on my mind now than it was then,' Norris went on, as though conscious that he might have asked Bellingham what he was doing, and thereby changed history. But, as he told the court, it was not the first time he had encountered the stranger. 'I had seen him frequently in the gallery of the House of Commons, and about the passages of the House.' Saying nothing to Bellingham, Norris had left the lobby, toiled up the stairs and was nearing the gallery when he heard the shot.

The evidence of Vincent Dowling, *The Day*'s reporter, turned the calendar back another week. He told of his encounters with Bellingham in the Strangers' Gallery when the tall man had come in and asked to have Perceval and other members of the government identified. 'On one occasion I sat immediately next to him, while the House was in debate,' Dowling said. 'I sat next to him about half an hour; I cannot say the precise time; there was a sort of general conversation between him and myself, and some other person that was sitting near me.'

Three more weeks dissolved away with the testimony of William Taylor, the aptly named tailor. On 25 April Taylor had been walking down Guilford Street, the commercial thoroughfare that cut across the end of New Millman Street. There he bumped into Bellingham, who 'informed me that he had a small job to do, and if I would step back with him he would give it me immediately'. At his lodgings, Bellingham produced a dark brown coat, and asked Taylor 'to make him an inside pocket on the left side, so as he could get at it conveniently; he wished to have it a particular depth; he accordingly gave me a bit of paper about the length of nine inches'.

At this point, the Attorney General paused, evidently to let the jury appreciate the significance of Taylor's evidence because he repeated the phrase, no doubt with slow import, 'He gave you a bit of paper about nine inches in length.' Using the paper as a pattern, Taylor sewed the pocket in place the same day, 'he was very particular to have it home that evening,' the witness confirmed.

The precise size of the pocket was significant because just four days earlier, on 21 April, Bellingham had gone to the well-known City of London gunsmith, William Beckwith, and purchased a pair of steel pistols. They were designed to be concealed, and used only at close quarters. The length of the grip and firing mechanism was seven inches, and each had a detachable screw barrel that added another two inches. Beckwith told the court he had charged Bellingham four guineas for the two pistols, together with bullets, gunpowder, a key for screwing the barrel into place, and a kit for casting more ammunition. He also advised him to practise with the weapon, since the short barrel and large half-inch calibre would be hopelessly inaccurate over any distance of more than a few feet.

The Attorney General was careful to draw the attention of the jury to the implications of the two witnesses' evidence. During the next few days, he pointed out, Bellingham had gone to the wooded land around Primrose Hill, and practised shooting at trees with Beckwith's pistols. The experience convinced him that he needed to hold the muzzle virtually against his victim to be sure of hitting him. It also demonstrated that precious minutes would be lost in screwing the barrel into place. The weapon would have to be prepared before he left home, and he would need a pocket exactly nine inches deep to hold it. In case of a misfire, he decided to carry the back-up pistol, loaded and cocked, in the pocket of his nankeen trousers, but the murder weapon would be concealed in his secret pocket, from which it could be drawn at the last moment.

With attention concentrated on the pistol, events were brought abruptly up to date by testimony from the Bow Street Runner, John Vickery. He confirmed that while searching Bellingham's rooms he had found in a drawer the gunpowder, ammunition and bullet moulds purchased from Beckwith. In court the murder weapon was now produced and, in a moment of theatre, one of the bullets was inserted into the barrel. 'This ball fits the barrel exactly,' Vickery announced. 'And it was made in this mould, I have no doubt.'

Finally, the prosecution demonstrated with elaborate care that the coat Bellingham was wearing in the dock was the one that Taylor had altered. None of the evidence was in question. Alley had only found it possible to intervene once, when by questioning one of the MPs at the scene of the murder, he tried to point out Bellingham's irrationality. He drew out the fact that Bellingham had expressed no personal dislike of Perceval, and that the only motive he had offered for his action was the lack of compensation for his losses in Russia. 'That is the reason he gave you?' Alley demanded, 'mere want of redress of grievance on the part of the government?'

It was a tiny pebble to rescue from the avalanche of evidence produced by the Attorney General. By launching it in such detail, the prosecution had illustrated how carefully, logically and cold-bloodedly the prisoner had planned his crime. When the Attorney General sat down, no one could seriously believe Bellingham to be a lunatic, or that for at least four months he had acted with anything but conscious intent to murder.

* * *

There was, however, a serious gap in the prosecution case, and one of its own making. The testimony of Ann Billett and Mary Clarke carried genuine significance. No one could have mistaken the frenzy of John Bellingham's behaviour two years earlier, in 1810. When the women described him as deranged at that time, they were undoubtedly using the word accurately. Had he determined to assassinate the prime minister when he first returned from Russia, or Lord Leveson-Gower, or anyone else he blamed for his misfortune, it would certainly have been the work of someone out of his mind.

The Attorney General, however, had equally good justification for stressing the normality of Bellingham's conduct in 1812. No one who met him in London during that time – including one crucial witness who knew him well in Liverpool, but was not called to testify – supposed that Bellingham was anything but sane. Everything he did up to the final moment appeared to be planned, self-contained and, in the way of life he established with Rebecca Robarts, comfortably civilised. Only at the very last did the beautiful plan begin to become so sublimely terrifying that, as he confessed to Sir William Curtis MP, 'I have been fourteen days in making up my mind to the deed.' Not until forty-eight hours before the murder did he finally screw up his courage to kill Spencer Perceval.

In other words, the pattern of John Bellingham's behaviour changed utterly between 1810 and 1812 – wild, excitable and deranged on his return from Russia, but calm, organised and sane while staying with Mrs Robarts. The anxieties that propelled him towards madness in the spring of 1810 were clear enough. But no one wondered why he behaved so differently in the spring of 1812. His goal had not altered – he still wanted compensation for his losses, although only £8,000 instead of the 'hundred thousand pounds' he had expected in 1810. And he still followed the same strategy of petitioning and interviewing ministers and their staff.

But his emotional state was transformed. Clearly something had happened to him.

What it was did not matter to Sir Vicary Gibbs or to Sir James Mansfield. They were intent on hanging Bellingham. The only motivation they suggested for his action was his wicked character. But to anyone interested in the truth, in how the Prime Minister really came to be killed, there had to be some reason for the murder – unless the prisoner really were insane. Even the spectators in court expected something more. When John Bellingham stood up to defend himself, there was a hushed air of expectancy.

The argument they heard from him was so bizarre that most of those present were left bewildered. The majority suspected that he might be mad after all, and a few thought he might be lying. No one could believe that he was being both rational and truthful.

Bellingham and the Absence of *malice prepense*

When a Minister is so unprincipled and presumptuous at any time, but especially in a case of such urgent necessity to set himself above both the sovereign and the law, as has been the case with Mr Perceval, he must do so at his personal risk, for by the law he cannot be protected. Gentlemen, if this is not fact, then the mere will of the Minister would be law, it would be this thing today and the other tomorrow. What would become of our liberties?

John Bellingham addressing the jury, 15 May 1812

Sprinkled among the spectators in court were five or six shorthand writers busily preparing records of the trial for immediate publication. As John Bellingham began his defence, they noted not just his words but his manner. They described his patched coat and short hair, his quiet, reasonable voice, his fluent delivery, broken by occasional tears and sudden flurries of emotion. They were trying to supply an answer to the question that their readers would certainly ask themselves – Was he sane? Whatever Vinegar Gibbs might assert, ordinary people wanted to come to their own conclusion.

The accused started by politely insisting on having back the papers that had been taken from him in the House of Commons. Without them he could not defend himself. These were his petitions to ministers and the answers he had received. They were duly handed over, although he only once consulted them. But with the papers in his hand he felt able to begin his defence. He did so by thanking the Attorney General for insisting on his sanity. 'That I am insane I certainly am perfectly ignorant, and I assure you that I never had an idea of it.' The only occasion when he thought he might have gone mad was when he lost control of himself in front of Archangel's military governor. As he said this, the shorthand writers noted that he choked up. 'Gentlemen, I beg pardon,' he said when he had wiped his eyes. 'This is the first time I ever was in public in this kind of way.'

So far from pleading insanity, he told the jury, his defence would be based on the proposition that the killing of Spencer Perceval was entirely lawful. 'Had I murdered him in cold blood, I should consider myself a monster, not only unfit to live in this world but too wicked for all the torments that may be inflicted in the next.' Not even Perceval's family could regret 'this catastrophe' more than Bellingham himself. From the start, he wanted to dispel any suspicion that he had some private motive for the killing. 'I had no personal or premeditated malice towards that gentleman; the unfortunate lot had fallen upon him as the leading member of that administration which had repeatedly refused me any reparation for the unparalleled injuries I had sustained in Russia.'

Unlike the backward pattern of the prosecution, his defence moved forward from the moment in 1804 when he arrived in Archangel. Step by step, he took the jury through the repeated imprisonments in Russia, through the barrage of appeals for justice in 1810 and 1812, to the point where Perceval denied him the chance to present his petition to the Commons.

Nothing the jury had heard from the prosecution could have illustrated Bellingham's self-possession more convincingly than the two-hour speech he delivered in his defence. His only aid was the bundle of papers that had been returned to him minutes before he began to speak. It was, however, a story he had told many times before, the epic narrative of his Russian venture. The detail of debts, and lawsuits, and petitions, and hearings, might confuse his listeners, but to Bellingham the thread of his argument was clear. He was being stitched up by the Dutch and Russians, 'and Lord Gower refused to interfere in the business, and the Consul [Sir Stephen Shairpe] told me I must pay the money'. Occasionally he broke down, overcome by his own descriptions of his suffering in St Petersburg. 'I had been but recently married to a wife, then only twenty years of age, with an infant at her breast, and pregnant with a second child,' he declared. 'Yet I was doomed to continue immured in a dungeon.' At such moments, he wept with self-pity while the court silently watched and the shorthand writers scribbled, but invariably he gathered himself together and continued his narrative.

His betrayal by Leveson-Gower – the refusal to come to his aid in Archangel, the decision in St Petersburg to hand him back to the Russian authorities, the indifference to his suffering – was what he kept coming back to. 'What must his heart be made of?' Bellingham exclaimed, once more on the edge of tears. 'Gentlemen, I appeal to you as men, as fathers, as Christians, if I had not cause of complaint.' As he neared the end of his speech, he gave vent to a damaging exclamation: 'If I had met Lord Gower, he would have received the ball, and not Mr. Perceval.' It was symptomatic of Bellingham's self-absorption that he should have looked round with surprise at the murmur of disapproval in the court. In his mind, his dispassionate execution of the prime minister was quite distinct from his passionate resentment against Leveson-Gower.

Finally he turned to the papers in his hand. In laborious detail, he read out the petitions he had presented in 1810 and 1812 to the Prince Regent and to the Privy Council, and the appeals he had then made to the Prime Minister and other members of the government to be allowed to petition Parliament, and the stone-walling replies sent by a succession of civil servants – 'I am to inform you that his Majesty's Government is precluded from interfering . . .', 'their Lordships do not find that it is a matter in which they can interfere . . .', 'the time for presenting petitions having elapsed . . .' The last of his letters was to the magistrates at Bow Street reminding them that the right to petition Parliament for redress 'is the birth-right of every individual'. It was to them that he made his intentions most obvious. The government had denied his natural rights, and denied him justice. He appealed to the magistrates to persuade ministers to grant what they had so far refused him. 'Should this reasonable request be finally denied,' he wrote, 'I shall then feel justified in executing justice myself – in which case I shall be ready to argue the merits of so reluctant a measure with his Majesty's Attorney-General, wherever and whenever I may be called upon so to do.'

The case he made explained why he felt so relaxed. In his view, everything was going to plan. He had executed justice, and here he was arguing the merits of the killing with the Attorney General. However skewed the steps of his argument, they followed a clear pattern. The failure of the government's representative in Russia to help him had cost him money. The refusal of the government in 1810 to compensate him for Leveson-Gower's failure to help was an injustice. By denying him the right to appeal against this injustice through a petition to Parliament in 1812, the government had prevented him exercising a basic civil right. 'Justice is a matter of right, and not of favour; and as such, I think it should be dispensed at all times . . . . Where can an injured subject appeal so justly as to Parliament? and if that constitutional door be shut against him, where is his redress?'

This was the very heart of his argument. It was for an abstract right rather than for a commercial loss that Perceval, the representative of unjust government, had to be killed. The difference constituted the core of Bellingham's defence. Because he was acting in the interests of natural justice rather than of personal revenge, the killing could not legally constitute murder. 'That my arm destroyed him, I allow,' ran the most eloquent recorded version of Bellingham's speech. 'That he perished by my hand, I admit; but to constitute felony, there must be *malice prepense*, there must be the wilful intention, and I deny that it has been proved. Unless proved, however, the felony cannot be made out; this you will shortly hear from the Bench, and in that case you must acquit me.'

He sat down, flushed, breathing hard, and once more on the verge of tears. Yet within minutes he had regained his calm self-control. Nothing else that happened in the trial shook his confidence in his line of defence. Up to the very moment that the foreman of the jury delivered his verdict, Bellingham was convinced that he would be found innocent. As the judge was summing up, Bellingham leant over to his solicitor, and whispered that Harmer should be sure to send a note in time for the evening mail coach to Liverpool to tell his wife, Mary, that he had been set free.

After Bellingham finished his long speech, Peter Alley attempted to repair the damage by demonstrating that despite his client's apparent coherence, his behaviour was indeed that of a madman. Although not allowed to plead, a barrister could examine witnesses. He called Ann Billett into the witness box. She was, the shorthand writers noted, 'very moved'. Since Alley's one convincing witness was evidently close to breaking down, he restricted himself to establishing that she had known Bellingham since childhood, thus giving weight to her opinion that he was deranged. He got her to say that Bellingham's father had died insane, then he sat down.

In cross-examination, however, Gibbs lured Ann Billett into asserting that '[Bellingham] has been more than three years in a state of derangement', then forced her to admit that she had not seen him for more than a year. Defiantly she recalled his wild behaviour in 1810, and the embarrassing encounter with Mr Smith of the Foreign Office who had implicitly confirmed her impression that he was out of his mind. But whatever might have been true about his traumatised state of mind at the time, she could offer no evidence about his behaviour in 1812. Step by step Gibbs chipped away at the picture of 'perfect derangement'. Had Bellingham ever been confined? Had someone else been put in charge of his affairs? Had his friends been forced to take care of him? Had Mrs Billett warned the government that he was mad? To all of which she answered with a monosyllabic 'No'.

Mary Clarke's evidence received the same treatment. She agreed that Bellingham had conducted business by himself in London. No doctor had been consulted about his state of mind, no restrictions had been placed on his movements, and when she unexpectedly met him in January 1812 he had behaved reasonably and appeared capable of looking after himself. In the absence of his two mental-health experts, Alley turned to his last witness. This should have been Rebecca Robarts. Calling her was a sign of desperation – she had already told Vickery of Bellingham's considerate, civilised behaviour – but there was no one else in London in a position to give evidence that the accused was prone at least to delusion. Even this forlorn hope evaporated when her chambermaid, a young girl called Catherine Figgins, stepped into the witness box instead. Mrs Robarts was too ill to attend, she explained, and so she had been sent in her place. Beyond being able to say that over the weekend Bellingham 'seemed confused' and 'not so well as he had been', the chambermaid's testimony shed no new light on his sanity, and in cross-examination she readily admitted that he was 'a remarkable, regular man'.

By the time the elderly chief justice came to sum up, there could not have been much doubt as to the outcome. But Sir James

Mansfield managed to screw down the lid of Bellingham's coffin with the way he delivered his opening sentence. 'Gentlemen of the jury,' ran the otherwise dry report of his performance in the *Old Bailey Sessions Papers*:

> you are now to try an indictment which charges the prisoner at the bar with the wilful murder (here the learned judge was so hurt by his feelings, that he could not proceed for several seconds) of Mr. Spencer Perceval, (in a faint voice) who was murdered with a pistol loaded with a bullet; when the prisoner mentioned the name of (here again his lordship was sincerely affected, and burst into tears, in which he was joined by the greatest portion of the persons in court) a man so dear, and so revered as that of Mr. Spencer Perceval, I find it difficult to suppress my feelings.

In this emotional atmosphere, it was surprising only that the jury should have taken as long as fourteen minutes to find the prisoner guilty of murder. Seven hours after his trial had begun, Bellingham was sentenced to be taken 'to a place of execution, where you shall be hanged by the neck until you be dead; your body to be dissected and anatomized.'

When asked whether he had anything to say, the prisoner remained silent, showing no apparent response. Disappointment was an emotion that he must have been used to, and he accepted the outcome stoically, as though he expected no less of a world that had always proved hostile. The only regret he ever expressed was that Alley had not called any of the witnesses, including Shairpe and Leveson-Gower, who Bellingham had hoped would testify to the injustice of his Russian treatment.

The kangaroo nature of the trial had made it obvious that the government intended to have Bellingham executed as quickly as possible. Yet the speed with which the foregone conclusion was reached not only left unexplored the problem of his motivation and passed over the transformation in his behaviour, it created a mystery of its own.

As Catherine Figgins concluded her evidence, Peter Alley made one final effort to win more time, and sent an urgent message to the doorkeeper asking whether any witnesses had arrived from Liverpool. Amazingly, Sheriff William Heygate returned to announce in open court that indeed two people from Liverpool had just turned up in a post-chaise and four 'to give evidence in favour of the prisoner'. They knew someone who matched Bellingham's description 'in whose conduct they had seen frequent marks of derangement'. Alley's hopes, however, were instantly dashed by Heygate's next words. Instead of producing the potential witnesses for examination in the witness box, the sheriff went on to say that having been shown into the court, they had decided that Bellingham was not the person they were expecting to see, and had left.

There was no quicker way to travel, and none more expensive, than in a speedy post-chaise, painted a distinctive yellow and drawn by teams of hired horses that were changed every twenty or thirty miles. The two potential witnesses probably took as little as twelve hours to come from Liverpool, fifteen hours faster than the mail-coach. The speed and the huge cost they had incurred showed how vital they believed their testimony to be. That they should have gone to such trouble and expense simply on a whim to help a stranger they only knew by sight is hardly credible. They must have come specifically to help Bellingham. His name appeared in Wednesday's *Liverpool Courier*, and his description was in the Thursday edition of the *Liverpool Mercury*. Alley's appeal for witnesses would have reached the mayor by Thursday afternoon, well before the pair left. Either they lost their nerve when confronted by the crowded courtroom or they were actively dissuaded by Heygate and the Attorney General from holding up the rushed trial.

As though their arrival were not dramatic enough, barely twenty minutes later the town clerk of Liverpool, Richard Statham, galloped up with three more witnesses, carrying 'papers which the Mayor of L[iverpool] thought would be material in the trial of Bellingham'. They too had come 'express' from Liverpool in order to give their testimony, and the expense was so great that Statham later asked the government to contribute towards the costs. Unfortunately their journey was also in vain. Despite the furious pace of their journey south, they arrived minutes too late to take part in the proceedings. By the time Statham hurried into the Old Bailey, the judge had completed his summing-up and the jury had retired to consider its verdict.

Nevertheless, the appearance of no fewer than six unexpected witnesses from Liverpool, all ready to testify at John Bellingham's trial, could not have been a coincidence. The Prime Minister's former colleagues might only have been interested in executing his murderer, but Perceval's friends, eager to understand *why* he had been killed, must have had an inkling that the answer was to be found in Liverpool rather than in a courtroom in London.

The Compelling Evidence of Miss Stevens

As a general minister Mr Perceval inflicted all the evils on the country which can result from the combined effects of boldness, ignorance and tenacity. Of the philosophical principles of law, civil policy or political economy, he knew very little, and rather piqued himself indeed upon despising them.

Edinburgh Review, June 1812

On the afternoon of Friday, 15 May, the day of the trial, Mary Stevens, Mrs Bellingham's business partner and closest friend, returned to Liverpool by the mail-coach from London. She went straight from 'The Golden Lion' inn, where the London coach terminated, to the Bellinghams' home at 46 Duke Street. Twenty-four hours earlier she had been with John Bellingham in his cell as he awaited his trial. Mary Stevens carried with her back to Liverpool two letters he had written, one for his business colleague, John Parton, and the other for his wife. She also brought a message from Bellingham telling his wife that he would be released the following day, and she could expect him home shortly, a free and wealthy man. The ensuing conversation between the two women must have been unimaginably fraught.

The first rumours of the murder might have reached Mary Bellingham as early as Wednesday as the brief notice in the *Courier* filtered through its readers to the wider public. But on Thursday both of Liverpool's papers carried detailed reports, and when the town clerk, Richard Statham, paid her a visit, she learned the full truth. Statham may not have told her directly of James Harmer's request for evidence of insanity, but he certainly let her understand that it was desirable to have evidence that his behaviour was irrational, obsessive, and had nothing to do with sentiment in Liverpool. The papers he subsequently carried south to Bellingham's trial were Mary Bellingham's statement, probably supported by written testimony from two further witnesses whose addresses she knew, Bellingham's business partner, John Parton, and his solicitor, Thomas Avison. Until Friday afternoon, however, Mary Bellingham had heard nothing that might have suggested why her husband had committed such a terrible deed. No one, however, was better placed to explain than Mary Stevens.

Between the two women, there was a bond closer than that of a business partnership. Together they rented the Duke Street house that served as both home and shop, and although Mary Stevens was the less well-educated, it was her unshakeable commonsense that anchored the pair. Perhaps most importantly, she helped look after the three Bellingham children with a fund of affection that made her, as even Bellingham himself recognised, a natural second mother to them. While Mrs Bellingham concentrated on hats, Miss Stevens clearly had a flair for designing dresses, and from the beginning of their partnership in 1806, the firm of Bellingham & Stevens, as they were listed in *Gore's Trade Directory*, had quickly found customers among Liverpool's wealthy inhabitants. Indeed Liverpool's love of fashion would soon earn it a reputation as the best-dressed city in England.

The arrival of John Bellingham two years after they started work together could only have appeared as an intrusion. In law, he owned his wife's share of the business, and although he evidently made himself agreeable, as he always did to women, and kept the accounts in order, Mary Stevens made it plain that her loyalty was always to his wife and children. Nothing he did ever quite won her over. That he appeared to contribute little financially to the household could not have helped his cause.

The Archangel disaster had, by his own account, left Bellingham almost penniless. As he explained to the jury, 'My affairs [were] ruined by my long imprisonment in Russia through the fault of the British minister, my property all dispersed for want of my own attention, my family driven into tribulation and want, my wife and child claiming support, which I was unable to give them, myself involved in difficulties, and pressed on all sides by claims I could not answer.'

His return to Liverpool in May 1810, six years after he had left, could not have been easy. His Irish business had disappeared and the city had undergone a radical change. The slave trade that had been the source of all its wealth for almost three generations had been made illegal, and the old financial and political networks were struggling to readjust. A sense of disorder was in the air. For lack of an alternative, Bellingham had set about resurrecting his former trade, and, according to Mary Stevens, 'he went over to Ireland for the purpose of re-establishing his connexions in Business'. Among those Bellingham met would have been John Neville, but his reprobate father-in-law had gone bankrupt again and, having moved from northern Ireland to Dublin, was no longer in the linen trade. Clearly Bellingham did find some customers – Mary Stevens referred to him as a merchant, and said that John Parton 'transacted business for Mr B in Liverpool' – but everything was on a small scale.

In Liverpool circles, John Bellingham was known mostly as an insurance broker, suggesting that he and Parton also acted as agents insuring the almost risk-free Irish trade where profits were pared to the bone. When Ann Billett visited the Bellinghams in 1811, she did not see him do any business during the week she was there. And he certainly did not earn enough to sustain the family, because his wife had to keep working at a business she found 'very uncongenial to my feelings'.

In the last half of 1811, their situation was made worse as the already wounded city was gripped by a national economic recession. By December 1811, half of all skilled workers in Liverpool – shipwrights, sailmakers, riggers and brassfounders – were out of work, and four out of five casual labourers such as dockers and porters had lost their jobs.

The Bellinghams were not immune. The Irish business suffered as people patched their own shirts, turned their own collars, and ate more bread in place of beef. At the Chester Fair, the great showcase for Ireland's exports, 'a vast deal of Irish linens' were left on the shelves, and there was 'little demand for cattle'. With the English market contracting, Irish demand for goods manufactured in the Midlands faded.

The pinch affected the fashion industry too, and fewer orders were placed for hats and dresses that winter. When Phillips & Davison, a London silk supplier, inadvertently delivered more ribbon than Mary Bellingham's hat-making business could use, and insisted on payment, she was distraught. 'It is their Traveller's mistake, and not any fault of ours,' she insisted. 'Miss Stevens merely ordered 6 or 8 yards for millinery as we had none in the house and they have sent a large quantity, we do not know how much as we never opened the parcel as we saw by the size of it it was not the order given.'

The mistake had a fateful consequence. Bellingham promptly seized on the need to sort out the problem as an excuse for travelling to London. At the same time, he intended to carry out a private business deal of his own. Before the trial, the London newspapers reported the interesting discovery, presumably made by John Vickery, that when Bellingham came to the capital it was to buy iron. This was an expensive commodity to purchase in trade quantities, and since he had no money he must have been acting on commission for another Liverpool merchant. But when he left Duke Street at the end of December 1809, his wife had every reason to believe that it was solely to sort out the family's financial problems.

Anxiety about their lack of money never left Mary Bellingham's mind. 'I think I need not intreat you to act with economy,' she wrote to him on 18 January 1812, more than a fortnight after he had left Liverpool, 'your feelings for your familly will induce you to keep to it.' But she could not help pointing out that their tiny business could not afford his absence. 'You will be there three weeks on Thursday, and you know I cannot do anything with regard to this business until your return. We have got in very little money since you left.' Although 'extremely surprized' that he had not come back, she was not yet alarmed. She could still persuade herself that he only had to be reminded how vital he was to the household – 'Pray let us know when you intend to return' – and he would hurry home.

Whatever their disagreements, John and Mary Bellingham were completely united in their love of Henry, the youngest of their three sons. His birth in the autumn of 1811 had set the seal on their reconciliation, and both doted on him. When Bellingham left for London, the baby was uncomfortable and crying, and the most urgent concern in his first letter home in early January 1812 was for Henry's health. Mary understood his feelings and her reply had begun, 'I am glad to relieve you immediately regarding darling Henry who is wonderfully recovered and has cut two teeth.' She ended it, 'The children send dear Papa each an affectionate kiss with one from Mamma' and a final 'yours very affectionately'.

Either his reply, which has not survived, or his failure to respond drove her to search his room. There, according to an affidavit from Mary Stevens, she 'accidentally discovered' a note referring to a petition asking for compensation for his Russian losses that he intended to present to the Prince Regent. The note also revealed that he had given the document to his lawyer, Thomas Avison, presumably for his expert advice since formal petitions had to be drawn up according to a specific formula. When Mary Stevens confronted John Parton, he confirmed that Bellingham had 'meditated such application [for compensation] for some time'. The solemn promise made to his wife had been deliberately broken, and his trip to London had been deceitfully planned for something other than business reasons.

The news had thrown Mary Bellingham into despair. She became physically ill and lost weight. Her letters blaming Bellingham for his bad faith no longer exist, but in reply he must have insisted he had a plan that made payment of the compensation a certainty. She did not attempt to believe him. Then in mid-April, when he was about to buy the pistol with which he would kill Spencer Perceval, he sent an extraordinary message addressed to the two Marys in Duke Street.

The covering note to his wife was brief, and mostly concerned business matters and the welfare of baby Henry: 'I could have wished when you had written, you had mentioned where and with whom Henry is, and let me know how the dear boy goes on.' But it enclosed a second, longer letter that began, 'My dear Miss Stevens, As my affairs in London are terminating according to wish, you may easily imagine it's my desire for Mrs B- to quit the Business as soon as possible and for you to come into full possession of it.' In other words, he was so certain of being paid a large sum in compensation that his wife could afford to retire, and he had decided to make over her share in the dress-making business to her partner. His proposal was as detailed and business-like as an accountant could make it. Mary Stevens was to have his wife's share debt-free; she was to come to London so that he could personally introduce her to 'the respective Trades people for the arrangements';

and finally she was to 'Bring the Books and [have confidence] in me to do what is right and proper – you will not be deceived.'

His announcement drove his wife to a new pitch of desperation. 'If I could think that the prospects held out in your letter receved yesterday were to be realized,' she wrote bitterly, 'I would be the happiest creature existing, but I have been so often disappointed that I am hard of belief.' Her husband's wild optimism must have brought back memories of her theatrical, self-deluding, twice-bankrupted father. Bleakly she reminded Bellingham of the financial reality of their situation. 'Be certain you can make good your intentions, for should you not ultimately be enabled to fulfill them, we would be sunk in ruin from not having sufficient means to meet the tradespeople.'

Poverty had forced her to send Henry and his middle brother out to an infants' nurse so that she and Mary Stevens could work undisturbed. James, the eldest, aged nine, should have been going to school but had to be kept at home because, in Bellingham's absence, she could no longer afford to pay the fees. But the house at 46 Duke Street doubled up as workplace and shop, and she confessed to being 'very uneasy at James being at home, having so much valuable Linen in a work room'.

Briefly she allowed herself to cling to a tiny sliver of hope that Bellingham's prospects were not entirely an illusion. Her first impulse was not to let Mary Stevens know of his offer because, as she told her husband, she wanted to allocate her share to her cousin, Eliza, who had helped her look after James when she first arrived back from St Petersburg in 1808. Then, as though her husband's attempt to take this decision for her was the last straw, she burst out:

I cannot help remarking that in writing to Miss Stevens you address her in the same manner as me, 'Oh my dear Miss Stevens & yours truly John Bellingham'. Now I cannot help feeling hurt that there is no distinction made between an indifferent person and an affectionate wife who has suffered so much for you and your children – it appears as if I was no more to you than any woman that you were obliged to write a letter to . . . . [To] a delicate & feeling mind: these are insults, more particularly as my indisposition seems to have been forgotten . . . . The change in my appearance will convince you that I have been very ill, as I am now as thin as I ever was. If I was to follow your example, six lines might fill my letter – but perhaps I am not worthy of more.

This time there was no 'very affectionately', only a cold 'yours truly'.

Almost certainly, she had no cause for sexual jealousy. Bellingham was too orderly in his ways to enjoy the messiness of an affair, but he liked to win affection. With the young widow, Rebecca Robarts, he presented himself as the ideal tenant, respectful, attentive, and always ready to take her to church services and museums. Mrs Robarts admired him enough to allow him more than two months' credit on his rent but, whatever warmer feelings she might have had and he might have encouraged, there was no indication that they led to any unbuttoned intimacy.

Equally with Mary Stevens, he acted the competent, masterful male, who examined the books of the women's business and kept them in order. He undoubtedly expected gratitude, even a certain tenderness, in return for giving her half the business free of charge, but by enclosing the letter to her in one to his wife he showed clearly enough that he wanted no more. However, he was to be disappointed even in that modest ambition. Mary Stevens, who probably saw him more clearly than any other woman close to him, refused to believe in his act of generosity. Her scepticism gave rise to a uniquely clear-eyed account, recorded later under oath, of his behaviour immediately before the murder.

* * *

Evidently both women must have discussed among themselves the contents of his letters to them, because on Tuesday, 5 May Mary Stevens travelled south on the overnight coach to London. The next morning, five days before the murder, she took lodgings with a Mrs Barker close to Hatton Garden. Bellingham had promised to meet her at the coaching inn, but failed to turn up. She sent a note for him at New Millman Street, and on Friday, 8 May he called round to see her. In evident irritation, she declared bluntly that 'she and Mrs B were very much hurt to find one of the Objects of his Journey was to continue his application to Government for redress. That she represented to him how he was [wasting] his time, and the loss his Children were sustaining in their education in consequence of [his] absence.'

Her accusation must have cut him to the quick. It precipitated an angry argument that he concluded by saying 'he would be undeserving the name of a parent if he did not endeavour to make some provision for his Children'. It was too late then to go through the accounts, but he promised to return the next day.

When she saw him for the second time, on the Saturday before the murder, Mary Stevens made her disbelief plain by asking about his plan on which the handover of the business depended. 'I suppose,' she said sceptically, 'nothing further has transpired?' He replied, with complete accuracy as it turned out, 'Nothing, for he had been rather dilatory that week in consequence of [her] arrival, but he determined to set about it vigorously on Monday.'

Bellingham then took her and Mrs Barker to see an exhibition of watercolours in Piccadilly. Afterwards he went away with the books of the millinery business, which he as an accountant had kept and, as even Miss Stevens admitted, 'with which he was very conversant'. On Sunday morning, one day before the assassination, he returned with them together with letters for her to take back to his wife and John Parton, his business partner. This time Mary Stevens was struck by the look of nervous strain on his face. She did her best to persuade him to return with her to Liverpool, and thereby came within a hair's breadth of uncovering what he intended to do the next day.

It was clear, she said, that Perceval's government would not give him what he wanted, to which Bellingham immediately replied there would soon be a new ministry. Not realising what he meant, she objected that the appointment of a new administration would 'retard your concerns. Would it not be better to relinquish it than try to oppose the powerful so much?'

Clearly stung, he snapped, 'I will not. If Ministers refuse to do me justice, I will do it myself.'

Mary Stevens refused to back off. 'How are you to obtain this?' she demanded. When he replied, 'I will bring it into a Criminal Court,' she pushed him harder, 'What do you mean? Is that the Court of King's Bench?' By now she had reached the homicidal heart of his plan, but at that point Bellingham clammed up. When she asked again, he refused to explain, only repeating that he would 'compel the Minister to do him justice'.

In her sensible fashion, Mary Stevens then ended the conversation by saying firmly that she hoped it would be over soon so that he could return to his family. She intended catching the evening coach back to Liverpool after a day in the country, and with what must have been frigid politeness he wished her good morning and a pleasant journey.

However foolish she judged him to be, Mary Stevens never thought he was mad. While making her affidavit, she was asked about his mental state on this last day before the assassination, and declared that he did not betray 'any symptoms of derangement nor has he done so during the time of [her] knowledge of him, but when speaking of his application to government he was very violent'.

It was probably as good a judgement as could be made. However deep-seated his obsession about the injustices he had suffered, the clearest indications of Bellingham's underlying sanity were the unmistakable symptoms of stress that he betrayed. At one point in their conversation, he placed his hand on his heart, and said, 'You do not know Miss Stevens, what I have endured the last 6 months. I would rather commit suicide than undergo it again.' For the first time, she believed what he said and was deeply alarmed. 'God forbid that you should come to such an act,' she had exclaimed. 'But your countenance shews what you must have suffered.'

A psychopath would have had no qualms about the murder. But it appalled John Bellingham. If there is a key to unlocking the mystery of the Prime Minister's murder, it lies here.

What struck all observers at the trial, and ensured that Bellingham would be condemned to death, was the coherence of his defence. However misplaced, his argument possessed a logic of its own. It hinged upon the legal understanding of what constituted murder. The vital ingredient that turned a killing into a murder was premeditated malice or, in the lawyer's Norman French used by William Blackstone in his classic definition of the crime in his *Commentaries on the Laws of England*, '*Malice prepense* is necessary to constitute murder.' Bellingham referred to this concept several times and in different ways during the trial. His last words to the jury were, 'I disclaim all personal or intentional malice against Mr Perceval.' He assured them that the judge would tell them 'you must acquit me' because there was no evidence of *malice prepense*. And in a phrase he had repeatedly used before, he told them that 'a refusal of justice was the sole cause of this fatal catastrophe'. It was an oddly legalistic argument, and even his use of the phrase *malice prepense* rather than the common English version, malice aforethought, was the wording that a lawyer would have chosen.

The *malice prepense* argument, as Bellingham understood it, depended on showing that there was no personal ill-will in what he had done. Justice was all he sought. Every level of government, from the Prince Regent to the Bow Street magistrates, had been tested to see whether the door of justice would be opened. Only when none of them responded did he proceed to his final option. It was there, clearly stated, in his letter to the magistrates, 'Should this reasonable request be finally denied, I shall feel justified in executing justice myself.'

There was a fundamental flaw in his reasoning. The requirement of *malice prepense* was designed to exclude an accidental or unintended killing from the definition of murder, rather than a judicial execution. As Mansfield pointed out in his summing up, 'If a man fancied he was right and, in consequence, conceived that . . . he had a right to obtain justice by any means which his physical strength gave him, there is no knowing where so pernicious a doctrine might end.' What Bellingham overlooked was that the mere act of planning someone's death was enough to constitute malice aforethought.

Nevertheless, his strangely formal defence points to the nature of the difference between his frenzied appeals for compensation in 1810 and his methodical behaviour in 1812. When he first returned from Russia, it is clear that, in his traumatised state, he was driven by demons. In 1812, as his argument in court revealed, he had a plan whose endgame was the execution of Spencer Perceval. Everything he did during his months in London, from the petition sent to the Prince Regent in January to the assassination in May, constituted a single process.

The killing would force the government to bring him into court where the jury would have no option but to acquit him of murder. Their verdict, the judgment of the ordinary people, would at last drive an unjust government to pay him proper compensation. In contrast to the wild demands made in 1810, the sequence of events he undertook in 1812 amounted to a business plan designed to bring a financial return. And instead of the hundred thousand pounds he had talked of to Ann Billett, he soberly estimated he would receive a sum of about £8,000.

Although her affidavit did not mention it, Mary Stevens had seen Bellingham once more. When she heard of his arrest, she went to visit him in his cell just before she caught the coach to Liverpool. It was there that he assured her that his plan had succeeded, and that he would be released the following day. In her anguished discussion with Mary Bellingham, this assurance must have had a hollow ring. Neither woman could have been unaware that his plan was about to leave his wife a widow, his children fatherless, and all of them in penury.

Yet as they agonised over the idiocy of his reasoning, both of them must have kept stumbling over a problem.

To show that every avenue to justice had been tried was not a quick process. Bellingham's plan of campaign had taken months to carry out. Somehow he had been able to afford to live in London all that time. Yet he had no money.

The Search for the Truth behind the Murder

In its magnitude, and its cruel effects, the slave trade stands alone among our national offences; defying, like Satan, in the foremost rank, the wrath of the Almighty.

James Stephen, *The Dangers of the Country*, 1807

In place of the comfortable room where he had been held before the trial, John Bellingham was taken back to a narrow, vaulted cell reserved for condemned prisoners awaiting execution. Barely nine feet long by six feet wide and lit by a small barred window high in the wall, it enclosed the prisoner like a stone coffin. As a good journalist, William Jerdan had once asked to be locked up there simply to experience the effect, but he was almost immediately suffocated by claustrophobia. 'I screamed for the gaoler,' he recounted, 'but no one answered my call; reason had not time to exercise its influence, and after another fruitless effort with hand and voice I fell insensible upon the pavement.'

According to the account fed to the press by the keeper, however, Bellingham never lost his sense of self-possession in this bleak hole. Newman also revealed that in the brief period between the sentence and execution, a series of visitors arrived attempting to understand what lay behind his crime. Although physically weighed down by chains, and destined for hanging on Monday morning, the prisoner greeted each newcomer respectfully, expressed sympathy for the children of the murdered Prime Minister, but remained obstinately convinced of the rightness of his action. 'Yet with all his expressions of sorrow for the fate of Mr. Perceval, and the misery of his family,' the *Annual Register* exclaimed in exasperation, 'neither Priest nor Layman, Churchman nor Dissenter could obtain from him any acknowledgement of guilt on his own part in the premeditated assassination by which he had produced so much and such wide-spread grief.'

Among the most persistent was the clergyman who would attend him on the scaffold, the Ordinary of Newgate, Dr Samuel Forde. As a priest he anted a confession for the sake of Bellingham's soul, but on Saturday morning he had to give way to magistrates from the City of London. The responsibilities once resting on Harvey Combe had passed to the City authorities, and they now pressed the murderer to explain what had really driven him to his crime. The attempt was fruitless. Bellingham refused even to admit that he had done anything wrong.

'Government think to intimidate me,' he replied when one of the magistrates tried to bully him into giving up his supposed secret. 'But they are mistaken. I have been guilty of no offence, having only done an act of justice.'

To the eminently rational Samuel Romilly, such an attitude was one further symptom of Bellingham's insanity. 'No person can have heard what the conduct and demeanour of this man have been since he committed the crime,' he wrote in his diary, 'without being satisfied that he is mad.' William Cobbett, whose conviction for libel made him a fellow inmate of Newgate with Bellingham, decided that 'he was one of those unhappy men who are driven to a state of insanity by not being able to bear misfortunes, and especially misfortunes proceeding from what they deem wrong'. In the views of these people, and probably of the majority of people who read the shorthand writers' accounts of his trial published in pamphlets and the weekend newspapers, the murder was simply the act of a lunatic in the grip of a delusion. It was a senseless accident, without purpose or wider significance.

For the Prime Minister's grieving family and friends, Bellingham's refusal to reveal some deeper motive was as frustrating as the public assumption of his insanity. Sharing Spencer Perceval's Evangelical belief that his career was the working out of Providence, they needed to understand the real purpose behind his assassination. At the time of his death, the Prime Minister headed the most powerful democracy in the world, and, should Napoleon be defeated as Daniel had prophesied, quite simply the most powerful nation on the globe. Still more importantly in Evangelical eyes, his government directed the most powerful Protestant state in creation, capable of putting an end to Catholicism, sending missionaries to every corner of the world, and bringing forward the arrival of the new millennium.

The Prime Minister had transformed these tenets into government policy, and the growing might of the British empire was proof that it was indeed acting as an agent of Providence. 'And whither can the fainting eye of human misery turn,' demanded the egregious Reverend Daniel Wilson, soon to become bishop of Calcutta, 'but to this great Protestant Empire, which God appears to have aggrandized, at the present momentous period, with the design of employing her as the herald of mercy to mankind?' At the head of such a nation, Spencer Perceval could have done more to improve the condition of humanity than anyone else on earth. That God should have brought him to such a powerful position, then used Bellingham to cut short his life when there was so much left to do, challenged one of the deepest tenets of their faith.

To one friend and ally, it was especially difficult. None of Perceval's political colleagues understood better than James Stephen the Prime Minister's unshakable conviction that he was both the instrument of Providence and a politician who needed guile to do God's work. Stephen was the master strategist of the campaign to abolish the slave trade, but he owed his greatest victories to collaboration with the murdered Prime Minister.

James Stephen was William Wilberforce's brother-in-law, and his renowned fierceness of character caused the great abolitionist deep anxiety when he learned who his widowed sister, Sarah, was about to marry. Stephen was, Wilberforce wrote, 'an improved and improving character, one of those whom religion has transformed and in whom it has triumphed by conquering some strong natural infirmities'. However, Stephen's chief infirmity, his feral temper, had clearly not been entirely defeated because Wilberforce forecast gloomily that this, his sister's second marriage, would be like 'going to sea once more in a crazy vessel'.

Fortunately Sarah turned out to be just as fierce as her husband. To save money for charitable purposes, she wore her clothes until they were patched and darned beyond further repair, and felt it dishonest not to express her opinions as directly as possible. Thus the marriage proved a surprising, if volcanic, success. In a paroxysm of grief after her death almost twenty years later, Stephen blurted out to Wilberforce, 'O she was a friend of my soul! She told me frankly all my faults.'

Since a single soul was worth more than an empire, the only conceivable explanation that Stephen could find for Perceval's murder was that Providence intended it to be the means of saving his murderer's soul. On Saturday morning, therefore, he also visited Bellingham in the condemned cell to persuade him that he had sinned. According to keeper Newman's report, the condemned man was 'composed, and even cheerful, but rather taciturn' that morning. He had asked for his usual basin of tea, but was told that, according to regulations, he would receive only bread and water until his execution. He received this news as stoically as he had the verdict in court. But to Stephen's suggestion that his killing of the Prime Minister was a sin, he flared up, exclaiming yet again that it was no more than an act of justice.

Frustrated by Bellingham's refusal to accept that he had done anything wrong, Stephen returned the next day with none other than the evangelical Reverend Daniel Wilson. For two hours, Wilson harangued Bellingham: 'O! what will be the misery you will endure, if you rush into [God's] presence in an impenitent state! How unspeakably solemn is eternity! Never-ending duration! And how soon will this overwhelming scene burst upon you!' Loaded down with heavy iron chains, Bellingham listened politely but remained obdurate. 'I confess my sins,' he answered calmly, 'but I cannot say I feel the sorrow you describe.' But Wilson wanted something more. Bellingham's action only made sense in a wider context, as a force of evil. Deep down in him there had to be some revelation that explained why the catastrophe had occurred. Wilson continued hammering away until he was exhausted, 'Let me again and again entreat you to confess and forsake your sins.'

The only concession Bellingham made was in response to Wilson's emotional description of the pale-faced widow, Jane Perceval, and her weeping children kneeling around the coffin of her dead husband. 'She must be a good woman,' he murmured, hanging his head. 'Her conduct was more like a Christian's than my own, certainly.' But beyond that he would not go. When the keeper at last entered the cell to break up the interview, Wilson had got no nearer to convincing Bellingham to say the one word, to confess the vital link, that proved him to be acting on behalf of the forces of evil.

The list of visitors did not end with Stephen and Wilson. Just before eleven o'clock on the last night of Bellingham's life, Joseph Butterworth, a government-subsidised bookseller in Fleet Street

The Right Honourable Spencer Perceval, Prime Minister, Chancellor of the Exchequer. According to his friends, 'a man more highly blest by nature was never known,' but in the view of his critics he was 'the most mischievous of all the bad ministers.' NATIONAL PORTRAIT GALLERY, LONDON

John Bellingham. Attested as a 'most correct likeness' by Newgate's priest or 'Ordinary,' the Reverend Samuel Forde, who knew the sitter well.

© TOPFOTO/THE IMAGE WORKS

The assassination of Spencer Perceval in the lobby leading to the House of Commons. This contemporary print accurately conveys Bellingham's fashionable clothing.

© TOPFOTO/THE IMAGE WORKS

ASSASSINATION OF MR. PERCEVAL.

We have the painful duty of communicating to our readers a most atrocious and afflicting event—the Assassination of the Right Honourable Spencer Perceval, under circumstances that find no parallel in history. Whether the horrid perpetrator were really insane, does not distinctly appear, but we are informed that he has been confined for some time in a receptacle for lunatics. The circumstances that have reached us are the following:—

Yesterday afternoon, at about a quarter past five, as Mr. Perceval was entering the Lobby of the House of Commons, he was shot by a person of the name of Bellingham, who had placed himself for that purpose at the side of the door leading from the stone staircase. Mr. Perceval was in company with Lord F. Osborne, and immediately on receiving the ball, which entered the left breast, he staggered and fell at the feet of Mr. W. Smith, who was standing near the second pillar. The only words he uttered were, " Oh! I am murdered," and the latter was inarticulate, the sound dying between his lips. He was instantly taken up by Mr. Smith, who did not recognize him until he had looked in his face. The report of the pistol immediately drew great numbers to the spot, who assisted Mr. Smith in conveying the body of Mr. Perceval into the Speaker's apartments, but before he reached them, all signs of life had departed. Mr. Perceval's corpse was placed upon a bed, and Mr. Lynn, of Great George Street, who had been sent for, arrived, but too late even to witness the last symptoms of expiring existence. He found that the ball, which was of an unusually large size, had penetrated the heart near its centre, and had passed completely through it. From thence the body was removed to the Speaker's drawing-room, by Mr. Lynn and several members, and it was laid on a sopha.

Headline and article in the *Morning Chronicle* the day after the assassination.

William Wilberforce MP, responsible for the 1807 law making the slave trade illegal, and an ardent supporter of Perceval's efforts to put the law into effect.
LIBRARY OF CONGRESS

James Stephen MP, architect of the anti-slavery campaign, who avowedly 'would rather be on friendly terms with a man who had strangled my infant son than support an administration guilty of slackness in suppressing the Slave Trade.'
NATIONAL PORTRAIT GALLERY, LONDON

Lord Granville Leveson-Gower, ambassador to Russia and, by coincidence, both the cause of Bellingham's sense of injustice and the object of Maria Perceval's dismissive judgement that he was 'handsome enough, but his features are too pretty for a man and he is rather silly looking.' NATIONAL PORTRAIT GALLERY, LONDON

General Isaac Gascoyne, MP for Liverpool, who 'considered the slave trade so great a blessing that if it were not in existence at present, he should propose to establish it.'

The Old Bailey, the central criminal law court where all important cases were tried. Newly modernised in 1774, it was designed to allow better reporting of proceedings, as the number of pamphlets on Bellingham's trial testified. NATIONAL PORTRAIT GALLERY, LONDON

The House of Commons as it was before being burned down in 1834: an airless, candle-lit cockpit where force of personality counted for more than reasoned argument. NATIONAL PORTRAIT GALLERY, LONDON

James Harmer, who undertook John Bellingham's defence, was the prototype of the new breed of professional lawyer, 'a worthy and a clever man' in the opinion of his colleagues.

One of the many pamphlets printed immediately following John Bellingham's execution, evidence of the popular interest in the mysterious motives that had driven him to murder the Prime Minister.

Aerial view of Liverpool and its numerous docks.

Liverpool from the River Mersey around the time of Perceval's assassination.

and a firm supporter of Perceval's anti-slavery policy, was allowed into Newgate prison with a pass from the City of London sheriffs. Like Stephen and Wilson, he too was an Evangelical, and he too prayed with Bellingham. With more sympathy than his predecessors, he recorded the condemned man's belief 'that in a few hours more he should be in a better country than this – for it was a miserable place'.

Butterworth, however, was not simply interested in the state of Bellingham's soul. He had a question to put on behalf of the government. Reminding Bellingham that he would soon have to answer for any untruths before God, he asked, 'Had you or had you not, some other person or persons concerned with you in the murder of Mr Perceval?'

'No,' Bellingham replied, 'I do most solemnly declare I had not.'

It was the answer the government wanted to hear. The lingering suspicion that Bellingham must have had someone to help him persisted right up to the moment the rope was placed around his neck, but this was the most convincing denial he ever issued. Once he had heard it, Butterworth slipped away into the night.

There is no reason to suppose that Bellingham was lying. Indeed in his adamant refusal to cave in to the pressure to 'confess' that he sinned in killing Perceval, he demonstrated his commitment to telling what he saw as the truth. Yet it is also apparent that his grasp of reality had a particular flaw. However his state of mind is categorised, as deranged, obsessive, or sinful, he had a remarkable capacity to see only that part of the world that made sense to him. The question of how he had financed his long stay in London lay outside its narrow scope, and in the haste to hang him, it escaped the attention of the authorities as well. The records, however, showed that he was not short of money.

Among the items that the Bow Street Runner, John Vickery, removed from the rooms in 9 New Millman Street was the murderer's blue-backed 'Washing book'. In it Bellingham recorded in typically neat detail his weekly laundry lists, and the prices he had paid for having his shirts, drawers, cravats, stockings and dressing gowns washed. His cravats were changed daily, his shirts at worst every other day, as were his stockings and handkerchiefs, and he often paid more than half a crown a week in laundry bills for the pleasure of being clean and well-dressed.

He took similar care in making himself comfortable. Mrs Robarts's lodging house was on the corner of Ormond Street – the modern Children's Hospital is barely three streets away – and his rooms on the first floor received light from two sides. The area was unfashionable, but quiet and respectable, a convenient place to stay for visitors consulting the high-priced lawyers in nearby Lincoln's Inn and Gray's Inn, and less than an hour's walk from the palace of Westminster. Rebecca Robarts charged half a guinea a week for her rooms, with luxuries such as a fire costing another 5s a week. Even when the weather grew warmer in April, Bellingham still chose to keep the expensive fire in his room rather than suffer from cold.

There were other receipts in the bundle of papers that Vickery took away. The printer who had produced Bellingham's pamphlet containing his petition and correspondence with the Privy Council and other government departments had charged almost £10 to run off no fewer than 660 copies. The two pistols from William Beckwith had cost four guineas. A new suit of clothes ran to £7 10s. On his last Saturday and Monday of freedom, Bellingham had taken Mary Stevens and Mrs Robarts to exhibitions where the entrance fee was not less than one shilling each. And, as the chambermaid, Catherine Figgins, explained, twice on the last Sunday he and his landlady went to the fashionable Foundlings' Hospital church in nearby Coram Fields where collections were taken up for the support of the foundlings, and worshippers were expected to give generously. Finally, Vickery noted that in Mrs Robarts's keeping was a pledge of £20 to Bellingham from a Mr Wilson.

Whatever else might be mysterious about Spencer Perceval's assassin, it was clear that he did not stint himself. While he was in London, at least £85 passed through his hands, and those who arrested him at the scene of the crime found another £2 9s 6d in his pockets. As a yardstick, £50 was the annual salary of the government law clerks who lived in the neighbourhood. The amount that Bellingham spent in less than five months would have paid the wages of a grammar-school headmaster for a year and a half.

It was not unthinking expenditure. On the very morning of the murder, the washerwoman had returned a dressing gown for which she had charged a shilling, a sum he had questioned, saying 'If he had known the price would be more than eight pence he would have washed the gown himself.' But Bellingham appreciated comfort, he had cultivated tastes, and he enjoyed the more refined pleasures of the capital. The real mystery was how he afforded them.

Although some newspaper reports alleged that he had received 'remittances' from his wife, they were almost certainly untrue. Mary was too hard pressed to find anything extra for him, not even earning enough to keep their eldest child in school. By April she was, as she told her husband, 'greatly distressed for money', and a few weeks later she was 'totally destitute'. Yet in London, her husband was living on an income equivalent to around £200 a year.

It is possible that only the highly experienced John Vickery saw all the receipts and thus had the chance to assess their significance against the widespread reports of the Bellinghams' poverty. With barely a week before the execution, he had no time to undertake the necessary enquiries, but the pattern of Bellingham's behaviour in the months before the murder would surely have aroused his suspicions. In the sixty or so Old Bailey cases in which he appeared as the arresting officer, Vickery showed himself to be an exceptional detective. He had a policeman's eye for the detail that did not fit – a badly loaded basket that turned out to contain stolen furs, the furtive behaviour of two men who were sharing out money after a robbery – and in a service often accused of corruption he was rare in being trusted by criminals not to plant evidence.

The salaried Metropolitan Police, who supplanted the Bow Street Runners in the 1840s, always disparaged their predecessors on the grounds that their income depended largely on the rewards paid for apprehending criminals and returning property, a practice that encouraged corruption. But it was also true that among their contemporaries the Runners enjoyed a high reputation for their professional expertise. They had contacts with magistrates' courts around the country, they were called in to help on cases far from the capital – Vickery himself went to Wiltshire to help in apprehending a murderer there, others travelled to Yorkshire and Scotland – and, as he himself told a parliamentary select committee in 1816, 'at Liverpool, Birmingham and Manchester, there was a Police office, and regular communication [was maintained] between the offices and Bow street'. With time, an officer like Vickery could certainly have tracked down the source of the assassin's funds.

From the evidence found in John Bellingham's rooms and from questioning witnesses, Vickery would have learned that the murderer arrived in London off the Liverpool coach on 27 December 1811 and paid for a week's lodging with Mrs Robarts. On 2 January he told her he was staying on, but without specifying for how long. Nor did he pay her any more rent. Soon afterwards in Red Lion Square he bumped into Mary Clarke, the friend of his cousin, Ann Billett, whom he had last seen in 1810. Their conversation was brief, but, according to her testimony, when she asked what he was doing in London, 'He said he came upon business, and he might not stay above ten days or a week.'

Up to that point, there was nothing extraordinary about Bellingham's behaviour. He visited General Gascoyne in his Mayfair home to discuss having his petition presented to Parliament, and was told that only a minister could introduce a petition concerning money. Some of his time must also have been devoted to meeting the appropriate brokers in the Baltic Coffee House to arrange the purchase of iron and its shipment to Liverpool. On 21 January he sent the Prince Regent his petition for compensation, and asked for royal permission to present it to Parliament. By rights the document should have been passed on to the Privy Council for its advice. But somewhere in the bureaucratic process his petition was mislaid. Bellingham did not learn what had happened until late in February. By then the fee for the purchase of iron and whatever other money he had been able to bring with him from Liverpool had run out. Significantly, he owed Rebecca Robarts more than two months' rent, and, as he told the jury, 'under these circumstances, I was plunged into ruin, and involved in debt'.

But at the very moment when poverty should have forced him to cut his losses and go home, Bellingham began to spend freely. He commissioned the expensive printing of his pamphlet on 28 February, and paid a substantial deposit. On 5 March afterwards he ordered a pay nine weeks' arrears of rent in fashionable toilinet waistcoat from a new pair of pantaloons completed payment on the printing order. tailor. On 12 M ght after he was plunged into ruin, he spent Altoge the same date in February, he began again his attempt to on Parliament. The Prince Regent was sent another memorial and when he refused permission on the advice of the Privy Council, Bellingham methodically set about approaching the ministers of all the relevant government departments – Home Office, Treasury, Chancellor of the Exchequer and Prime Minister – and making personal visits to each. He spoke to the clerk of the Privy Council, the solicitor for the Treasury, and to Spencer Perceval's secretary whose written reply summed up all the others, 'Mr Perceval thinks [the petition] is not of a nature for the consideration of Parliament.'

Having exhausted the executive branches of government, Bellingham appealed to the legislature by distributing the pamphlet to every Member of Parliament. When that achieved nothing, he turned to the judiciary in the shape of the magistrates at the Public Office in Bow Street. On 23 March he sent them a bundle of papers – the petition accompanied by copies of all the ministerial rejections, together with a letter explaining that by refusing 'to permit my grievances to be brought before Parliament for redress' the government was closing 'the door of justice'. But this time, because he had by now completed his appeals to each branch of government, he outlined the shape of his plan. 'Should this reasonable request be finally denied, I shall then feel justified in executing justice myself.' Such an outcome would be, he said, an 'abhorrent but compulsive alternative'.

In a sense his plan was mad. To channel his desire for justice into a yes/no choice, with death as the penalty for a wrong answer, was crazy. But it wa~ ~~o beautiful in the sense that Goethe's Werner found beauty in do~~~~ ~~~~. Bellingham's plan lay an a~~try bookkeeping. At the heart of in a Russian prison where the be~~y system that set his sufferings a hive against an ambassador's refus~ ~~~tered as thick as bees in Minister's denial of his right to petition for ~~~~ne, and a Prime called justice. When the columns were totalle~ ~~~~~, imbalance between personal pain on one side and~~stem was indifference on the other. The deficit could be cancelle~ ~~n £8,000 in compensation – or by death.

In Bellingham's mind, this automatic outcome ensured the absence of *malice prepense*. Because payment or execution were simply consequences of the system, devoid of human emotion, the assassination could not be termed murder. But first the injustice of the government had to be made clear. Hence the need to approach every branch of government, and to demonstrate its refusal to do him justice. That took time, and Bellingham needed money to live. To be precise, to live by his standards, he needed £20 a month.

In his April letter to Mary Stevens promising to give her half the business free of charge, Bellingham offered a curiously phrased reason for his generosity. He could afford to do so because 'my family has had the benefit of a maintenance'. Bellingham liked to use precise, technical terms – *malice prepense* rather than 'malice aforethought' – and the *Oxford English Dictionary* defines a maintenance first as 'the amount provided for a person's livelihood', but this is followed by a secondary meaning: 'aiding and abetting litigation . . . undertaking to indemnify the Plaintiff against the costs in the case'. An investment in a plan that depended, as Bellingham himself put it, on a 'point of law', would have exactly fitted such a definition.

Vickery had one real lead to the source of the money, the £20 that Mr Wilson had promised to pay Bellingham. Although his report gave no further details, circumstantial evidence suggested that it was drawn on Thomas Wilson & Co., a London company with a particular expertise in providing finance for the Baltic trade. Wilson's services were used by many Liverpool merchants, but especially by the agents of United States exporters who wanted to trade with Russia. It need not have taken Vickery long to find out on whose behalf the letter was issued. But lack of time crippled his investigation. The discovery of the £20 promissory note was made on the evening of the assassination. He and the two other Runners assigned to the case had just three days before Bellingham's trial opened. The Attorney General, Sir Vicary Gibbs, required evidence that showed premeditation and sanity, and the officers had concentrated on assembling a picture of the accused, and tracking down and questioning witnesses who would substantiate the government's case.

The rush would have unsettled Vickery. The hallmark of his detective work was a slow, methodical approach. At the start of his career, he once let a man escape from a yard by rushing in to arrest him before a back-gate had been secured, and the lesson was not forgotten. The evidence suggests he was a big man – he was the one posted at the rear of a house when the Bow Street officers were making a raid, and criminals did not resist once he had his hands on them – but with his size went patience. He would note every detail at a crime scene; it was his habit to tag the evidence carefully or to mark it with a knife so that it could be identified in court; and he checked every alibi in person. It was typical of Vickery that he should have made a physical test to ensure that the ammunition in Bellingham's rooms fitted his pistol. And his unhurried manner encouraged suspects to trust him. When he arrested Robert Watkins, who turned out to be the Wiltshire murderer, Vickery noted that he 'seemed disposed to talk', and in relaxed conversation coaxed from him a full if inadvertent confession.

No doubt he sent a request for information to the Liverpool magistrates and to the police office attached to the court but, like James Harmer, Vickery would have been frustrated by the slowness of communication. The annual government grant of £600 that covered the cost of the Bow Street Public Office did not run to hiring post-chaises. When Sir Vicary Gibbs stood up in the Old Bailey on Friday morning, he had the evidence he wanted – the premeditated purchase of a weapon, the intent to conceal it, and proof that Bellingham 'was a man of sense, capable not only of carrying on his own business, but that he was entrusted with the business of others'. In the rush, however, Wilson's name had clearly dropped off the list.

The evidence from Bellingham's room that his sudden expenditure began in late February might have prompted Vickery to consider the wider significance of the date. Given the identity of the victim, he could hardly have avoided being aware of the political context. In February all the London newspapers, from the Whig *Morning Chronicle* to the Tory *Morning Post*, had chronicled the outcome of a power struggle between the Prime Minister and the Prince Regent. A month earlier, the doddery old king, George III, had finally gone irredeemably mad, and the prince seized the chance to try to remove from office the man who had humiliatingly forced him to take back Princess Caroline as his wife. Acting in concert, Lord Wellesley, the Foreign Secretary, resigned from the government, on the grounds that Perceval had unconstitutionally taken over 'the Supreme Command of the Cabinet', while the Prince Regent appealed to the Whigs to support a new, coalition ministry with Wellesley as Prime Minister.

The attack rebounded badly. First the Whig grandees, Grenville and Holland, refused the prince's offer because they recognised that without Perceval they had no hope of commanding a majority in the Commons. Next, the entire cabinet, at Perceval's suggestion, promised a mass resignation rather than serve under Wellesley. To establish his mastery beyond doubt, the Prime Minister then drafted what amounted to a surrender document for the Prince Regent to sign. It publicly declared that the prince was 'well satisfied with the principles upon which my present servants have acted, and with the success which has attended their measures'.

From late February 1812 Perceval's position as supreme commander of the government could no longer be doubted. He appointed the cold and serpentine Castlereagh in Wellesley's place, and recruited to the cabinet two of the nation's most efficient vote-gatherers – in England, Henry Addington, now Lord Sidmouth, and in Scotland, Henry Dundas, now Lord Melville – tossing offices and sinecures to their hangers-on to secure their loyalty. That was the only way in which contemporaries could see the unreformed constitution working, as a spoils system – 'without corruption,' observed Alexander Hamilton, secretary of the United States Treasury, 'it would fall apart'. With the king mad, the Prince Regent neutered, the country gentlemen loyal, Spencer Perceval's position as Prime Minister was not just impregnable, but he was close to exercising a parliamentary despotism.

His dominance should have given an investigator pause for thought. William Pitt had used the system to hold office for fourteen years, and the next Prime Minister, Lord Liverpool, would last for seventeen. At the age of forty-nine, Spencer Perceval could expect a similar span in office. Anyone hoping for a quick change of government policy could abandon the thought as unrealistic. In his memoirs, Henry Hunt suggested that this political shift was what lay behind the assassination – Bellingham realised that his petition would never be accepted while Perceval was alive. Hunt was wrong. But February's events might have provided a motive for the person paying the killer's maintenance.

Choking to Death the Illegal Slave Trade

The boxes in the front room and in the back room I have no doubt but they were broke open by these tools, we fitted them; this tool has a jagged edge, there is the impression of this tool on the box exactly, this tool was rusty, and on the box the rust was left, and it fitted the impression exactly, it was a strong elm box, it took some force to open it.

Evidence of John Vickery, Bow Street officer, in the trial of
William Askew for burglary, 1806, *Old Bailey Sessions Papers*

Had John Vickery been given more time to consider the source of the assassin's money, he would have begun his investigation with the classic question asked in the investigation of every crime with no obvious suspect: *Cui bono?* – Who benefits? Once posed, the question would have thrown up a surfeit of possible suspects. The *Morning Chronicle* named only the most obvious when it declared just before Bellingham's trial opened, 'It indeed afforded some relief to the agitated feelings of the community to find that the assassin was neither a Roman Catholic nor a Manufacturer – that he had nothing to do with the Orders in Council – and was not a Reformer of Political Abuses.'

Its readers might have expected the list of those with a motive for murder to be longer still. Wherever little Perceval had turned the paralysing beam of his boundless energy and narrow mind, he had made enemies. His indifference to the suffering of those he opposed ensured that their hatred took on a murderous quality, observable in the wild jubilation that greeted his assassination. 'He was a bitter persecutor,' judged the Whig magnate, Lord Holland, 'of such political and religious principles as he, without much painful inquiry or dispassionate reflection, disapproved.'

Two groups could be eliminated at once. Whoever backed Bellingham had money, and this took out of the reckoning both the Luddites who had publicly proclaimed their desire to see Perceval shot, and the London radicals who wanted his ribs to be broiled with the lardy flesh of the Prince Regent. Catholics could also be excluded from the list of suspects. However much they might want to see Perceval replaced by someone like George Canning who was sympathetic to their cause, there was no guarantee that a new government would enact any measure of religious emancipation – in fact the Prince Regent's opposition frustrated all attempts at toleration.

A detective who examined the scene of a crime closely enough to note how the rust on a jagged tool matched the rust and jagged marks on a broken box would surely have paid particular attention to the setting of the House of Commons at the moment when Perceval was shot. At first glance there might appear to be no great significance to the bad-tempered crowd of strangers who milled around the lobby and filled the gallery, but most were there for the same purpose, the inquiry into the Orders in Council. And it was remarkable how many of them were prominent in the abolition of the slave trade – Francis Phillips and William Smith in the lobby, Thomas Babington chairing the committee in the chamber, and Spencer Perceval himself. But perhaps Vickery might have been most interested in the man selected to lead the government's defence of the Orders, James Stephen, widely praised and reviled as the master strategist who had made the Abolition Act of 1807 possible. There was something about his character that would have attracted the sharp attention of anyone concerned with law and order.

Unlike his morally upright companions in the Saints, James Stephen was, as he himself confessed, a torn soul. Born in 1758, he grew up tall and good-looking, with dark, sensual eyes, attributes which allowed him to become a serial seducer in early life. Although he attended various schools, including Winchester College, his most important education came from Fleet prison, where his father was held as a debtor after his business collapsed. His experience in that unforgiving environment, including a daring jail break that his father organised, taught Stephen a bandit's view of conventional society that he never entirely lost.

He chose to practise law, motivated by a desire to avoid becoming its victim, and he first became interested in the abolition cause as a way of meeting girls. Having delivered a bravura speech as a teenager at a public debate in order to impress Maria, his best friend's girlfriend, he seduced her and made her pregnant, then set up house with her and his own girlfriend Anna Stent, while also having a child by someone else's wife. 'I have been told,' he said at the time, 'that no man can love two women at once, but I am confident that this is an error.'

The cost in lies and deceit, and other people's pain, caught up with him, however. 'I was in consequence plunged into a labyrinth of guilt and misery, from which my extrication was to human eyes almost impossible,' Stephen wrote in an uncompleted autobiography; 'and but for the infinite mercy of God, I should at this moment have been the Author of the destruction, the temporal destruction at least, if not the eternal, of more than one fellow being who fondly loved me, and whom I fondly loved.' This referred to a suicide attempt by Anna Stent, who had loved him since he was fourteen, and the nearness of her death was a turning point for Stephen. 'A sense of dependency on Providence for averting those dreadful consequences with which others were imminently threatened brought me to true repentance,' he confessed, 'and gave me a victory over those guilty passions by which I had been so long enslaved.' His transformation also awakened in him an awareness of other people's suffering that became remarkable in its passion.

Bringing his tangled love life to an end, he married Anna and in 1783 left London to practise as a lawyer in St Kitts in the West Indies. On the way the ship called in at Barbados, and he took the opportunity to visit the local court. There he found two slaves being tried for assaulting an overseer. Stephen watched the mockery of justice as they were found guilty after a brief hearing. Then, with a horror he never forgot, he heard them sentenced to be burnt alive. As he later learned, the verdict might either mean that they were consumed in flames or more probably baked on a red-hot sheet of iron laid over an open fire. During the eleven years he worked in the West Indies, he realised that there was nothing extraordinary about the barbarity of the sentence. It sprang naturally from the routine cruelty that was meted out every day to slaves wherever they were held.

Little had changed since Sir Hans Sloane's visit to Jamaica in the early eighteenth century when he observed that a rebellious slave was punished by 'applying the Fire by degrees from the feet and hands, burning them gradually up to the head, whereby their pains are extravagant . . . For crimes of lesser nature, Gelding, or chopping off halve of the foot with an Ax . . . . For Negligence, they are usually whipt by the overseer with Lance-wood Switches, till they be bloody . . . . After they are whip'd till they are Raw, some put on their Skins Pepper and Salt to make them smart.' In 1756 Thomas Thistlewood, a Jamaican slave owner, boasted in his diary of the refinement he added to the usual punishment: 'Derby catched by

Port Royal eating canes. Had him well flogged and pickled, then made Hector shit in his mouth.'

By the time James Stephen and Anna returned to Britain in 1794, his hatred of the planters and slavers had reached such a pitch that, as he confided in his autobiography, 'I would rather be on friendly terms with a man who had strangled my infant son than support an administration guilty of slackness in suppressing the Slave Trade.'

Back in London, he chose to specialise in marine law, and in particular the abstruse law that governed privateering. The rules that decided whether a vessel taken by a privateer could be treated as a prize or had in fact been seized illegally were arcane. But with the disposal of cargoes worth £10,000 or more riding on the result, tempers ran high, and the furious atmosphere gave the court its nickname, the Cockpit. Within its precincts, there was a general recognition, however, that Stephen's mastery of detail and savage determination to win at all costs made him cock of the walk.

He naturally gravitated towards the Clapham Sect and, after Anna's death in 1797, his marriage to William Wilberforce's sister, Sarah, cemented his position at the heart of the abolitionist cause. With this ferocious, driven man, Spencer Perceval developed a political partnership that was in many ways closer than a friendship. They were bound together by a passionate detestation of slavery, a conviction that their lives served a higher purpose, a background in the law, and a readiness to use any means to achieve their ends. Yet their collaboration lacked personal warmth.

Perceval shared the values of the Clapham Sect, but never belonged to their social circle. It was partly because the Percevals divided their time between Downing Street and their Ealing home west of London, but it was also a matter of temperament. The Saints were wealthy, convivial, and at the tolerant end of the Evangelical spectrum. Spencer Perceval had had to work for his money, he lacked time for partying, and he was unrelenting in his hostility to any form of Christianity that differed from his own. Soon after her father became Prime Minister, Fanny Perceval conveyed the underlying irritation the Percevals felt about Wilberforce's unpredictable views: 'Mr Wilberforce I do not think has behaved at all well,' she wrote to her eldest brother. 'Papa has hardly proposed a single thing that he has not objected to, and all for the pleasure of contradicting . . . I wish he would not "Friend" Papa any more, and go over [to the opposition] at once.' Yet where slavery and the trade in captive Africans were concerned, those doubts vanished, and, in Stephen, Perceval found a Saint whose outlook was even harder and more urgent than his.

Their first success had been to push William Pitt into stopping the importation of slaves to Guiana, but their mission to make the Act abolishing the slave trade effective united them till the day that Perceval was shot. Initially both men, in common with other abolitionists, imagined that the measures contained in the Abolition Act would in themselves bring the slave trade to a halt. At the moment of victory in Parliament, Wilberforce had turned to his fellow Saint, Henry Thornton, and gleefully exclaimed, 'What shall we abolish next?' His mistake was understandable. No one had tried to abolish the trade in slaves before. It was a skill that could only be learned from experience.

The Act had made it a crime punishable by confiscation of goods or a fine of £100 to engage in any activity concerned with the purchase, transport or sale of slaves. To enforce the law abroad, a garrison and a court were established in the British colony of Sierra Leone in west Africa to capture and convict traders who entered that corner of the empire.

Optimistically the abolitionists at once moved on to the next stage, building an African society that would resemble Europe's. In

1807 Perceval and Stephen became co-founders, with Wilberforce and others, of the African Institution whose goal was to 'introduce the blessings of civilization' to Africa by fostering the spread of education, of smallpox immunisation and of trade. It took time to realise that slaving had not gone away, only underground.

Hints of what was happening appeared in the 1809 report of the African Institution, but the following year the grim reality became unmistakable. 'It has been discovered, that in defiance of all the penalties imposed by Act of Parliament,' the report commented, 'vessels under foreign flags have been fitted out in the ports of Liverpool and London, for the purpose of carrying Slaves from the Coast of Africa to the Spanish and Portuguese Settlements in America.'

Under the laws of Spain and Portugal, the trade in captive Africans remained legal. It was easy for a Liverpool shipper to recruit a partner from one of these nations to become the nominal owner of a slave cargo ostensibly destined for Spanish and Portuguese colonies, in particular Cuba and Brazil. But the illegal trade took many forms. It registered Liverpool ships under foreign flags. It provided crews and skippers for genuinely foreign ships in exchange for a share of the profits. It dealt in equipment, such as that carried by a ship stopped in the Thames in 1810 whose cargo included 660 padlocks, 93 pairs of handcuffs, 197 shackles, almost six tons of chains and 'one box of religious implements'. But the most pervasive aspect of the illegal trade was participation through investment.

Bankers in London and Liverpool made credit or cash available to equip slaving voyages originating outside the British empire, or furnished vessels with papers identifying them as foreign-registered. Once the ship had taken on its human cargo, it might land them anywhere, not just in Spanish Havana or Portuguese Rio de Janeiro, but in American New Orleans or British Trinidad. So long as

Britain's financial web reached there, any port could be a market, and any investor could be sure of a return.

To abolish such a deeply established, highly profitable trade called for prolonged government commitment. Legislation turned out to be no more than the overture. From the day of his appointment in 1807 as Chancellor of the Exchequer in the duke of Portland's ministry, Spencer Perceval threw his growing political authority behind the persistent, aggressive policy needed to kill slave trading. The Bible-driven persistence that kept Wellington in Portugal, the blackmailing ruthlessness that forced the Prince of Wales to take back his wife, the bigoted contempt that swept Catholics to the margins of society and William Cobbett into prison – all were focused against illegal slavers. He began by persuading the cabinet to authorise the Sierra Leone court to pay a bounty of £40 to priva-teers and ships' captains for each slave they liberated. In 1809, again at his urging, a deeply reluctant Admiralty agreed to send two Royal Navy vessels, regarded as superfluous to other requirements, on a permanent patrol of the west African coast. Then the cabinet issued an Order in Council requiring the administrators of recently acquired colonies in the West Indies, still under direct control from London, to begin registering their existing populations of slaves in order to make it more difficult to smuggle in more. The legal and financial arguments needed to win the support of other ministers for these measures were supplied by James Stephen. The remorse-less Perceval hammered them home, but Stephen dug out the facts, and in return the Chancellor of the Exchequer used his powers of patronage to find his colleague a safe Irish constituency so that he could become an MP. To give Stephen more time for his anti-slavery research, Perceval also appointed him to a well-paid job as a master in Chancery.

* * *

The partnership acquired greater momentum with Perceval's appointment as Prime Minister. His first step was to force the Admiralty to provide a beefed-up squadron of five ships including frigates to patrol the African coastline constantly. This was the true beginning of what became known as the 'West Africa squadron', a unit periodically riddled by disease and despair, but one that grew into the emblem of the British empire's ideological commitment to the eradication of slavery.

At home, Perceval's government drastically strengthened the penalties for breaking the law. In 1811 any connection to the slave trade, including financing and equipping a ship, became a felony punishable by imprisonment and up to fourteen years' transportation to penal colonies in Australia. In place of the voluntary register of slaves, his cabinet passed Orders in Council imposing a mandatory registration of all existing slaves in Trinidad, followed by similar orders for other new colonies such as St Lucia, and Mauritius in the Indian Ocean. Step by step these measures squeezed each aspect of the trade and reduced its profit. Yet as significant as any legislation was the unremitting political support the Perceval government gave to the remarkable judge in charge of the Sierra Leone court.

What Oskar Schindler did for Jews in Nazi Germany, Judge Robert Thorpe accomplished for slaves in west Africa. Using his small base of power in Sierra Leone, he confiscated the ships of slavers found on the high seas, regardless of their nationality, and released their captives. Then he went further, actively encouraging Royal Navy squadrons and privateers to mount raids on slave stations along the African coast far outside his jurisdiction. At Goree and on the Pongus river hundreds of miles away, ships' captains used Thorpe's written authorisation to free slaves who were being assembled for transportation across the ocean, and to seize the ships in which they were about to be carried to the Americas.

Thorpe had a tiny legal justification for this flagrant abuse of international law. When slavery was made illegal in Britain in 1772 by the *Somerset* case, the judge, an earlier, better Mansfield, declared that the natural right to liberty made slavery 'so odious, that nothing can be suffered to support it, but positive law'. The lack of any such explicit statute making slavery legal under Spanish or Portuguese law was Thorpe's excuse for freeing their slaves. Only while he had the backing of the government could he make this vestigial argument stick. But during Perceval's lifetime he had that unconditional support, and Thorpe's unilateral action along the west African coast resulted in the release of almost four thousand Africans destined for slavery.

In this unremitting struggle against the illegal trade, the partnership between Perceval and Stephen was so close that it became impossible to say who took the lead. The Whig, Henry Brougham, asserted that 'the influence of his friend, Mr Stephen, over [Perceval's] mind was unbounded'; and in terms of intellect and intensity, he was undeniably Perceval's superior. On the other hand, Stephen lacked the confident charm, ambition and inborn political instinct that made Perceval so formidable. Certainly John Quincy Adams, the well-informed American Minister in St Petersburg who kept a close eye on London politics, thought that 'Mr. Stephen echoed back the word of Mr. Perceval', and did not hesitate to hold the latter responsible for the consequences of their alliance. In ruthlessness, however, they were almost a match. To choke the hydra-headed trade to death, they were even prepared to use what turned out to be a doomsday weapon.

The weapon was designed by James Stephen, and was originally intended for use against the French. Its purpose was outlined in a pamphlet published late in 1805 called *The War in Disguise*. Drawing on his experience as a maritime lawyer, Stephen showed that from the outbreak of the war with France in 1793, the enemy had gradually transferred all its trade from its own vessels to ships flying a neutral flag, predominantly that of the United States. Because neutral shipping was allowed free passage, this had rendered the existing blockade maintained by the Royal Navy round the coast of France utterly ineffective. Sugar from French Martinique and cotton from Guadaloupe were exported to the United States, then carried as American produce under the Stars and Stripes across the Atlantic to European ports. On the return voyage, their cargoes consisted of French weapons, pottery and wheat, carried in American-flagged ships ostensibly to the United States but in reality to French colonies.

When Holland and Spain fell under French control, those two countries adopted the same policy. 'Spain and Holland have totally ceased to trade under their own flags, to or from the ports of any of their colonies,' Stephen claimed. 'In short, all the hostile colonies . . . derive from the enmity of Great Britain, their ancient scourge and terror, not inconvenience but advantage; far from being impoverished or distressed by our hostilities, as formerly, they find in war the best sources of supply, and new means of agricultural as well as commercial prosperity.' It was time, he argued, for the Royal Navy to stop and search neutral vessels in order to control the trade of Britain's enemies. And the news of Admiral Horatio Nelson's crushing victory at Trafalgar, which arrived as Stephen was correcting the proofs of *The War in Disguise*, showed that Britain had the overwhelming naval supremacy to make such a policy work.

In 1807 the Chancellor of the Exchequer presented Stephen's theory to the cabinet, and asked for a more stringent blockade that required all neutral ships carrying cargoes to Europe to register them at a British port. Since Napoleon had proclaimed a blockade on Britain in 1806 with a decree from Berlin, the cabinet welcomed the chance to retaliate. The president of the Board of Trade, Lord Bathurst, presciently warned that the hostility created in the United States might lead to war, and 'an American war would be severely felt by our manufacturers'. But no other minister anticipated the ramifications, both intended and unintended, of a trade war.

Certainly Perceval himself did not understand the gigantic market forces that were beginning to drive international commerce. The purpose of the blockade, he told his colleagues, was not to stop trade with Europe but to force it to go through British ports: 'either these countries will have no trade, or they must be content to accept it through us,' he said. During November 1807 no fewer than nine Orders in Council were issued requiring a neutral ship with a cargo for the European mainland to register it first at a British port, paying a British tax of up to 15 per cent. To put this policy into effect, the Royal Navy was authorised to board any vessel under any flag that was encountered on the high seas to check its cargo and its papers.

The blockade against France was the weapon that Stephen wanted to use against the illegal slave traders. William Wilberforce, who knew him better than most, believed that he had always intended to employ the Royal Navy to prevent slaving. But it was the Prime Minister who wielded the weapon. Under Spencer Perceval's direction the Royal Navy was transformed into an international police force to combat an international crime. In his diary Wilberforce recorded tersely that Stephen 'agrees with Perceval *passim*, and with the government as to their grand scheme of policy – Order in Council; indeed it is his measure.'

Yet there was a difference between them. Whereas Perceval understood that success depended upon nurturing political loyalties and keeping personal ambitions well-regulated, the ferocious Stephen was ready to sacrifice everything to demolish the slave trade, 'and in its associated iniquity, the dreadful slavery of our colonies'. Not to do so was to risk God's goodness being withdrawn from the British. 'Who are the people that have provoked God thus heinously,' he demanded, 'but the same who are among all the nations of the earth, the most eminently indebted to his bounty?' Together, politician and firebrand made the extermination of the slave trade a crusade.

No other place suffered more grievously from their onslaught than Liverpool. For fifty years, most of its wealth had come from the West Indies trade – the profitable triangle that carried leg-irons, jewellery and axes to Africa, humans to the West Indies and sugar or cotton to Liverpool, and the less profitable but healthier triangle that took Cheshire salt to Newfoundland, salted cod to feed the West Indies slaves and Caribbean produce to Britain. For almost as long, these merchants had run the city's government, its common council, and used it to finance the massive public works – the docks, warehouses and canals – that had made it the second largest port in the country. But the West India group also represented the slave trade. Until 1807, the most prosperous, most respectable members of the oligarchy that ruled Liverpool had been the merchants who sent almost two hundred ships a year to the African coast, the Gascoynes, Gladstones, Pennys, Leylands and Aspinalls. Until 1807, they had invested about £1 million a year in the business of buying and transporting captured Africans to the West Indies and to north and south America.

In the last eighteen months before the legal ending of the trade on 31 December 1807, Liverpool's slave traders had shipped across the Atlantic 49,213 captive Africans for a return of more than £2 million. George Case, a former mayor, sent out no fewer than eight slaving expeditions in that time; others managed five or six. The chance of a final profit produced a kind of feeding frenzy that brought in outsiders such as James Bibby from the Irish trade and

Atlantic traders like Joseph McViccar, whose vessels were usually bound for the United States. No one quite knew what so many shipowners would do when this lucrative business became illegal.

John Aspinall, a former mayor of Liverpool, its deputy mayor in 1812 and a member of the West India group's inner circle, represented the respectable choice. In the wake of the Abolition Act, he changed the cargo of his two ships. West Africa remained their destination, but instead of loading slaves they brought back palm oil for the rows of lamps that lit Liverpool's grand mansions. Of twenty-two ships carrying palm oil in 1809, seventeen were former slave ships. Other slavers who decided to go straight after 1807 turned to the Baltic trade, importing Russian products through St Petersburg or Archangel. This was where John Gladstone, another former slaver and owner of a reputed one thousand slaves in the West Indies, sent three of his ships. But the movements of at least fifty former slave vessels, and as many as one-third of the original two hundred-strong fleet, were unaccounted for.

Some, if not most, had gone illegal. Although the participants concealed their identities, clues could be found in the blue pages of the Liverpool ships' registry where the fate and changing ownership of each one had to be recorded. It was striking how many left the registry in the years of Perceval's premiership, and astonishing what bad luck suddenly afflicted Liverpool's shippers in places where slaves might be traded. Vessel after vessel was reported 'lost off the coast of Africa', 'lost off Cuba', 'lost off Brazil', but whether in storms or by transfer to a more slave-friendly flag could not be established.

No fewer than four vessels belonging to William and James Taylor were reported as being 'lost off the coast of west Africa' between 1809 and 1812. Despite losses that should have driven them into bankruptcy, the Taylor brothers continued to prosper, almost certainly from slaving profits made under another flag. Just months after buying out the partner of his new vessel, the *Nile*, James

Penny, the millionaire slave trader who gave his name to a lane and a Beatles hit, found it necessary to remove *Nile* from the registry in 1811 because it was discovered to be 'unserviceable' while in the West Indies. Either the shrewd Penny had been duped by his partner or he found it more convenient to register the ship under a more tolerant regime. In transferring the *Amelia* to a Brazilian owner in 1811, Samuel Holland hardly bothered to conceal the fact that he was continuing to conduct his business under the flag of the most slave-friendly nation in the Americas. Suspicions even hovered around John Gladstone, father of the upright W. E. Gladstone, who supposedly had transferred all his ships to the Baltic trade but reported that his ship *Blanchard*, a well-known slaver, had been 'lost off the coast of Brazil' in 1811.

Driven out of a formerly respectable trade by Spencer Perceval's zeal, these owners, together with their investors and crew, had been transformed into felons liable to fines and confiscation, even transportation to Van Diemen's Land. The illegals had every motive to hate the Prime Minister who persecuted them so vengefully. It was Perceval who had championed the cause of abolition, introduced punitive measures for infringements of the Act, and ordered the Royal Navy to hunt down their vessels like terriers after rats. In February 1812 they must have feared that his basilisk hatred would pursue them for decades.

For such people, any Prime Minister would have been better than Perceval, but when Lord Liverpool was appointed to succeed him in June 1812, the illegal slavers must have felt themselves blessed. Until 1807, the new Prime Minister had been a staunch advocate of the slave trade, to the point of receiving a vote of thanks from the Liverpool council for his support. Although declaring himself opposed to the trade following its formal abolition, his government's lax policy contrasted sharply with Perceval's moral fervour.

It immediately dropped the compulsory registration of existing slaves in the West Indies that Perceval and Stephen were preparing to push through against the wishes of planters. The measure was not needed, Lord Liverpool blandly assured the abolitionists, because 'there was no evidence of smuggling [slaves]'. The voluntary code that was substituted became, as James Stephen angrily predicted, a dead letter. At the same time as the market in the West Indies was being relaxed, Judge Richard Thorpe in Sierra Leone was crippled by a withdrawal of political support for his extra-legal onslaught on international slavers. Far from urging the lords of the Admiralty to greater efforts, Foreign Secretary Castlereagh asked them in 1813 'to instruct His Majesty's cruizers not to molest Portuguese ships carrying Slaves *bona fide*'. And Thorpe's campaign was finally halted in 1815 when Spanish claims against his arrest of two hundred of their slave ships were upheld by the Privy Council.

By no coincidence, the number of slaves shipped across the Atlantic in that year jumped by almost twelve thousand to more than forty-eight thousand souls. This represented an increased return of about £600,000 for the illegal slavers, or very approximately £60 million in purchasing power today. Murder has been committed for less.

But the slave trade was not the only business in Liverpool to be hit by the Orders in Council.

Richard Statham, the town clerk, had impressed on Mary Bellingham the importance of distancing her husband's action from Liverpool affairs. Accordingly, soon after her return to Liverpool, Mary Stevens went to the council chambers to pass on her own information about Bellingham's behaviour. Her testimony was deemed of such importance that in Statham's absence her affidavit was taken personally by the deputy mayor, John Aspinall. Apart from the general desire to protect Liverpool's reputation,

Aspinall's particular interest was the West India trade. It was important to know whether there was any connection between the assassin and the disgruntled slavers.

Mary Stevens's commonsense and tone of unremitting scepticism about Bellingham's plans showed her to be a reliable witness. Aspinall would have been alert to any hint of collaboration, and relieved that nothing in her affidavit implicated the West India trade. That, however, was not the sum of Miss Stevens's information. She also had Bellingham's letter to his business partner, John Parton. What it revealed was the scope of his interests during his time in London. He had not simply expected to buy iron while he was there, he had hopes of returning to the Russian trade.

To a Liverpool insider like Aspinall, the implications would have been immediately apparent. Although Gladstone and other former slavers were involved with the Baltic trade, they all used their own, British-flagged vessels, and thus were unaffected by the Orders in Council, indeed they benefited from the restrictions put on neutral shippers. However the huge bulk of Russian iron, hemp and tallow shipped through Liverpool was destined for the United States. Almost certainly, whoever commissioned John Bellingham to buy iron in London was not a slaver, but someone engaged in the American trade.

Since the beginning of the war with France in 1793, American business had grown phenomenally, until it was worth £18,000,000 a year to Liverpool shippers. In effect Liverpool had become the hub of a trade that involved not just Britain, but every part of Europe, with the Russian portion growing faster than any other. The interests of traders shipping goods to and from the United States made them bitter rivals of the West India group. What the former wanted was free trade, and an end to the special privileges and monopolies of colonial trade that every sugar dealer and slave dealer had depended upon.

Generating more profits and attracting more participants, Liverpool's United States traders were already challenging the West India group for control of the city's council in 1809 when Spencer Perceval became Prime Minister. That challenge abruptly ended with the detonation of the doomsday weapon that he and James Stephen had devised against the illegal slave trade. Paradoxically, it hit no one harder than the merchants trading with the United States.

In February 1812, their own spokesman had publicly estimated their losses from the Orders in Council to be more than £1 million, or roughly £100 million in modern money. It dwarfed any motive for murder the illegal slavers might have had.

How to Kill an Economy

He never knew trade to be so bad, that he had never known so many failures in the same space of time, nor so many capitalists decline business, or fall off in their capital. The failures, he said, had arisen principally from the non-intercourse of the United States of America.

Evidence of Joseph Yates, Liverpool merchant, to the
House of Commons, June 1812

At 11 o'clock on Sunday night, 17 May, after James Stephen and the Reverend Daniel Wilson had left the condemned cell, John Bellingham set himself to write a last letter to his wife. His mood was curiously serene. His only real concern was for her financial security after his death, but Newman, the keeper, must have told him of the widespread sympathy for him, and of plans to raise money for her. 'My Blessed Mary,' he began, 'It rejoiced me beyond measure to hear you are likely to be well provided for, I am sure the public at large will participate in, and mitigate your sorrows.'

Money had always been his anxiety. He had been brought up to expect a standard of living that he could rarely afford. Temperamentally, he enjoyed being neat, fashionable and having women admire him. His clothes and his preferred way of life were those of a gentleman. But in Liverpool, where status was determined by how far above the

River Mersey you lived, the Bellinghams' home was rather too close to the squalid houses jumbled round the docks, rather too far from the substantial dwellings at the top of Mount Pleasant.

His taste in entertainment, as Rebecca Robarts could testify, ran to theatres, exhibitions and concerts. But his preferences were all expensive, and with three young sons to provide for, the struggle to climb further up the hill, away from the Mersey and towards the respectability of Mount Pleasant, cost more than he could afford. It was his desire for the security that money could bring that had driven him to take the gamble in Archangel.

'I assure you, my love,' he went on, 'my sincerest endeavours have ever been directed to your welfare. As we shall not meet any more in this world, I sincerely hope we shall do so in the world to come.'

The sentiments and loving tone were at variance with rumours of a rift in their marriage. Several newspapers had claimed that before the assassination the Bellinghams were about to separate. Undeniably tensions existed between the two. Ever since Bellingham had returned to Liverpool in May 1810 and won his way back into the family by promising to give up any further attempt to get compensation from the government, his Russian experience had haunted the couple like an infidelity. It was something both knew of but dared not mention. 'It is always a matter of dissension between me and Mrs B,' Bellingham admitted to Mary Stevens, 'and we never shall be happy until it's settled.' Ann Billett who visited the Bellinghams in Liverpool in 1811 went so far as to say that he became 'violent' whenever the matter came up. And anxious to preserve the peace, Mary Bellingham remarked that 'she had decided never to raise the subject of Russia because it so clearly upset him'.

Yet the tenderness in his final letter was not invented. Friends in Liverpool described him as 'a most affectionate husband and father, particularly fond of his children'. And Bellingham himself, in a rare moment of revelation, declared that 'no person was more inclined to be domestically happy than himself'. Even James Nevill, Mary's uncle and rescuer after her return from St Petersburg, who publicly declared him to be 'uniformly cruel' in failing to look after his wife properly, admitted that 'In his manners he was kind to his family.'

Of all his children, it was baby Henry to whom Bellingham was most devoted. And his love for the boy must have starkly emphasised his own incapacity to provide adequately for the family. The timing of his son's birth made it worse. The arrival of a new mouth to feed in the late summer of 1811 coincided with the dramatic collapse of Liverpool's trade. Throughout Henry's first months of life, the economy of the city was in free-fall. By the end of the year so many people had been thrown out of work that more than sixteen thousand people, a fifth of Liverpool's population, were dependent on free food and clothing handed out by the churches. Holding baby Henry in his arms that winter may well have been the trigger that prompted John Bellingham to think once more of the riches he had lost in Archangel, and the injustice of being denied compensation for what had been taken from him.

The recession was a direct consequence of the Orders in Council. Every kind of trade suffered, but none more heavily than that with the United States. In part this was an inescapable consequence of the size of the United States merchant fleet, which had captured the bulk of trade in the northern hemisphere since war broke out between Britain and France in 1793. From about £9 million in that year, the value of goods carried by US-registered vessels had multiplied phenomenally to more than £60 million by 1807.

As Stephen's *The War in Disguise* had revealed, much of that growth came from carrying the produce of French, Spanish and Dutch colonies to their home countries, and returning with cargoes of European goods needed in the Caribbean and South America. But close to £40 million came from a rocketing growth in trade between Britain and its former colonies, with almost half passing through the port of Liverpool.

The two countries made a perfect match. On one side of the ocean, the first industrialised nation in the world, on the other a gigantic, undeveloped, rural economy with a limitless appetite for manufactured goods of every kind – metal, machinery, glass, pottery, jewellery, even toys – and producing an infinite supply of raw cotton, tobacco and wheat for trade in return. As early as 1790, just seven years after the United States won its independence, the importance of Liverpool to its trade led to the appointment of James Maury as American consul there, the first time the young republic had created such a post.

Unlike the West India merchants who shipped cargoes in their own vessels, those engaged in the United States trade acted primarily as agents, arranging ships, cargoes, and warehouses for importers and exporters. They warehoused wool from the West Riding, textiles from Manchester, ironwork from Birmingham, linen from Ireland, until they could be loaded on a ship bound for the United States. Other warehouses held Massachusetts timber, cotton from the Carolinas, and Pennsylvania wheat for British customers. And from 1803, the traders had increasingly begun to arrange the import of consignments of iron and hemp from Russia for onward sale to American merchants. Each ton of goods sweated money into Liverpool pockets. Fees were charged for storage, for finding a vessel, for letting it enter the port, for loading, for shipping, for insuring, for extending credit, and – if necessary – for forging the appropriate papers. And the fees were high enough to bring complaints from the future president, Andrew Jackson, then exporting cotton from deep in Tennessee on the far side of the Appalachian mountains.

As early as 1801, an American Chamber of Commerce was set up in Liverpool, the first to be established abroad. Most of its members were British traders engaged in the usual two-way exchange of goods with the United States. But as the trade developed, a growing colony of American citizens came to do business in Liverpool, either trading on their own account or more often acting as agents for merchants and shippers in the United States. Many of these agents, such as Richard F. Breed from Massachusetts, William Brown from Baltimore, Elisha Peck from Connecticut, and Thomas Hazard were also involved in a complex three-way trade including Russia.

In 1800, when Tsar Paul officially banned trade with Britain, American-flagged ships exploited the opportunity to move into the Baltic trade carrying the iron, hemp and tallow that was so desperately wanted in Britain. After the tsar's assassination in 1801, British traders, including John Bellingham, returned in force, but American ships continued to carry Russian goods, only now they took them across the Atlantic for their own home market. For the agents of United States companies in Liverpool, it offered a third opportunity to make a profit – raw cotton or tobacco to Liverpool, then woven textiles, processed tobacco, or refined sugar for Russia, where the commodity could be exchanged for iron and hemp in St Petersburg or Archangel for shipment back to the United States. So rapid was the growth of Russian business that in addition to its St Petersburg embassy, the United States had to appoint a consul in Archangel, who happened to be Sam Hazard, Thomas's brother.

This mushrooming activity signalled the arrival of a modern way of conducting trade. Instead of the mercantile model, followed by the West India group, that prized trade between the home country and its colonies as the main source of a nation's wealth, the Atlantic trade responded simply to supply and demand. As Adam Smith explained in *The Wealth of Nations*, mercantile trade not only created an inefficient market because it restricted trade to the colonial power and its dependencies, but it also fundamentally misunderstood the nature of wealth, imagining it as a static value that could be accumulated behind trade barriers. The Atlantic business, by contrast, was virtually free of restraint, a marketplace for goods of all kinds, open to merchants, bankers and shippers of every nationality. In this context, wealth was made up not just of the capital value of the goods, but of the accompanying investment and income that flowed between customers, suppliers, shippers and financiers in pursuit of greater returns. This market-driven trade behaved in ways that few anticipated.

One surprising characteristic was pointed out in a petition protesting against the Orders in Council that was presented to Parliament by the manufacturers of Birmingham in 1808. Despite the war with France, the petition explained, Britain's exports to French-dominated Europe were worth £10 million a year. Napoleon's blockade made it difficult for the manufacturers to send these British goods directly to Europe, so instead they were first despatched to the United States, then carried in American-flagged ships to France. In the words of the petition, 'the neutrality of America has been the means of circulating, to a large amount, articles of the produce and manufactures of this country in the dominions of our enemies'. In the more vivid language of the law lord, Thomas Erskine, 'America . . . continued to smuggle [our] goods into France, for her own interest, and France contrived to buy them for hers. The people huzzaed their emperor in the Tuilleries every day, but they broke his laws every night.' Clearly, if the Royal Navy prevented American vessels reaching Europe, the damage would not be confined to the United States and Europe.

In response, Perceval's government reshaped the economic blockade in April 1809. New Orders allowed United States vessels to trade in the Baltic without registering at a British port, and, at the same time, made it simpler for individual traders to apply for special licences to trade with Europe. During 1810, more than eighteen thousand legitimate permits were issued for voyages to Europe, enough to meet the needs of the manufacturers. Napoleon's troops in Spain were largely clothed in uniforms made of British cloth and fed on American wheat carried by licensed vessels, while two million boots made of English leather were exported to Poland so that his army could march into Russia. Meanwhile eight thousand tons of wheat from northern France came through British ports, including Liverpool, to feed British soldiers preparing to sail for Spain. But as well as the official licences that made this trade legitimate, an uncountable amount of forged paperwork was also in circulation.

When John Bellingham returned to Liverpool in early 1810, the city, although still prosperous, had begun to be infected by a dangerously anarchic mood. Significantly, but not surprisingly given the example set by illegal slavers, the Atlantic traders decided to break the law en masse rather than observe the Orders in Council. False papers were routinely provided for American vessels bringing in cotton and tobacco, so that if stopped by the Royal Navy when sailing to Europe, they could show that their ship was British, or had called at a British port and paid British taxes, and was thus free to pass.

By the summer of 1811, about the time baby Henry Bellingham was born, the policies of Spencer Perceval's government had driven a large number of otherwise respectable Liverpool merchants to break the law and use false papers, false registration documents, false inventories, false bills of consignment. 'Not only are the names forged,' Henry Brougham told the House of Commons in 1812, 'but the seal is also forged, and the wax imitated. But this is not enough. A regular set of letters is also forged, containing a good deal of fictitious material.' As evidence, he quoted the advertisement of a Liverpool company which announced that 'we have established ourselves in this town, for the sole purpose of making simulated papers'. They promised to provide perfectly forged ships' papers and licences needed to carry goods to twenty different ports, based on 'the original documents'.

Yet despite Liverpool's best efforts, almost one thousand United States vessels were seized by the British between 1807 and 1812 to be sold as prizes, and countless more were stopped and searched. Although the French, Dutch and Danish navies subjected American ships to similar searches and took more than five hundred as prizes, it was the actions of the Royal Navy that rubbed rawest on American nerves. Influential voices in the United States soon began to talk of war as the proper response.

Whenever a Royal Navy boarding party inspected the cargo and papers of a United States vessel, it took the opportunity to press-gang into its service any seamen regarded as British subjects. The practice had begun in June 1807, when the British warship HMS *Leopard* on patrol in the waters off Norfolk, Virginia, battered the United States frigate *Chesapeake* into submission so that the crew list could be inspected for possible deserters. Three of the four sail-ors arrested by *Leopard*'s boarders turned out to be American citizens. The fury caused by the incident was rekindled every time another seaman was taken off an American ship.

Both President Thomas Jefferson and his successor in 1809, James Madison, tried to retaliate by imposing a trade embargo on Britain. Faced by the prospect of bankruptcy if they obeyed the law, most United States merchants preferred to turn smuggler, and the embargoes failed. But in the 1810 Congressional elections, the repeated humiliations produced an upsurge of political fury. Led by two of the giants of nineteenth-century American politics, James Calhoun of South Carolina and Henry Clay of Kentucky, a lobby demanding an armed response to what Clay called 'British slavery upon the water' began to influence the new Congress. The manifesto of the War Hawks, as they were dubbed, was summed up by Tennessee congressman, Felix Grundy: 'we will resist by force the attempt made by [the British] Government to subject our maritime rights to the arbitrary and capricious rule of her will'.

In May 1810 Congress gave the president what turned out to be an effective weapon against the two European predators, France and Britain. Under the Macon Act, complete freedom of trade with Europe would be permitted, but Madison could impose a total ban on one European power, if the other lifted its blockade before March 1811. In response Napoleon publicly announced that France intended to comply – covertly he instructed officials to continue to seize American vessels bound for Britain – but in London the United States ambassador, William Pinkney, found Perceval intractable. The Prime Minister declared point-blank that he was utterly opposed to 'courting of negotiations or explanations with Mr Pinckney [sic] of what England will do if America shall do this or do that'.

Henry Brougham blamed Perceval's attitude on his 'scorn of the Americans, whom he disliked with the animosity peculiar to all the courtiers of George III'. But the roots went deeper than snobbery. Intelligence gathered by the African Institution had identified the nationality of the ships, owners and crews that had taken over Britain's leading role in the slave trade. From agents on the ground in Africa and from the courts where privateers took slave ships they had captured to be condemned as prizes, the Institution concluded in 1810 that 'The persons who are by far the most deeply engaged in this nefarious traffic appear to be citizens of the United States of America.'

It had become illegal to import slaves into the United States in January 1808, but without a navy capable of enforcing the law American slavers operated without fear of the consequences. James

Stephen had already suspected they were proliferating from the number of cases in the Cockpit that involved American slavers sailing under false colours. And he had powerful support from Judge Robert Thorpe in Sierra Leone. 'The Americans swarm on the Coast,' he wrote, 'their Factors and Agents are evidently spread, and with Spanish or Portuguese Flags, papers and citizenships they still carry on the Slave Trade extensively.'

Whatever papers it carried, there was no disguising a slave ship, with its fast, narrow lines, foul smell and rows of shallow decks, like a chest of drawers, suitable for shipping humans lying prone. Unpredictable though the effects of the blockade might be on international trade, it was undoubtedly having the intended impact on the slave trade. From 1807, the court in Sierra Leone had dealt with several hundred slave ships boarded by British warships and privateers. Although some were captured by the West Africa squadron near to the coast, many were taken on the high seas, often close to Cuba or Brazil. No fewer than two hundred were flying the Spanish flag, although many were owned and crewed by Americans, and probably financed by British money. The mounting losses not only hit the illegal slavers hard, but undoubtedly deterred other shippers and financiers from fitting out ships for the trade. The impact of this onslaught was evident in the dramatic reduction in the number of slaves taken from Africa. From a peak of about eighty thousand slaves transported in 1807, the number had fallen to around forty-two thousand in 1810.

Perceval's obstinacy in the face of United States pressure to withdraw the Orders in Council was grounded in the belief, fostered by James Stephen, that the illegal slave trade was covertly dictating American policy. The War Hawks, it was noted, were dominated by representatives from the slave-owning states of South Carolina, Kentucky and Tennessee. All had a direct interest in relaxing restrictions on the illegal trade. To emphasise the hard line the British government intended to take, Stephen published a pamphlet in 1810 with the belligerent title, *Coup d'oeil on an American War*, arguing that hostilities with the United States would be in the national interest because it would leave trade routes free for British vessels.

Nevertheless, in their combined zeal, Perceval and Stephen were creating the conditions for the first worldwide economic depression of the industrial era.

In March 1811 the United States prohibited all trade with Britain. This time the ban held. In Liverpool the effects were immediate. Over the first six months of the year, the revenue from harbour dues dropped by a third. In September the United States consul, James Maury, could count no more than seventeen American vessels in port compared with nearly a hundred the year before. By the end of 1811, exports formerly running at close to £10 million had been cut to £1.4 million. The *Liverpool Mercury*, newly launched that year to represent the voice of reform and the interests of the Atlantic trade, warned that 'the distress in this town has been excessive, and it seems impossible to impute this to any other cause but the great reduction of trade with America'.

Those engaged in the Atlantic trade could not afford hold-ups in the flow of business. As agents, they depended on high volumes and long lines of credit from London banks so that they in turn could extend up to eighteen months' credit to their clients. The speculator Richard Breed, for example, could get immediate credit of £16,000 from Hughes & Duncan, Liverpool financiers, but his wish to make a long-term speculation in wheat for twice that sum required approval from Barings in London. These characteristics made the Atlantic trade uniquely vulnerable.

Suddenly, like a sub-prime housing crisis, confidence in United States business evaporated, and credit from the London banks dried up. Liverpool's warehouses were quickly crammed with exports that could find no ships, and imports that no one could buy for want of money. On the west African coast, the incidence of illicit slaving was falling, but in Liverpool the American trade was dying. In September the *Mercury* called for a mass petition to the Prince Regent demanding that the Orders in Council be lifted. But when the matter was raised in Parliament, Perceval's government swept aside the objections.

Significantly, the government spokesman was James Stephen, who defended the Orders as an essential weapon in the war against Napoleon. The *Mercury* angrily noted that he had 'the temerity in a moment of premature triumph to boast that the Orders in Council were the production of his brain . . . many a poor, starving family may lay their distress at the door of that gentleman'.

As it spread, the credit crunch hit trades that had nothing to do with exports to the United States. Organisers of the Chester fair where there was normally brisk demand for Irish goods like linen, beef and butter reported that 'the general stagnation of every species of trade was never more severely felt than at our present Fair'. Even the Baltic and West India merchants began to feel the pinch. And looming over the depression was the growing threat that the trade dispute with the United States would escalate into war.

When Congress reassembled in November 1811, the War Hawks immediately pressed for a rearmaments programme, including the building of new frigates and the recruitment of an army of twenty-five thousand men. The report of the Foreign Affairs committee, packed with hawks, recommended that 'the Orders in Council, so far as they interrupt our direct trade . . . ought to be resisted by war'. Summing up the political mood, Felix Grundy declared to his fellow slave owner, Andrew Jackson, 'Rely on one thing, we have War or Honorable Peace before we adjourn.'

There was little popular enthusiasm, and none in New England, for fighting what was generally thought to be a southern planters' war. Thus the New York and New England merchants, whose sufferings were being used as the excuse for belligerence, were the most vociferous in opposing the hawks. A writer to the New York *Evening News* declared that out of $45 million worth of United States exports, $37 million went to Britain. 'Now, after this,' he concluded, 'let me ask you what you think of making war upon Great Britain and her allies, for the purpose of benefiting commerce?' As the War Hawks gained influence in Congress, American business sent increasingly anxious messages to its agents in Liverpool urging them to find a way of having the Orders in Council removed.

To traders in Liverpool who could see the economic devastation before their eyes and at the same time heard from their partners in Boston, New York and Philadelphia of the rising threat of conflict between Britain and the United States, it was peculiarly obvious that Spencer Perceval had to be made to change his mind. And if he refused, to some of them at least his removal appeared preferable to war.

The *Mercury* columnist who described Perceval as 'the cadaverous looking, little gentleman on the green benches' was not alone in blaming the Prime Minister for the economic crisis that engulfed the town. The belief was shared by almost everyone engaged in the United States trade. Bankers such as William Roscoe and Hughes & Duncan had seen their profits slashed – the latter slumping from £32,000 to £13,000. The value of imports and exports tied up in Liverpool's warehouses was estimated in 'millions'. A single cargo of Virginia tobacco was worth up to £5,000, and a speculator like Richard Breed was ready to invest £35,000, or almost $200,000, in American wheat on the expectation that trade would be resumed. For such merchants, it was becoming obvious that the riches they might make or lose depended solely upon the will of Spencer Perceval.

When Bellingham began to plan how to force the government to pay him what he deserved, he found himself in the company of people whose ideas were running in the same direction. The focus of all their frustrations was the unyielding intransigence of one man.

In this bitter, desperate atmosphere, many Liverpool merchants, accustomed to breaking the law to make a profit, must have talked of the simplest solution to their troubles, the elimination of the man responsible for all the town's woes. The idea of political assassination was certainly current. A columnist claimed in the *Mercury* that 'we have ourselves heard persons who did not hesitate to declare that the assassination of a tyrant may on some occasions be a meritorious action'. The argument had originally been put forward by a government-financed newspaper, with Napoleon as the proposed victim. But, the *Mercury* pointed out, the principle could equally well be applied to other targets closer to home.

No doubt in Liverpool's salty fashion, loud voices declared that killing Spencer Perceval would be for the good of the country, and whoever did it would be a hero. And in the heat of the discussion, someone with a smattering of legal knowledge could have claimed that in the circumstances it would not even constitute murder, because it would be a patriotic act, committed without *malice prepense*. Whether he heard it casually, or someone deliberately suggested it to him, the idea remained firmly in Bellingham's mind.

That winter he broke the promise to his wife, Mary, to give up all thought of compensation. But when he returned to thinking about it in 1811, he did so less like a refugee from Russia, and more like the man he was, a hard-pressed merchant of Liverpool. He had a realistic target of £8,000 compensation, and a plan that would force the government to pay it. The process would involve approaching ministers as he had in 1810, but this time he intended to work his way methodically through each arm of government. If at the end he was still refused what he wanted, the injustice of it would be obvious to everyone. Out of Liverpool's fury and his renewed desire for compensation, a plan evolved whose endgame was assassination.

Even at that early stage, he probably voiced something about it in public. 'I was very well known in Liverpool,' Bellingham assured the jury, 'I could have got the signatures of the whole town [for my petition].' It may have been an exaggeration, but his obsession was certainly familiar to many people. The witnesses who rushed down to testify at his trial to his derangement had clearly heard some of his contributions to the wild discussions. Unfortunately, they realised too late that while others had given vent to pure rage, Bellingham had expressed serious resolve.

The Russian Connection Returns

He has not been shaved. He complains seriously of this last
prohibition, as he thus will not be able to appear as a Gentleman!

Report in *The Times* referring to Bellingham's protest against
prison regulations forbidding condemned prisoners the
use of a razor, 18 May 1812

In his memoirs, Lord Holland recorded his distasteful encounter
with a Birmingham manufacturer a few days after the Prime
Minister's murder. 'With a demure countenance and a subdued
voice,' Holland wrote, the Birmingham man condemned the public
displays of joy at Perceval's death. ' "It is indeed disgusting, and
yet," added he with an arch, puritanical smile, "it proves the sad
condition of the poor manufacturers, and it cannot be denied that,
in the present critical state of the question on the Orders-in-
Council, the finger of a benevolent Providence is visible in this
horrible event." '

Leaving Providence out of it, the manufacturer was undeniably
right about a sense of popular relief, amounting almost to achievement, among wholly respectable people at Spencer Perceval's
elimination. Everyone had suspected that he alone was responsible
for keeping in place the Orders in Council, and his murder supplied
the proof. So long as he existed, the Orders were invulnerable;

without him they simply evaporated, and almost at once the recession began to lift. An investigator like John Vickery, doggedly determined to understand why the Prime Minister was murdered, would have been intrigued by the widespread schizophrenia, deploring the murder but rejoicing that it had happened.

In June Lord Liverpool was appointed to succeed Perceval as Prime Minister, and at the first opportunity Henry Brougham then tabled a motion in the House of Commons calling for the Orders' repeal. Twice before while Perceval was alive, Brougham's attacks on the Orders had been defeated by large majorities. This time, despite vehement opposition from Stephen and Wilberforce, he found himself pushing at an open door. Perceval's former cabinet colleagues had already decided the Orders were to be withdrawn.

During the debate Castlereagh tried to justify this abrupt reversal of policy by pointing to Napoleon's announcement in April of a second decree withdrawing the French blockade. But in private he agreed with Wilberforce when the veteran abolitionist objected that the decree was spurious and French policy was unchanged. 'Aye,' Castlereagh admitted, 'but one does not like to own that we are forced to give way to our manufacturers.'

Had Vickery travelled to Liverpool in June 1812, he would have found its most civilised Mount Pleasant citizens caught up in celebrations at the withdrawal of the Orders in Council. 'The town,' declared the polymathic banker, William Roscoe, 'had arisen from the dead.' Anticipating the restoration of the multi-million pound, American trade, and a general slackening of controls on shipping everywhere, Roscoe and his wealthy friends raised enough money to present a solid silver plate to Henry Brougham.

Attempting to justify what looked uncomfortably like pleasure at the Prime Minister's death, the Atlantic trade's own newspaper, the *Mercury*, went out of its way to insist that Bellingham's action played no part in this triumphant outcome – 'the petitioners [against the

Orders],' it editorialised soon after the Prime Minister was shot, 'must [have] be[en] ultimately successful whether Mr Perceval be minister or not.' The *Mercury's* denial of the obvious demonstrated how the national schizophrenia could be resolved – by presuming that the Prime Minister's personality and policies had really been irrelevant to the grand sweep of events, and that his murder was therefore no more than an aberration. It marked the beginning of what became a national amnesia about Spencer Perceval's premiership until his very name slipped out of history. In fact, the reverse was true. Spencer Perceval's central position in the grand sweep of events – the war with Napoleon, the fight against the slave trade, the arrival of industrialism and the emergence of a trading pattern driven by market forces – explained why he had to die.

Amongst the citywide euphoria, Vickery, that careful detective, would surely have noted the exceptional satisfaction felt by the American trade. At a special session of the American Chamber of Commerce, convened on 25 June to hear about the withdrawal of the Orders, no fewer than thirty-seven members turned up, and in their relief they voted the generous sum of £500 towards the expenses of those engaged in lobbying against the Orders.

The minute books of the chamber, a volume the size of a small suitcase, showed how desperate conditions had become before the assassination. So few of the fifty or more members turned up for meetings that most had to be cancelled for lack of a quorum. Its chairman, John Richardson, estimated that his members had goods worth 'about a million in money' held in warehouses awaiting import or export. He had personally lost £20,000 when two cargoes he had tried to smuggle into the United States were confiscated. By contrast, in the summer after Perceval's murder members of the chamber shipped out more than £1.5 million of goods, worth roughly £150 million in today's prices.

Within the American trade, however, one small group not only shared in these unquestionable benefits from the removal of Spencer Perceval, but were engaged in the three-way Russian trade that would have brought them into contact with John Bellingham. Several of their names appear repeatedly in the minutes of the chamber of commerce – Tom Hazard, brother of Sam, whose partner Henry Cabot took care of the agency in Boston; Abraham Barker, whose brother Jacob handled the New York end of the business; and Elisha Peck, whose partner Anson Phelps had also remained in New York. The nature of their trade not only gave them an interest in removing the multiplicity of blockades that choked their business, but a passionate concern to preserve the peace between their native country and their adopted home.

At the hub of Liverpool affairs was the enigmatic figure of Richard Statham. While mayors came and went every year, the town clerk was permanent. An attorney-at-law with many wealthy clients, Statham had served a long apprenticeship on the town council before his appointment as clerk in 1807. He was efficient and generally well-regarded by the ruling Tory and West India group, except in one regard. Large sums of money passed through his hands, both as a private solicitor and as a public official, and much of it stuck to Statham's fingers. His business files were thick with letters of complaint from clients about his slowness in paying out funds that he controlled. Twice he had to be sued in order to force him to disgorge money belonging to other people. But the habit had helped him grow wealthy, and presumably he knew too many secrets to be forced out of office.

Statham's overriding concern at the time of the assassination had been to protect the town's reputation. He had raced south with testimony to suggest that an obsessed Bellingham had acted alone, and he had raised money for Mary Bellingham with the clear understanding that she supported this view. He was unlikely to have preserved any papers that suggested the contrary.

Nonetheless, had John Vickery been given access to Statham's private papers, the detective might have found overlooked among the thousands of documents in the town clerk's files a scruffy affidavit on rag paper dated 18 March 1810 attesting that William Gee 'was a fit person' to be considered for the post of keeper of the King's Dock timber yard. Three people had signed it – T. Browne, J. Parton and E. Peck. Browne was a Liverpool merchant who traded with Scandinavia, later to be Swedish consul in Liverpool, but of no immediate interest to an investigator. J. Parton, however, was John Bellingham's business partner, and E. Peck's cramped handwriting had inscribed the name of Peck & Phelps in the minutes book of the American Chamber of Commerce as one of its founding members in 1801.

It was a tenuous link at best, but it took on more significance when seen in the context of the extraordinary letter that Bellingham wrote to Parton just before the murder. Although dated 11 May, the very day he killed Perceval, it was clearly the letter given to Mary Stevens on Sunday, the previous day, when Bellingham brought her the account books. On 25 May the *Mercury* printed a copy of it provided by 'a friend' who, unmistakably, was Parton himself. The critical passage, according to the *Mercury*, was the last, chilling paragraph, which demonstrated Bellingham's indifference to the shedding of life. To avoid embarrassment, Parton blanked out all names connected to Liverpool, but it is still possible to fill in the spaces, at least in general terms:

London May 11 1812. Dear ——— [*Parton*], I have to acknowledge your favour of the 4th. Ten days ago I wrote to ——— [*presumably a merchant*] to forward the ——— [*some form of goods*] which suppose he will do without loss of time. As you have not mentioned any thing about the Russian ship, suppose nothing has been done by you; or that —— [*someone interested in the Russian trade*] has procured one through another channel. Herewith a letter to —— [*probably his solicitor, Thomas Avison*] and get the —— [*terms*] explained. —— [*a merchant, possibly Russian given the context*] had returned home some days before your letter came to hand, as you must most likely be apprised. £17 is the price here, six months credit out of the yard for duty paid; that is to say for such as has paid duty, and the seller retaining the drawback; so that it ought to be £2 less at least. If —— [*the Russian merchant*] is inclined for it, the strong (quality) would be objectionable to him but that can be given off to advantage at home. A Russian friend has offered me the loading of four vessels to —— [*presumably Archangel or St Petersburg*], and to receive the return cargo on consignment.

I wish my affairs were come to a conclusion; everything in point of law is in my favour; but Mr Perceval and the ministry have shewn themselves more inclined to favour Lord Gower than do justice to me; however as I am resolved on having justice, in case of need, I will very shortly play a court card to compel them to finish the game. I am yours sincerely John Bellingham.

To the *Mercury*, the final paragraph's throwaway allusion to murder as the last play in a card game was truly shocking. On the face of it, this was the outlook of a psychopath. But, as Mary Stevens had witnessed, Bellingham was undoubtedly repelled by the thought of murder. Thus what is most striking about the casual tone is how completely Bellingham had grown accustomed to thinking of Perceval's assassination as part of a legal process. Once it had come to a conclusion, he could concentrate all his attention on business. And, despite all the woes he had suffered in Archangel, that business was almost exclusively concerned with Russia. For Bellingham, trading there was not history, but the future.

Clearly he did not have the money to get back into the business on his own account but, as his instructions to Parton showed, he hoped to do so by finding a suitable ship for another Liverpool merchant interested in the country's products. Nor could he take up his Russian friend's offer of four cargoes of goods, or finance the complex deal concerning a commodity – possibly Burton's beer, much in demand at the time in Russia – whose price was £17 duty paid, but £15 with the 'drawback', or repayment of duty. Nevertheless, his tone indicated that they were live projects and that his partner needed to be told what was going on.

For any investigator, the letter radically changed the context of Bellingham's visit to London. Throughout his time in the capital, he was pursuing two objects at once, the quest for justice and a return to the Baltic trade. As Vickery had already discovered, his original commercial intention was simply to purchase some iron. This must have been a commission from a client since he could not afford it on his own behalf. In London Bellingham would have been expected to deal with a specialist Baltic broker, negotiate a price, and arrange the means of shipment to the customer. It was certainly within his competence, but, given his uncontrollable urge to rant about the injustices done to him whenever the subject of Russian trade was raised, the client who commissioned him could not have escaped hearing about his past and his plan for getting compensation. A Liverpool businessman only interested in acquiring iron would hardly have commissioned as his agent a man with such an unreliable history and so obsessive a frame of mind. Yet someone did. At which point, the question becomes inescapable – why deliberately choose Bellingham?

From Bellingham's blinkered perspective, the answer would have been because he was a merchant with unique experience of Russia, eager to get back into his old business. In the longer term, as he frequently indicated when writing to those closest to him, including his wife and Mary Stevens, achieving justice was only a step towards the larger goal of escaping poverty. His reference to finishing the game with 'a court card', a pun meant in the legal as well as high-ranking sense, made this explicit. The assassination was the last move in a play that would inevitably bring his legally watertight case into court, where he was bound to be paid compensation of £8,000. All he needed was some time in London.

No businessman interested purely in its money-making potential would have been attracted to such a scheme, but at the end of 1811 with trade in ruins other priorities came to the surface. Like the Birmingham businessman who regarded the murder of Perceval as providential, a Liverpool merchant could well have learned of Bellingham's plan for forcing the government into court by means of killing the Prime Minister, and wondered whether this was Providence at work.

Bellingham's client evidently did think like this. There would be no direct involvement. The commission to buy iron would merely set matters in motion. But anyone who knew about the mad obstinacy with which Bellingham fought to obtain compensation from the tsar's despotic rule could be sure that he had the crazy determination needed to carry out the plan. At which point, a second question must be asked – what sort of person would make it possible for John Bellingham to assassinate the Prime Minister?

The pre-eminent London bank dealing with American affairs was Baring Brothers. It was used by both British and American citizens. Barings had financed the Louisiana Purchase by the United States from France in 1803 with a loan of $15 million, and was deeply involved in lending to the booming market in American land speculation. For many United States merchants, trading in anything from salt fish to slaves, Barings was the banker of choice to provide the necessary finance. But in Liverpool, one particular section of those in the Atlantic trade preferred another London banker when they needed long terms of credit.

Thomas Wilson of 98 Leadenhall Street in the City of London, once a partner of William Roscoe, certainly understood the risks of the agents who ran the Atlantic trade. In normal times, Wilson & Co. advanced the money to pay Liverpool exporters for their goods when they left the port, and passed on to their American customers the price plus interest at 6 per cent for the six weeks or so it took for the shipment to arrive. On the other side of the Atlantic, the bank did the same for American cotton exporters, but billed the Liverpool importers who settled up more quickly something nearer 5 per cent. As Wilson's reputation grew, a network of New York merchants and financiers including Jacob Barker and Gabriel Shaw sent business his way. Wilson's Russian connection, however, was what chiefly attracted the agents of United States merchants in Liverpool.

Russian producers insisted on being paid in advance for ore and timber, and so not only was local knowledge essential but also a line of credit that might have to stretch from the import of goods in one season through the winter freeze-up of the Baltic and Archangel until the waters opened up six or seven months later. It was useful, therefore, that Wilson's cousin, John, a longtime resident of St Petersburg, happened to be a partner in the brokerage agency of Porter, Brown & Wilson. As a result, Thomas Wilson & Co. could guarantee both to find a market for rice or tobacco or calico sent on from Liverpool, and to arrange the finance for a cargo back to the United States where the American merchant fleet was as desperate for Russian produce as the Royal Navy. 'The hemp, iron and duck [sailcloth] brought from Russia have been to our navigation and fisheries like seed to a crop,' exclaimed George Cabot, brother of Sam Hazard's former partner.

To underfunded American shipowners, the backing of such a well-connected banker was essential. Thus when Henry Ladd, a New Hampshire merchant, discovered that the value of the barrels of sugar in the hold of his vessel, *Hannah*, was not enough to pay for a full load of hemp in St Petersburg, he turned to Wilson who advanced the credit to cover the shortfall. The advantages of Wilson's deep pockets and good contacts made it doubly attractive for American shippers to ship goods first to Liverpool rather than directly to Russia. They were paid immediately for the first leg of the voyage, and they were then safeguarded against emergencies in a distant country.

John Bellingham could have used such backing in Archangel instead of relying on his own credit and his own contacts. When he went to London in 1812, the banker providing the finance for the purchase of iron would most probably have been Thomas Wilson & Co. Not only was the commodity Russian, but among Liverpool's merchants the only sector with a strong interest in buying iron was the American trade. On both counts Wilson was the financier most likely to be used. And of all his clients, the one most in need of iron was Elisha Peck.

In the United States, Phelps & Peck specialised in importing metal. Other companies might ship linen or flax or hemp, but theirs concentrated on pigs of iron, lead ingots, copper, brass and tinplate, the hard materials that the rural economy of the United States needed for its growth. Eventually they would establish a near monopoly in the United States as metal merchants, paying fees of around £12,000 a year to Thomas Wilson & Co., and earning fortunes for the two principals, Elisha Peck and Anson Green Phelps. Although they rarely saw each other, Peck and Phelps acted like brothers, tied to one another by religion and upbringing.

Peck was a Baptist, born in 1781, who came originally from New London, Connecticut, whereas Phelps was a Presbyterian, but they shared the same stern understanding that their faith was a covenant demanding conditions of behaviour as strict as those of a business contract. The ruthlessness with which each of them drove bargains and enforced contracts was equalled by the ferocity of their interior battles against temptation and idleness. Phelps's account books showed him by day suing his debtors for every penny they owed, while at night he berated himself in his diary for allowing 'the variety of business and cares for the present life' to distract him from the renewal of his 'covenant of faithfulness with God'. He and Elisha Peck had grown up together in Connecticut, and been friends since boyhood.

As adults, each felt a compelling desire to obey God's will and to make money. The solution was to go into business together, and to trust no one except themselves. At first the pair specialised in leather goods – saddles in particular that they made and sold in the south – but they did not take long to realise that there was more profit in metal. This had to be imported from England, and so at the age of twenty-one, Elisha Peck moved to Liverpool. There he set up the company of Peck & Phelps, the reversal of names reflecting the fact that it was simply the other side of the American coin.

Initially he engaged in the classic two-way trade, American raw materials, mostly cotton shipped out of Savannah and Baltimore, in exchange for tinplate, nails, lead and brassware shipped back to New York. But at some date before 1811 he had added the third leg that took Peck & Phelps into the Russian trade, and led him to employ Thomas Wilson as his banker.

By December of that year, in common with other American merchants in Liverpool, Phelps had certainly come to realise that one man was single-handedly driving the United States and Britain into war. That conclusion was obvious to every American on the eastern side of the Atlantic. Even in distant St Petersburg, the ambassador, John Quincy Adams, expressed conviction that 'the

British Orders in Council unless abandoned would inevitably produce a war between us and England', and that 'the most powerful patron and supporter of the Orders in Council [is] Mr. Perceval, First Lord of the Treasury and Chancellor of the Exchequer'. In December 1811, American expatriates learned from the newspapers that Congress had told President James Madison that Britain's economic blockade would justify a declaration of war. That recommendation was hammered home by hawkish supporters.

'We must now oppose the farther encroachments of Great Britain by war,' insisted Congressman Richard Johnston of Kentucky. Only by a drastic change of policy could bloodshed be avoided. 'I wish to see Great Britain renounce the piratical system of paper blockade,' he demanded, 'liberate our captured seamen on board her ships of war; relinquish the practice of impressment on board our merchant vessels; repeal her Orders in Council.'

So long as Perceval remained alive none of those measures would be taken. Thus hostilities would break out, thousands would be killed and many more horribly mutilated. Homes would be destroyed, towns burned, trade brought to a standstill, and the affairs of Peck & Phelps ruined. It was apparent to anyone whose prosperity depended on keeping the peace that the time had come to intervene.

Where the Money Came From

I consider his Majesty's Government to have completely endeavoured to close the door of justice, in declining to have, or even to permit, my grievances to be brought before Parliament for redress, which privilege is the birthright of every individual.

John Bellingham to the Bow Street magistrates, April 1812

When he left Liverpool, three days after Christmas 1811, Bellingham apparently allowed only a few weeks for the operation of his plan to wring £8,000 from the government. From the delivery of his petition to the head of state, the Prince Regent, in January, he evidently expected to have reached the endgame by late February. Either his petition would have been presented to Parliament, or he would be ready to play 'the court card'.

Through no fault of his, however, the original timetable immediately fell apart. The inefficiency of the prince's office in losing his letter, and the delay in discovering the mishap, meant that by the middle of February the first card in the game had not even been played. It would take at least another month to carry out his plan, and already he owed six weeks' rent. Without new funds, he would shortly be forced to return home.

In the United States the military clock was ticking faster. In January news arrived in Liverpool that Congress had voted $11

million for armaments and authorised the establishment of a
militia army of fifty thousand men. No one yet believed the
United States to be prepared for hostilities, and its armaments
budget was dwarfed by Britain's annual expenditure on the army
and navy of almost £40 million, equivalent to about $200
million. Nevertheless, the War Hawks were gaining support,
and not only from those infuriated by the Royal Navy's repeated
press-ganging of American citizens. In the western states, settlers
moving into the prairies joined the call for war when they
discovered that the Native Americans resisting their advance
had been armed by the British.

For Americans who did not share the interests of slave owners,
these were powerful arguments, but not yet decisive. Thus in
February 1812, the outcome still hung in the balance.

That same month, Spencer Perceval won his power struggle with
the Prince Regent, guaranteeing that his policies would not be
changed for the foreseeable future. And in February John
Bellingham also ran out of money.

What Bellingham needed was a maintenance until his case could
be heard in court. Whoever put up the money would be an investor
to be paid back out of the compensation Bellingham would receive
from the government. The possibility that this person might be
considered an accomplice never entered Bellingham's precise
mind. What Elisha Peck needed was someone to save the world
from war. Whether Peck was indeed the person who commissioned
Bellingham to buy iron in London and subsequently paid his
maintenance is impossible to know. All that can be said is that he
fits the profile better than anyone else. What little is known of his
character shows him to have been a typically stubborn, flinty-
souled Yankee trader. His handwriting is small, spare and tucked-up,
his religion was strict, his education minimal, his domestic situation solitary – he was thirty-seven when he married – and his

accounts meticulous. He regarded making money as next to godliness, and nothing would shake him from a bargain once made.

Either Peck, or someone remarkably like him, already had a commercial arrangement with Bellingham. Now he promised to pay a maintenance of £20 a month drawn on his bank, Thomas Wilson & Co. But the schedule was to be unshakable. The case must be brought to court without delay.

Bellingham's acceptance of the contract was rewarded with a first payment at the end of February 1812. He celebrated with a spending spree, and at the beginning of March began the process of winning justice again, with another petition to the royal household.

The need for haste had become urgent. On 3 March, Henry Brougham presented a motion in the House of Commons calling for an inquiry into the effects of the Orders in Council. James Stephen led the government side, blandly declaring in the face of the nation's appalling economic distress that the Orders had actually led to an increase in trade. In reply, an outraged Alexander Baring came close to calling him a liar, exclaiming 'Nothing could more surprise him than to hear an honourable and learned gentleman . . . asserting that they had produced great commercial prosperity'. Even General Gascoyne, a lifelong supporter of Pitt's Tories, broke ranks and voted with Brougham and the Whigs. His defection showed that the West India lobby, once supporters of the economic blockade, had been engulfed like the rest of Liverpool by the trade recession.

At the end of the debate, however, Perceval made it plain that no criticism, either British or American, would shake him. 'As England is contending for the defence of her maritime rights, and for the preservation of her national existence which essentially depends on the maintenance of these rights,' he explained in his dull, persistent voice, 'she could not be expected, in the prosecution of this great and primary interest, to arrest or vary her course to listen to the pretensions of neutral nations.'

Sitting in the gallery listening to the debate was Jonathan Russell, the United States chargé d'affaires. The following day he wrote to James Monroe, the Secretary of State: 'If any thing was wanting to prove the inflexible determination of the present ministry to persevere in the orders in Council, without modification or relaxation, the declarations of leading members of the administration on these measures must place it beyond the possibility of a doubt. I no longer entertain a hope that we can honorably avoid war.'

The eleventh hour had come, and all hopes of peace and prosperity now lay in Bellingham's hands. On the surface, his justice programme was going according to the worst-case expectations. The Prince Regent rejected his petition, followed by the Privy Council, and the Foreign Office, and the Treasury. But during those fraught days, as one department after another refused to allow him to petition Parliament, the conflict in John Bellingham's nature between the beautiful and the sublime became extreme. By early April every avenue had been explored. The Bow Street magistrates had not responded to his clear threat to execute justice himself. A perfunctory note from them told him his letter would be forwarded to the Home Secretary, but nothing more. That marked the end of what was small and beautiful. He had now reached the endgame that consisted of one terrifying, sublime act.

His first instinct was to find some way out.

In mid-April, he sent a second, written appeal to the Treasury, fielded again by John Beckett. He followed it up by going in person once more to Downing Street to plead his cause. There he met yet another civil servant, a Mr Hill, who, failing to realise that he was dealing with a man at the end of his tether, replied that he was at liberty to take 'such measures as he thought proper'. It was intended as a brush-off, but to Bellingham, who believed he had given clear warning of his intentions, it sounded as though he had been given 'carte blanche to act in whatever manner I thought proper'.

In that agonised state of mind, he went to see General Isaac Gascoyne again, this time in his Mayfair house. It was a strange encounter that lasted, according to the general, for about an hour. By Gascoyne's account, he recommended that Bellingham again ask the ministers to present his petition to Parliament. Each of them knew this to be a pointless exercise that had already been tried, and that Perceval's mind was unchangeable. But the general's advice was not entirely neutral. He was about to present a massive petition from Liverpool against the Orders signed by more than six thousand people, and knew that Perceval already regarded him as a turncoat. True to his instinct for personal abuse, Perceval publicly labelled Gascoyne a subversive troublemaker, lumping him in with factory-burners, machine-breakers and those responsible for 'exciting outrageous spirits through the country including the Luddites'.

At their lengthy meeting, it is possible that, like Mr Hill, the peppery general told Bellingham to do what he felt he had to do. Unlike Hill, however, the general was familiar with Bellingham's implacable obstinacy and with the anger in his Liverpool background. Exasperated as he was with both Perceval and Bellingham, Gascoyne might have suspected the consequences, and wished the worst on both of them.

Shortly after this meeting Bellingham went to purchase a brace of pistols from William Beckwith. But even then, he could not force himself to take the last step.

The strain in his face immediately struck Mary Stevens when she saw Bellingham on 8 May 1812. For more than three weeks he had put off playing the final fatal card. He had bought the weapons, a concealed pocket had been added to his coat, and he had familiarised himself with the Prime Minister's appearance. Then nothing.

Bellingham understood acutely the obligations of a contract. His entire campaign for compensation sprang from his resentment at the government's failure to perform the reciprocal duties it owed to its citizens. Now, having promised to bring the business to court, he had failed to carry out his side of the bargain. On the weekend of Mary Stevens's arrival he suddenly broke down, and admitted that he was close to suicide. He had been so forthright about the infallibility of his plan, and so direct in telling his wife of its impending success. Mary Stevens herself must have added to the nightmare by her unmistakable scepticism. But, as his behaviour was to demonstrate, it is also evident that the source of his maintenance had lost all patience with the delay. A contract had been made, Bellingham had been paid, and the case needed to be taken to court at once.

Information from New York made it clear that the absolutely final second was approaching before war was declared. On 2 April, Congress took the long-discussed measure of forbidding all shipping to enter or leave United States ports for ninety days. This was seen as the last step before a declaration of war. By 1 July, therefore, either the embargo would have been lifted or war would have been declared.

Information took four to six weeks to cross the Atlantic from east to west. A United States sloop, *Hornet*, carrying diplomatic despatches from London had sailed early in April, and was generally thought to be the last official carrier of news about the British government's intentions. Its message was simply that no change had taken place. But conceivably an unofficial courier could have left with good news as late as the first week of May, and still have been in time to prevent war breaking out.

During these last moments, Perceval and Stephen were becoming more isolated. In the Commons, Henry Brougham was finally granted the House of Commons inquiry he had pressed for into the economic effects of the Orders. Even former hardliners like the new Foreign Secretary, Lord Castlereagh, now argued for concessions. On 21 April the Prime Minister gave way sufficiently to allow the Prince Regent to announce that the Orders in Council might be withdrawn on condition that Napoleon publicly revoked the 1806 Berlin decree without secret caveats. Beyond that Perceval would not yield a step, and no one had the power to make him.

The stakes could not have been higher. In the United States, there was growing opposition to the war from New York merchants like Anson G. Phelps and Jacob Barker, and from New England shippers like Henry Cabot. A writer to the *New York Evening Post* appealed to the hawks to draw back from a declaration of war: 'The measure is perfect madness. You will lose millions when you will gain a cent. The expense will be enormous. It will ruin our country.' In Congress a substantial minority of congressmen and senators were adamantly against hostilities.

A handbill circulating in New England condemned the war as a device by rich, southern slave owners to gain control over the yeomen farmers and shopkeepers of the north. 'Ye who live by farming, by the mechanic arts, and by commerce,' it demanded, 'where and what would you be, at the end of a five years war with England, directed by Southern planters? If you escape a war, you are doomed to be deprived of your commerce; and with your commerce goes your freedom.' So deeply did this suspicion run that Governor Caleb Strong of Massachusetts refused to participate or even let the state's militia be called up for service. Nationwide, less than one-fifth of the expected volunteers had come forward to enlist. It only required the removal of the Orders in Council and the fragile momentum for war would collapse.

By Sunday, 10 May, John Bellingham was at breaking point. Psychologically, he still recoiled from murder. But there was nowhere else to go. He had broken his contract. As a result April's maintenance had not been paid. And now his money had run out.

Mary Stevens's arrival exposed his desperate position. The whole point of her coming to London was to be given the business free of debt, and an essential part of the process was for Bellingham to introduce her to creditors and suppliers so that they knew the arrangement. Have confidence in me 'to do what is right and proper', he had told her in his letter. 'You will not be deceived . . .' But he had deceived her.

Instead of meeting Miss Stevens off the coach as he promised, Bellingham avoided her for two days, and only made contact at the weekend when businesses were closed. Although he examined the accounts she had brought, there were no introductions to trades people, and no handover of half the business. Evidently he could no longer afford to do so and, since a husband was responsible for his wife's debts, presumably he himself could not face Mary Bellingham's creditors. On top of that, he owed his landlady for a further five weeks' rent and firing. Rebecca Robarts was prepared to extend him credit, but Bellingham's display of anger at the shilling charged by the washerwoman on the Monday morning showed how thin his well-disciplined nerves were stretched.

Dire though Bellingham's financial situation was, his sponsor evidently refused to pay him another penny until the contract was fulfilled. Yet with so great a prize so close at hand, he clearly hoped that even at the very last second Bellingham could still be persuaded to play 'the court card'. As much as any other detail, this adamant insistence on the terms of the deal points to Elisha Peck as the paymaster. That weekend he must have been in London because only his presence would explain Bellingham's extraordinary behaviour on the day of the assassination. Everything Bellingham did was dictated by the need to ensure that on Monday evening, as John Vickery could testify, Rebecca Robarts would be in possession of Wilson's note promising to pay £20 to John Bellingham.

Manifestly Bellingham could only have acquired the note just before the killing, otherwise he would immediately have turned it into cash. In court, Mrs Robarts's chambermaid Catherine Figgins testified that he left the lodging-house at noon on the day of the assassination for about an hour. Presumably that is when he met his investor, and secured an agreement that he would be paid April's maintenance, on the strict condition that he carried out his side of the contract that very day. While the American, if that's who he was, went off to 98 Leadenhall Street to make arrangements with his banker, Bellingham returned to New Millman Street and suggested to his landlady an expedition to the European Museum. Of all the strange events of that day, their last outing together was in many ways the most curious.

At about one o'clock on Monday afternoon, John Bellingham took Rebecca Robarts and her young son to an exhibition at the museum in King Street, next to St James's Square. They walked there from New Millman Street, a journey of about forty minutes. Tucked into the secret pocket of his coat was a primed and loaded pistol, while another bulged in his yellow ochre, nankeen pantaloons. The inconvenience, danger and sheer eccentricity of going so far for such a trivial reason, armed with two loaded weapons that were to be used to commit murder immediately afterwards, would have struck a mind far less fastidious than Bellingham's as bizarre.

It is impossible to suppose that he undertook the expedition simply to entertain a landlady who had been remarkably forbearing about his rent. At that moment, worlds kept apart in his viscous mind were in gross danger of colliding. The self-possessed, gentlemanly Bellingham, appreciative of beauty, of well-fitting, well-laundered clothes, and of the discreet affection of a young mother, was threatened by the terrifying reality of Peck's contract – the 'abhorrent but compulsive alternative' of killing the Prime Minister.

The trio spent more than two hours enjoying the exhibits at the European Museum. When they came out, it was some time after four o'clock. Hearings into the Orders in Council organised by Henry Brougham were publicly scheduled to begin at 4.30 p.m.

Bellingham should have chosen the direct route from St James's Square to Parliament Square, cutting through St James's Park. It takes about fifteen minutes. He would have arrived shortly before the start of the hearings, in good time for the appearance of the Prime Minister. Instead, he, Mrs Robarts and her son walked away in almost the opposite direction towards Leicester Square.

They went to Sidney's Alley, a short street leading into the square, where a row of smart shops sold jewellery, lace and silk. Bellingham would have needed some privacy for his last transaction with his sponsor. At 7 Sidney's Alley, Thomas Challenier offered fine linen for sale, material that came from both Russia and Ireland, and he might once have been one of Bellingham's customers. On this occasion, his flinty-souled sponsor had with him a note promising to pay £20, issued by Thomas Wilson. No doubt Bellingham had to prove that he did finally intend to carry out his plan. In the back of Challenier's shop, out of his landlady's sight, a glimpse of the two pistols would have carried conviction. The note was handed over. Bellingham rejoined Mrs Robarts, gave her the promise of £20, then politely excused himself, saying, as his landlady recalled, that he had to go to Westminster to buy a prayer book. Rebecca Robarts and her son would have arrived back at the lodging-house at about quarter past five, just as Spencer Perceval was being murdered.

He could not have avoided the detour. Indebtedness made it necessary. But it could have ruined everything. Had Spencer Perceval left 10 Downing Street at half past four for the start of the hearings on the Orders in Council, or at ten minutes to five to see his friend James Stephen open the defence, John Bellingham's plan would have collapsed. The promissory note would have been revoked, Rebecca Robarts would reluctantly have been forced to admit that her finely dressed lodger could not pay his rent, and a homeless

Bellingham would have had to return to Liverpool. Mary Stevens would not have been surprised.

As it was, anxiety must have squeezed the air from his lungs all the way down crowded Whitehall and up the steps into the lobby of the Houses of Parliament. The deep gasping for breath that struck William Jerdan when he caught Bellingham testified to the tension he had been under. At no time in all his tense life had John Bellingham been so completely alone with his fear of the sublime.

It is possible that one other person was also suffering from a similar degree of anxiety.

At the moment John Bellingham fired his shot, General Isaac Gascoyne sat in an upstairs committee room with yet another Liverpool petition against the Orders. He had made a private appointment to go through its terms with Perceval, and having been savaged for his irresponsibility in presenting the previous peti-tion, he was presumably prepared for a bruising exchange. Like Brougham, he had expected Perceval to arrive earlier, and, when he did not turn up, Gascoyne had walked upstairs to the committee room which opened onto a balcony overlooking the lobby.

Despite his distance from the scene, the general claimed under oath that sounds travelled so clearly, 'it was nearly the same thing as to hearing, as to being in the lobby of the House'. Accordingly when he heard the pistol shot followed by cries to close the door, he 'rushed down stairs, through the House into the lobby'. There someone said to him, 'that is the man who fired the pistol', and he saw a crowd gathered around Bellingham, whom he either did or did not recognise according to the particular version of the story he told. But there was one obvious flaw in every version.

While those in the lobby had seen Perceval fall dead, Gascoyne had only heard a shot. He could not have known that anyone was killed, still less that it was the Prime Minister.

The natural reaction to the sound of a pistol shot would be to step out onto the balcony and look down to the lobby to see what was happening. The general never explained why he decided to rush directly to the scene without looking, nor did he ever reveal at what point he discovered the identity of the victim. His testimony always implied that he knew immediately that it was Perceval who had been shot.

The most innocent explanation is that his knowledge of Bellingham, and especially the tone of their last encounter, had given the general some inkling of what he intended to do. Thus, when he saw Bellingham pointed out in the lobby as the man who had fired the shot, he instantly realised what must have happened.

A less innocent explanation is that Gascoyne had more than an inkling of Bellingham's intentions, but did nothing about it. Unlike the London magistrates and civil servants, he was aware of Liverpool's hatred of the Prime Minister, and the risk of it taking violent form. The fury with which Gascoyne attacked Bellingham, like his pretence at suddenly recognising him in the Commons, could be taken to be the result of bad conscience.

The least innocent explanation is that he had prior knowledge. Bellingham's story was sufficiently remarkable, and his persistence sufficiently irritating, to ensure that Isaac Gascoyne would have talked about him to friends in Liverpool, and especially to the Atlantic traders whose petition he had just presented in Parliament. Conceivably, they discussed the steps that Bellingham was prepared to take, and both the traders and the general had concluded, like Elisha Peck, that it might be providential if one life were sacrificed *pro bono publico*. In that case, there would have been no need to step out onto the balcony to find out who had fallen victim to a pistol shot. Only the pressing urgency to show that he was in no way complicit.

* * *

The relief that everyone noted in the assassin after his deed was not one that came from killing the Prime Minister, but from being able to return to the world of beauty. Convinced that the justice of his action would be recognised and that the government would have to pay the compensation he demanded, Bellingham was at last free from anxiety. His triumph would soon be known to his wife and to Mary Stevens, and beyond that there extended a limitless future as a successful Russian merchant, growing in wealth and basking in the affection of his three sons.

The first indication of this brighter future arrived in his cell on Thursday afternoon, just before the trial. While Mary Stevens was visiting him, *The Times* reported, the prisoner 'received a small box, containing one fifty, one twenty, and several Bank-notes for smaller sums, amounting altogether to about an hundred guineas [£105]. It was not ascertained whether this sum was an anonymous gift, or came from a known friend to meet the expenses of the trial.'

The report was not published until Monday, 18 May, and the paragraph was crammed into the foot of the right-hand column well away from the main story, clearly provided by Newgate's Keeper, John Newman, that on his last full day alive Bellingham had complained that he would not be shaved before his execution and 'he thus will not be able to appear as a Gentleman!' The item about the money came from a different source, and appeared at the last moment as the paper was being made up late on Sunday night. By any journalistic standards, however, it should have been the headline news. The thirty or so pounds in coin and small notes might well have been contributions from anonymous sympathisers, but the two large-denomination notes, for £50 and £20, represented something quite different. Such sums could only have come from one or more wealthy individuals.

The smaller note was presumably from his sponsor and represented May's instalment of the maintenance. In strict justice, it was not due until the end of the month, but even the moralistic, materialistic Peck could have guessed that Bellingham was not going to live that long.

The origin of the larger note can only be conjectured. But the one other person who knew of Bellingham's contract was Thomas Wilson himself. The banker shared to the full Alexander Baring's hatred of the Orders in Council, and his bitterness at James Stephen's dishonest attempt to justify their continued existence. Wilson understood better than most the catastrophic economic effects of a war with the United States. He had already warned his American clients of the difficulties they would face, and his prescience would be confirmed in 1813 when the war forced him to suspend all financial business with them. But Wilson had another reason for wanting to express his appreciation of what Bellingham had done.

In common with other British financiers, he had expanded his operations into South America, and Brazil's slave economy in particular. It was impossible for Thomas Wilson & Co. not to be involved with the ramifications of the illegal slave trade because every aspect of Brazil's cotton plantations, copper mines and coffee farms depended on slave labour. Brazil had no banks of its own. Its development could not take place without British finance. Wilson, Baring and their banking colleagues paid for everything, from government bonds to ships and the gaudy produce used in barter to buy the slaves in Africa. The more Spencer Perceval choked the slave trade, the tighter the bankers' profits were squeezed. Among those who gained most from his assassination were the mandarins of the City of London.

Late on Sunday, 17 May, John Bellingham finished his last letter to his wife. 'My blessing to the boys,' he wrote, 'with kind remembrance to Miss Stevens, for whom I have the greatest regard in consequence of her uniform affection for them.'

All that remained was to tell their mother his last thoughts. 'As we shall not meet any more in this world, I sincerely hope we shall do so in the world to come.' John Newman, the keeper, made copies of his letter for sale to the newspapers, and so this most intimate communication was quickly made public. There was just one backward look at his failures – 'With the purest of intentions it has always been my misfortune to be thwarted, misrepresented and ill-used in life . . .' – but in general the tone of Bellingham's final words was that of a soul at rest. Although he had never quite arrived at security, he was consoled by 'a happy prospect of compensation in a speedy translation to life eternal'.

Compensation was all he had ever wanted. It would have balanced the books between his suffering in Russia and the failure of the government to protect him. It was the lack of it that had forced him to execute justice. But his reward was now to be eternal freedom from penury and misrepresentation. The hangman's rope carried no terrors. A divine accountancy would ensure that the deficits of mortality were cancelled out: 'It's not possible to be more calm or placid than I feel, and nine hours more will waft me to those happy shores where bliss is without alloy. Yours ever affectionate, John Bellingham.'

Then, after laying the letter aside, he recalled some practical details and added what amounted to a will disposing of his worldly goods:

Sunday Night 11 o'Clock
Dr Ford [the prison chaplain] will forward you my watch, my prayer book with a guinea and note. Once more, God be with you, my sweet Mary. The public sympathise much for me, but I have been called upon to play an anxious card in life.

Of the hundred guineas delivered to his cell before his trial, no trace remained. With luck the money travelled north with Mary

Stevens, otherwise it would probably have been confiscated by the City of London sheriffs responsible for his custody. For an hour or so he dozed. The money no longer bothered him, but he was kept awake by a sense of the unfairness that had cheated him of the reward his meticulous plan deserved. Eventually he sat up and added a final postscript:

> Twelve O'Clock I lost my suit solely through the improper conduct of my Attorney and Counsel, Mr Alley, in not bringing witnesses forward (of which there were more than 20); in consequence, the Judge took advantage of the circumstance, and I went of [*sic*] the defence without having brought forward a single friend – otherwise I must inevitably have been acquitted. – J Bellingham

An Execution Ends all Cares

The police officers and the Secretary of State might have known
what would happen a fortnight past. I have obeyed them. I have
done my worst, and I rejoice in the deed.

John Bellingham before the bar of the House of Commons,

11 May 1812

Conscious that he was in a way blameless, both for what he had
done and for what was about to happen to him, John Bellingham
behaved in his last hours with an inner dignity that impressed all
those who observed him. Even the solidly Tory *Morning Post*
remarked that 'his deportment was calm, manly, and even at times
dignified; and had he perished for almost any other crime than that
of assassination, he would justly have excited the pity and respect,
if not the admiration, of everyone who beheld this extraordinary
close of his wretched career'.

He was woken early, and William Cobbett, sharing the same
prison, recorded that Bellingham had been 'sleeping sound in his
cell, and upon being called between six and seven, said he was
called too soon'. It was a justifiable complaint. Having washed and
dressed, he read his prayer book for half an hour, then took holy
communion, and still there was time to wait. Meanwhile in the
dark grey light of a rainy dawn, large crowds had been gathering

outside Newgate prison. They surrounded the scaffold that had been constructed opposite the debtors' door in the prison wall, and were soon filling Newgate street for a hundred yards in either direction. More spectators packed the windows and rooftops of nearby houses, among them Lord Byron, who had sat up all night in order to see 'Bellingham launched into eternity'.

There had been a riot the previous month at a double hanging, and posters warned spectators in large black letters of the danger they faced. 'Beware of entering the crowd! Remember! thirty poor creatures were pressed to death by the crowd when Haggerty and Holloway were executed!' Some latecomers were deterred and walked away, but unlike most execution crowds, this one's mood was subdued rather than excitable. It might have been the result of the steady downpour – 'the Old Bailey,' said the *Public Ledger*, 'seemed to be paved with umbrellas' – but it was also because, as Bellingham had said, 'the public sympathise much with me'.

Exactly a week had passed since the mob had taken to the streets celebrating Perceval's assassination as an act of liberation, and applauding the murderer as a hero. The authorities were taking no chances. There were constables and bludgeon men posted around the scaffold, and along the walls of the prison, while soldiers were posted in backstreets out of sight. The fear of revolution had not disappeared.

At about half past seven the two sheriffs, William Heygate and Samuel Birch, followed by the lord mayor, and about twenty official guests all dressed in black, assembled in the prison yard. Bellingham was told that they were waiting, and replied clearly, 'I am perfectly ready also.' He was still wearing the double set of fetters at wrist and ankle, and these had to be struck off before his execution. As he was led towards a small anvil in the middle of the yard, the watchers noted that he walked 'with a firm and intrepid pace, and looking up, he observed, with great coolness – "Ah! it rains heavily." '

He placed first his hands then his feet on the anvil so that the rivets could be driven out of his fetters, and it was only as the inexperienced jailer began to hammer at the chains close to his feet that he showed any sign of nerves, crying out 'Mind, mind – take care, take care.' With the chains struck off, he was taken to the condemned prisoners' room by the two sheriffs. Although he had not been allowed to shave, he had dressed with the care of a gentleman – the chocolate-brown greatcoat he had worn on the day of the assassination, a buff and blue-striped waistcoat in kerseymere, clay-coloured pantaloons, white stockings and, unfortunately, a pair of down-at-heel prison shoes made necessary by the iron rings around his ankles. But once the shackles had been removed, he and the sheriffs went into the executioner's room accompanied by a few of the dignitaries. There, he kicked off the shoes and pulled on his smart hessian boots. So far as he could, Bellingham remained stylish to the end.

With the hanging rope coiled on a table next to them, the law officers returned to the one question that still nagged at the authorities. Sheriff Samuel Birch voiced again the government's haunting anxiety that he might have had an accomplice in the murder. For the last time, as every newspaper reported, Bellingham 'solemnly assured the Sheriff that the act of killing Mr. Perceval was entirely his own'.

According to one of the black-clad witnesses in the room, someone called out, ' "Then it was your own affair; it was from personal resentment." Bellingham appeared hurt at the latter expression, and after repeating the words "personal resentment" with an indignant or rather dignified tone, said, "I bore no resentment to Mr Perceval as a man; and as a man, I am sorry for his fate . . . It was my own sufferings that caused the melancholy event, and I hope it will be a warning to future Ministers, to attend to the applications and prayers of those who suffer by oppression." '

It was a remark that suggested he had come to see the assassination as more than a balancing of the books, and something closer to a political act. At one point during the trial, he had demanded 'What is my crime to the crime of government itself?', language that would not have been inappropriate to Thomas Paine, or even to a late nineteenth-century anarchist like Prince Peter Kropotkin. Sensing that even on the verge of his execution, Bellingham's inner convictions represented some sort of challenge to the society they lived in, those in the executioner's room began to throw jibes at him. 'I hope you feel deep contrition for the deed,' Sheriff William Heygate exclaimed. Gracefully, Bellingham deflected the remark. 'I hope, sir,' he replied, 'I feel as a man ought to do.' And when someone from the surrounding group called out that he hoped he had repented so that 'you will meet the Almighty with a pure soul', Bellingham responded, 'No one can presume to do that, sir. Only our Saviour went from this world with a pure spirit.'

As the hour hand neared eight, the executioner, William Brunskill, entered the room. Bellingham turned to the table where the thick hanging rope lay. Beside it were two thinner cords to tie his wrists and arms. 'Gentlemen,' he said, 'I am quite ready.' Then he rolled back his sleeves and held out his clasped hands to the executioner. 'So?' he asked. He waited like that while his wrists were pinioned, then asked for the sleeves of his coat to be turned down neatly to cover the ties.

The second rope went around his elbows, and was passed behind his back to prevent him scrabbling upwards to loosen the noose as he swung. When it was tied, he tested to see how high he could reach, and asked for the cord to be tightened. 'I wish not to have the power of offering any resistance,' he explained. As the executioner left the room with the hanging rope, Bellingham asked whether it would be strong enough to bear his weight. Brunskill, by then in his late sixties, promised him with all the authority of almost thirty years' experience in the business that it would not break. Bellingham thanked him for that assurance. His composure and unfaltering voice astonished those present. He seemed to have no fear of what lay ahead. If so, it was not from a lack of feeling. As the procession walked out of the room into the prison yard, it was observed that the condemned man ducked his head down to his shoulder as though to wipe away a tear.

Cobbett, who was standing by the window of his cell, watched Bellingham emerge into the street and step lightly up the stair to the scaffold. But his attention was immediately diverted by the reaction of the crowd. 'I saw the anxious looks,' he wrote, 'I saw the half-horrified countenances; I saw the mournful tears run down; and I heard the unanimous blessings. What then, were these tears shed, and these blessings bestowed by Englishmen upon a murderer!' Searching for an explanation for this surprising, even shocking, display of sympathy, Cobbett decided that people felt grateful to Bellingham for having 'ridded them of the leader amongst those whom they thought totally bent on the destruction of their liberties'. Cobbett was not unbiased, but it was clear to him that in the public mind Perceval's murder had indeed been a political assassination.

On the scaffold, Bellingham looked about him with a lively interest, much as he had at the Old Bailey. William Brunskill, who had knotted one end of the rope around the beam above him, now removed Bellingham's cravat, and placed the noose over his head. Standing near to him, Dr Samuel Forde, the Newgate Ordinary, or chaplain, asked him whether he had any last words. Almost as a reflex, Bellingham once more began to tell the story of his Russian experience, but stopped when Forde reminded him that he had no more time left. Then he joined Forde in a short prayer. When it was over, Brunskill placed a white cap over his head. Bellingham asked to have it removed, but was told that it was obligatory.

This, the last stage, provoked more cries of 'God bless you!' and 'God save you!' from the crowd. Forde asked Bellingham whether he could hear them. Bellingham said he heard the shouting but could not make out the words. Then he was asked how he felt, and replied that he thanked God for enabling him to meet his fate with fortitude and resignation. Brunskill had done his job with swift efficiency, and for a long minute John Bellingham stood there on the trapdoor, blindfolded, noosed and pinioned, before a crowd that had fallen utterly silent.

Then the Newgate clock began to strike eight o'clock and, according to the *Edinburgh Annual Register*:

> while it was striking the seventh time, the Clergyman and Bellingham both fervently praying, the supporters of the internal square of the scaffold were struck away, and Bellingham dropped out of sight down as far as the knees, his body being in full view, the clergyman being left standing on the outer frame of the scaffold. When Bellingham sunk, the most perfect and awful silence prevailed, not even the slightest attempt at a huzza or noise of any kind was made. He did not struggle at first, and but little afterwards, the executioner below pulling his heels that he might die quickly.

Except for the clues left by his spending, that might have been the final act in a murder that seemed to make no sense. Bellingham's body swung on the rope till nine o'clock and was then taken down to be dissected by Sir William Blizzard at St Bartholomew's hospital. According to the *Annual Register*, when the chest was opened, Bellingham's heart was observed to be still beating. 'The expanding and contracting powers continued perceptible till one o'clock in the day,' it reported, 'a proof of the steady, undismayed character which he preserved to the last gasp.'

It was the sort of mythical detail that should have entered folk-lore. But with astonishing speed, the existence of John Bellingham was erased from public memory, until only a faint shadow labelled 'a deranged merchant' remained to show where he had been. 'You'd be astonished to find how shy people are of speaking on the subject,' an anonymous letter-writer reported from Liverpool just weeks after the execution. Obliterated with him were the mysteries of the crime, the bizarre motivation, the intricate planning, and the finances needed to carry it out.

Yet in his fumbling, anguished, obstinate way, Bellingham truly was someone who changed the course of history. Had he missed his encounter with the Prime Minister, the campaign to choke off the illegal slave trade would have continued, Judge Thorpe would have remained dispensing rough justice on slavers of every nationality, compulsory slave registers would have been extended to every West Indian colony, and as many as forty thousand Africans a year would have been saved from slavery.

Had Bellingham brought himself to carry out his plan as he intended and shot the Prime Minister in April, the news would have reached the United States in time to prevent the outbreak of war. Instead, Perceval's successor, Lord Liverpool, was not appointed until 8 June, and although the Orders in Council were withdrawn at the first opportunity, on 16 June, war had already been formally declared two days earlier. Only in August did James Madison's government learn that the Orders had been withdrawn. By then, the first American troops had invaded Canada and Fort Detroit was under siege by Canadian forces. On 19 August the humiliating surrender of the United States garrison in Detroit under General William Hull left such a wound that there could be no pulling back until honour had been regained.

Elisha Peck sailed back to the United States before the end of 1812. Reunited, he and Phelps moved the company headquarters to a prominent location in Manhattan, and set about creating a company that eventually held a virtual monopoly on the import of sheet metal into the United States. Once peace returned, Elisha Peck went back to Liverpool where he continued to make money until his retirement in 1834. By that year, the annual turnover of Peck & Phelps had reached £270,000 a year, and in the village of West Haverstraw beside the Hudson river Bellingham's paymaster had built a rolling steel mill imported from England, which he named Samsondale. Not far away, he constructed a massive mansion looking over the Hudson with a Palladian entrance modelled apparently on Liverpool's Athenaeum. He spent his remaining years there until his death in 1851.

After his retirement, Phelps & Peck changed its name to Phelps, Dodge and Co., eventually metamorphosing into today's Arizona-based mining conglomerate of the same name whose annual sales amount to more than $7 billion. Anson Phelps died a year after his partner, and was buried in the odour of sanctity despite having participated with Thomas Wilson's sons, Melvin and Fletcher, in an elaborate scam to milk more than three million dollars from investors following the bankruptcy of Thomas Wilson & Co. in 1837.

Although no one in Liverpool wanted to remember John Bellingham, the newspapers made it clear that Mary Bellingham was an innocent bystander to her husband's crime. In Liverpool, the West India group ensured that she was looked after, and authorised Richard Statham to set up a fund to support her and the boys. In response to an anonymous letter revealing that she was suffering from shock and was 'left totally unprovided for, with three helpless children dependent upon her', a surprisingly generous donation of £50 came from the good-looking Lord Leveson-Gower. The money was delivered in person by Peter Bourne, son of the mayor, together with an explanatory letter from the former ambassador.

Aware that Bellingham's accusations implied 'gross neglect of my duties', Leveson-Gower had written to the Foreign Secretary even before the trial, to defend himself and the consul, Stephen Shairpe. His need to send this document to Mary Bellingham, with a sum of money large enough to keep her family for a year, suggested at least the hint of an uneasy conscience. Publicly, however, he insisted there was nothing he could have done to help Bellingham. Once more he went through the sequence of events – Shairpe's discovery that Bellingham was undeniably Dorbecker's partner, Bellingham's refusal to accept the arbitration award made by Archangel's commercial court, the *duma*'s requirement that he pay the 2,000 roubles, and Bellingham's subsequent committal to prison. Gower ended the letter by claiming to have given Bellingham 'small sums of money' while in prison, and to have secured his release after a private talk with the minister for foreign affairs.

Peter Bourne reported back that Mary Bellingham did not feel inclined to blame Lord Leveson-Gower. She said that while she was in St Petersburg, Stephen Shairpe had explained the background of the case and convinced her that the ambassador was unable to help. As Bourne and Mrs Bellingham talked, the protective Mary Stevens appeared and, with her friend beside her, Mary Bellingham went on to explain that 'she did all in her power to persuade her husband of the folly and impropriety of his claims for remuneration'.

But money alone could not alleviate Mary Bellingham's distress. 'Her delicate frame has received a blow,' the anonymous writer to Gower revealed, 'which totally incapacitated her to attend to her affairs for the present in order to procure immediate Subsistence of Herself and her Family.' And when Mary Stevens announced the display of her summer collection, 'a new and elegant assortment of Millinery, dresses &c' in early June, she also had to declare that her partner would not be participating. She hoped that their clients would sympathise with them 'under their very peculiar situation'.

Six months after the assassination, Mary Bellingham still had not recovered. In November a sad little advertisement appeared in the *Liverpool Mercury*: 'M. Bellingham presents her best respects and sincere thanks to the Ladies of Liverpool and its Environs who have favoured her and her Partner, Miss Stevens, with their Orders; she is sorry to inform them that she has been reduced by unprecedented misfortunes and distress to the necessity of compounding with her Creditors for ten shillings in the pound . . .' In other words, she was bankrupt.

The two Marys may simply have decided to put Leveson-Gower's money aside, including perhaps the hundred guineas sent to Newgate prison, and start afresh somewhere else. Mary Bellingham's disreputable father, John Neville, had caused her deep embarrassment by advertising a fund-raising concert to celebrate Spencer Perceval's assassination, and to raise money for 'the widow of the assassin'. She wanted no publicity of that kind. The concert was condemned, and in search of anonymity she reverted to her maiden name but spelling it 'Nevill', the form used by her uncle, James, in Wigan. It is probable that she and Mary Stevens returned to live in the town together.

Although their subsequent history disappeared into obscurity, one intriguing glimpse remained. In 1875 the death was recorded in London of Henry Stevens Neville, who was married to James Nevill's granddaughter. Almost certainly, this was former baby Henry whose welfare had so concerned John Bellingham. That Henry should have taken the name of Miss Stevens as his own would seem to point to a continuing and happy partnership between the two Marys. And, given the anxieties of his ever insecure father, it is worth noting that Henry died prosperous.

Understanding Why it Happened

With every private virtue however which could adorn an human being, he was unquestionably the most mischievous of all the bad ministers who for these thirty years past have been placed at the head of affairs in this country; – and with totally opposite intent the political years of his life were employed in bringing this empire to the brink of ruin.

Edinburgh Review, June 1812

The body of Spencer Perceval had been carried to 10 Downing Street early in the morning of Tuesday, 12 May, after the last rioters had left the area. It was laid out in what had been his dressing room, surrounded by tall candles and attended by members of his family. The jibes that Sydney Smith once made about his pallor – 'the sepulchral Perceval', 'the sallow surveyor of the meltings' – were now literal description. His wide eyes were closed and his expression had taken on the peaceful indifference of death. 'Nothing could be more calm and undisturbed than his countenance,' wrote his sister Frances.

At the time of his murder, Jane Perceval had been visiting her closest friend, Frederica Ryder, wife of the ineffectual Home Secretary. The Ryders lived in Great George Street, opposite Parliament Square, and their house must have resounded to the cheers and jubilant cries of the mob as they too learned of her husband's death. The news, and perhaps the glee outside, left her too shocked for tears. Jane's dazed, dry-eyed calm lasted until the next morning when she was taken in to see the body. She had spent all her adult life with him. He was not yet fifty, and in less than a week the youngest of their twelve children would celebrate his fifth birthday. It was then, confronted by his familiar appearance and strange stillness, that she burst into uncontrollable weeping.

The backbenchers who had followed him so loyally wanted a public funeral, and a monument in Westminster Abbey, but Spencer Perceval's grieving widow was adamant about her husband's resting place. Parliament was informed that the family would have a private funeral, and early on Saturday morning – to avoid hostile crowds according to Cobbett – a hearse drawn by six, black-plumed horses and bearing the 'very superb' lead-lined coffin moved out of Downing Street followed by five mourning coaches carrying the Prime Minister's children, and most of the cabinet. The procession crossed Westminster Bridge, and followed the course of the Thames down towards its mouth until they came to Charlton where Jane Wilson had fallen in love with an impoverished young lawyer twenty-two years before. In the little church of St Luke's, Spencer Perceval was buried in the Egmont family vault beside the father who had taught him too well to resist all change.

The plain ceremony was in keeping with the way they had lived their lives. Already in the days following the murder, details had emerged that pointed up the simplicity of the Percevals' family life compared with the self-indulgent dedication to expense and pleasure that characterised fashion in the Regency era. The last meal shared by the Prime Minister and his wife had been a family lunch eaten at 2.30 with the daughters and youngest sons present. At this sort of occasion, said Robert Plumer Ward, 'Perceval was never more easy or more cheerful.' The previous day he had been present when two of his daughters were confirmed by the bishop of London, and the following day he was due to take part in his eldest son's speech-day celebration at Harrow school. Nothing could have been more domestic.

Returning home on Sunday, he had asked his valet whether he had any further engagements that day, and when told there were none, he had replied, 'What none to dinner? Then I am happy for I shall have a pleasure I very seldom enjoy, of dining alone with my family.' And, Ward said, after family prayers that evening, the Prime Minister had begged Jane to let the children linger a little longer before going to bed. At last they had gathered round and kissed him in a family ritual they would never know again.

As Perceval's family and companions looked back at the quiet flow of his private life, they felt sure that he had some premonition that it would be cut short. During the spring, he had scribbled a makeshift will on half a sheet of paper leaving all his possessions to his wife. A friend, Matthew Montagu, testified that he had 'strong apprehensions of his impending fate for several days before it took place'. Much earlier, soon after he became Prime Minister, he had written to his eldest son about his conviction that his life must serve some purpose, and his 'sense of the improbability of its long continuance'. Almost inevitably reports of similar clairvoyance came from around the country, as though so great an event must throw out a warning bow-wave before its actual occurrence. The best attested of them was that of John Williams, a famous Cornish mining engineer, who dreamed of a small man that he subsequently felt to be Spencer Perceval being shot dead in the House of Commons, and told friends of it, ten days before John Bellingham pulled the trigger.

The 'murder money', as frivolous-minded descendants of the Percevals referred to the £50,000 grant from Parliament, ensured that well into the twentieth century most of the Prime Minister's vast dynasty were preserved from poverty. But the immediate family had to find ways of coping not only with grief but the shock to their belief in the workings of Providence.

The option chosen by his widow, Jane, aroused profound, and almost universal disapproval. In the words of Henry 'Orator' Hunt, self-appointed voice of the people and enthusiastic scandalmonger, 'in a very few months after the decease of that best of all possible husbands, that nonpareil of married males; yes, in a few short months after her irreparable loss, his disconsolate widow concealed herself in the arms of another and a younger husband!' This was not entirely accurate – she did not remarry until January 1815, more than two and a half years after the assassination – but it was certainly true that at thirty-seven years old, her new husband, Lieutenant-Colonel Sir Henry Carr KCB, was eleven years younger. As would happen after President Kennedy's widow remarried, Jane Perceval's choice of partner was widely condemned as a betrayal of the memory of her murdered husband.

Yet becoming Lady Carr did provide a means of escape from the burden of being the widow of a political martyr. Her second husband was the younger son of the vicar at Ealing, and a wounded hero of Wellington's Peninsular War. In caring for him, Jane Carr no doubt found distraction from her own wounds, and relief from the demands of public life. Henry Carr died in 1821 and, during their short life together, he and Jane lived in Elm Grove, the plain, stuccoed, three-storey building surrounded by parkland that Perceval had bought when he was still a high-earning lawyer. It was the family home, and for some of her children the presence of the lieutenant colonel in their father's place was hard to bear. But they too were burdened with the problem of making sense of the tragedy of their father's murder.

Some of the younger children followed their mother's example by stepping away from the problem altogether. Isabella, the ninth child, married Spencer Walpole, a middle-of-the-road politician who became a progressive-minded governor of the Isle of Man, and betrayed no tendency to mysticism. Ernest, the youngest, took to being a country gentleman, strolling his estate with a terrier named Slut bouncing at his side. But at least four of the daughters, including the sharp-tongued Fanny, never married, and most, like the elder sons, were gripped by religious fervour.

Unable to find comfort in an Evangelical reliance on the Bible, they followed the lead of their eldest brother, Spencer Perceval junior, who left the Church of England altogether. Influenced by his wife, Anna MacLeod of MacLeod from Skye, he joined one of the earliest Pentecostal churches in Britain, the Catholic Apostolic Church. This was led by Edward Irving, who opened a chapel in a former art gallery near Portland Square in London, where speaking in tongues was encouraged.

The fashion-seeking MP, Charles Greville, went there in 1833 to hear Spencer Perceval junior speak, significantly about the fragility of human government. To Greville's annoyance, Perceval's sermon was almost immediately interrupted by several women moaning and crying out aloud. Perceval covered his head in his hands and fell silent, except for occasional exclamations of 'Hear the voice of the Lord', until Irving took over and began preaching in 'a mystical, incomprehensible rhapsody with extraordinary vehemence of manner and power of lungs'.

To his credit, Perceval did not restrict his preaching to the converted. He also made William IV and the Privy Council listen to a charismatic sermon on the degeneracy of the times, which began unpromisingly, 'You are aware that God has been pleased to make especial communications of His will to certain chosen instruments in a language not intelligible to those who hear, nor always to those by whom it is uttered. I am one of those instruments.' Appointed an 'angel' of the Catholic Apostolic Church with a particular duty to convert Italy, Perceval went to Rome where, helped by Henry Drummond, a fabulously wealthy banker who had married a Perceval sister, he delivered a similar sermon to the Pope. When he visited Lord Holland for the same purpose, Lady Holland placed two pageboys outside the study door with orders to scream for help in case the unpredictable preacher attacked his lordship.

What the charismatic movement offered was an escape from rational to revealed truth. It accepted that the human mind could not comprehend the working of Providence. To understand how the murder of a Prime Minister fitted into the improvement of the world was not necessary. A believer had only to receive the Holy Spirit whose message was true but incomprehensible. Taken to extremes, such an assumption might propel a fragile mind towards insanity. This was the fate of John Perceval, the Prime Minister's tenth child.

He was eight when his father was murdered, and approaching puberty when his adored mother married again. Weighed down by this Hamlet-like legacy, he was determined to wring from heaven some understanding of what it all meant. Bypassing the Catholic Apostolic Church, he went north to Scotland in search of the origin of Irving's charismatic beliefs. In the reformed Presbyterian kirk at Rhu in Dumbartonshire, he found the remarkable source of the modern tradition of speaking in tongues. In 1825 Isabella and Mary Campbell, the two sisters of the minister John McLeod Campbell, had both begun speaking when possessed by the spirit, and the practice quickly attracted an enthusiastic following, including Irving.

For John Perceval, it seemed to offer the way to ultimate truth, and he followed it with deadly passion. When Mary Campbell tried to moderate his zeal, he left the congregation to take his own extreme route. After a ferocious regime of fasting, praying and speaking in tongues, he went mad in 1830. Like John Bellingham senior, he became so violent he had to be restrained in a strait-jacket, and was occasionally chained up. For four years, he was incarcerated in two of the most advanced lunatic asylums in the land, Brislington near Bristol and Ticehurst in Sussex, before recovering almost spontaneously.

Although he remained as obsessive about the truth as Bellingham was about justice, John Perceval was helped to recovery by the gradual realisation that he had been too serious. God was the god not just 'of the sincere, the grave, the sober and chaste . . . but also of fun, of humour, of frolic'. Neither reason nor revelation was sufficient for understanding. At times John Perceval seemed to reach an almost Buddhist sense of detachment from material events, and a corresponding appreciation for the cosmic joke of existence. But in the agonising memoir he wrote about his lunacy, he confessed, 'I fear the death of my poor father was at the root of all my misfortune. I was then a little boy. But . . . I do not YET understand his loss.'

In 1832 the Reform Bill became law. Industrial towns such as Birmingham were allowed to return their own Member of Parliament, many of the urban middle-class were given the vote for the first time, and the sort of parliamentary seats that were controlled by a single noble family were abolished. It represented the first small expansion of democracy in a system that Spencer Perceval would have kept unchanged until the Book of Revelation came true. With the Bill's passage, the political ice age that he had inaugurated started to come to an end. In this new climate, it became possible to discern another, more political explanation of what had happened twenty years earlier.

What emerged was the uncomfortable realisation that the Evangelical Prime Minister had broken the constitutional rules.

Convinced of the truths revealed to him, he ceased to take account of other opinions. Nor could any power in the unreformed parliamentary system force him to do so. His predecessors, from Lord North to Pitt and Portland, had all been subject to the moods of the country gentlemen and the prejudices of George III. By coincidence, both these restraints were removed while Spencer Perceval was Prime Minister. The country gentlemen increasingly identified their interests with his, and the king went mad. Supreme authority allowed Perceval to exercise powers that were close to autocratic.

'If the laws had been made by persons chosen by the whole people, Mr. Perceval would not have been shot,' argued Henry Hunt. 'It was the want of an honest House of Commons that made Mr. Perceval a tyrant.'

Yet that cannot be quite the last word. Spencer Perceval's life and death would have been very different had they been shaped simply by politics. Without his obstinacy, guile and faith there would have been no heroic efforts to keep an army in Spain and to kill the slave trade. Nor would there have been his contemptible desire to silence Catholics, factory workers and political reformers. An older model offers a better way of explaining why the arc of his life should have ended as it did.

No Prime Minister should claim a monopoly on rightness. Perceval's hubristic conviction that he acted as a providential agent ensured that he would be met by nemesis, because sooner or later he was bound to encounter someone else whose conviction of his own rightness was equally fixed. In John Bellingham, with his single-minded conviction that he was owed justice and could achieve it with a pistol shot, the Prime Minister met that person.

Notes

Every modern account of the assassination of Spencer Perceval has rested on the indefatigable researches of Mollie Gillen, an Australian-born Canadian and self-taught historian, whose *Assassination of the Prime Minister* will always remain essential reading for anyone interested in the subject. She uncovered in the Public Records Office the cache of documents, now labelled BM Add Mss 48216, containing the vital information of Mary Stevens's affidavit and Bellingham's financial accounts and personal receipts that make it possible to link his plan for justice to the pattern of his expenditure and the political events of the day. The other substantial source of information is Denis Gray's assiduous and now somewhat outdated biography, *Spencer Perceval: The Evangelical Prime Minister*. The time is long overdue for a new look at Spencer Perceval's political leadership.

Chapter One: A Horrible Event

p. 1   'The assassin was late.' John Bellingham's movements were minutely recorded in contemporary pamphlets and newspapers. Bellingham himself, his landlady Mrs Robarts in evidence to John Vickery, the Bow Street officer, and her maid, Catherine Figgins, in court, were the prime sources. From 1760 to 1833 the House of Commons usually sat at 4 p.m., according to the 2009 House of Commons Factsheet 'Sittings of the House'. To accommodate the hearings when outsiders presented petitions against the Order in Council, the Commons designated itself a Committee of the whole house whose proceedings began at 4.30 p.m. after the attention to routine business. Most people had expected Spencer Perceval to be present from the start. A week earlier, on 5 May, he had actually arrived before hearings into petitions took place. In *Evangelical Prime Minister*, p. 457, Gray explains that Perceval 'was so absorbed [by work] that he was late starting for the Commons'. His lateness provoked the anger of Henry Brougham at his absence.

p. 1   'Prime Minister'. Throughout the book, Perceval is designated as the Prime Minister, but it should be noted that this title had only recently come into use. In parliamentary reports, he was commonly referred to as the Chancellor of the Exchequer, and elsewhere as the First Lord of the Treasury. Critics of his dominance in cabinet dubbed him 'the Supreme Commander'.

p. 2   'His anxiety would have triggered self-pity.' Bellingham's psychology became the focus of intense speculation following the murder. In his Russian pamphlet and all public utterances after the murder, he invariably portrayed himself as a victim of personal injustice. In private, however, he saw himself as someone who was dogged by misfortune in general and, having been dealt a poor hand, was required, as he put it in his last letter, 'to play an anxious card in life'.

p. 3   'The pavements were obstructed . . .'. In 1809 a complaint that the Privy Council offices at the lower end of Whitehall were 'in a very bad and even dangerous state' (PRO, P.C. 2/184) was symptomatic of a general stress on existing accommodation, as the civil service began to grow beyond its eighteenth-century limits. Parliament had already authorised the redevelopment of buildings around King Street next to Parliament Square in 1806, and, according to the Public Survey of London, buildings were being worked on in Great George Street, Whitehall Gardens, and other streets close to the Houses of Parliament.

p. 3 'his brown coat . . .'. The assassin's clothes were minutely described in newspapers and pamphlets, a tribute to the care he clearly took in choosing them.

p. 4 'The lobby of the Houses of Parliament . . .'. The scene in the lobby of the Houses of Parliament was described in detail by eyewitnesses at committal proceedings, the coroner's inquest and Bellingham's trial. The crowd had gradually dispersed, many to the Strangers' Gallery to listen to the hearings. According to estimates, around twenty or thirty remained when Perceval was murdered.

p. 5 'The anger in the chamber . . .'. The ideological split over the Orders in Council, and their underlying purpose in repressing the illegal slave trade, was apparent in the selection of Thomas Babington, a vehement anti-slaver, as chairman of the committee, and of James Stephen, the policy's architect, as its chief defender. Although no slaver, Henry Brougham, in leading for the opposition to the Order, inevitably was supported by those favourable to continued involvement in slave trading. For the mood of the committee and Babington's exchange see Gillen, *Assassination*, pp. 13–15.

p. 6 'He still sweated . . .'. Bellingham's physical state, the gasping breath and pouring sweat, was noted especially by William Jerdan in personal testimony, and *Autobiography*, vol. 1, pp. 133–41.

p. 6 'He had studied . . .'. Vincent Dowling, parliamentary reporter and government spy, revealed in testimony to the coroner's inquest and in court that Bellingham had appeared in the gallery at least three times.

p. 6 '"I thought he appeared . . ."'. John Norris's testimony in court.

p. 6 'Other people would also remember . . .'. Henry Burgess, William Smith and General Gascoyne all gave testimony at the inquest and in court. Gascoyne also testified at the committal proceedings, changing his account on each occasion.

p. 8 'the most powerful politician . . .'. The power vacuum that occurred after Perceval's death, with the initial paralysis of the cabinet and later the collapse of his policies, testified to the extent of his personal and political influence.

p. 9   'With genuine affection . . .'. A recollection of Wilberforce's friends, cited in J. C. Colquhoun, *William Wilberforce – his Friends and his Times*, London, 1867, p. 27. Wilberforce himself expressed his feelings in his private diary a few hours after the murder: 'Perceval had the sweetest of all possible tempers, and was one of the most conscientious men I ever knew; the most instinctively obedient to the dictates of conscience, the least disposed to give pain to others, the most charitable and truly kind and generous creature I ever knew.' *Life*, vol. 4, p. 95.

p. 9   'Spencer Perceval started up the steps . . .'. Jerdan, *Autobiography*, vol. 1, pp. 133–41.

p. 9   'he had no intention . . .'. Bellingham made this clear when questioned in Newgate prison by City of London magistrates on 12 May 1812.

p. 9   'The Prime Minister said something . . .'. The various witnesses agreed only that he uttered some words, not on what he said.

Chapter Two: The Identity of an Unfortunate Man is Revealed

p. 13   The scene after the murder was minutely described in newspapers during the following days, and recapitulated by witnesses at the inquest and trial.

p. 13   William Smith's testimony. He later admitted to William Wilberforce that he thought for a moment the victim was Wilberforce himself.

p. 13   '"If he had risen in a minute . . .", "'Large drops of agonizing sweat . . .'". Jerdan, *Autobiography*, vol. 1, pp. 133–41; William Jerdan was born in the Scottish Borders, but lived most of his life in London, falling into journalism having failed as a poet, and later becoming editor of the *Literary Gazette*. Despite a tendency to snobbery, he was much loved by authors for his enthusiasm in promoting early Victorian fiction. Even today most writers will sympathise with his assertion that 'the uncertainties and disappointments incident to a life entirely dependent on literature, in 99 out of 100 cases render that life to be at the best precarious and unproductive, and at the worst impoverished and wretched'.

p. 14   General Isaac Gascoyne's behaviour before and after the assassination was riddled with contradictions. Although not physically present, he apparently knew the identity of the victim without being told. He initially affected not to recognise Bellingham despite frequent meetings, the latest having continued for about an hour. Finally his evidence changed repeatedly to present himself arriving on the scene earlier, and taking a more pre-emptive role, than any other witness recalled.

p. 16   The Houses of Parliament lay within Middlesex, hence the lead role taken by the Middlesex magistrates. Once Bellingham was held in Newgate, he fell within the jurisdiction of the City of London.

p. 17   '"he considered the slave trade . . ."'. Lord Howick, later the 2nd Earl Grey, having debated the subject with Gascoyne, 23 February, 1807; 'The Liverpool Abolitionists' by F. E. Sanderson, in *Liverpool, the African Slave Trade, and Abolition*, ed. Roger Anstey and R. E. H. Hair, Historic Society of Lancashire and Cheshire, Occasional Series, vol. 2, 1976.

p. 17   '"he had seen Bellingham often . . ."'. *The Times*, 12 May 1812.

p. 17   'Jerdan found himself doubting . . .'. Jerdan put it politely, 'the consternation that prevailed might well excuse imperfection of memory and the blending of hearsay with what was actually seen and done'. *Autobiography*, vol. 1, pp. 133–41.

p. 18   '"I have been denied the redress . . ."'. *The Times*, and other newspapers, 12 May 1812.

p. 19   New Millman Street. In *The Adventures of Philip*, serialised in *Harpers* in 1862, W. M. Thackeray wrote 'Millman Street is a little cul-de-sac of a street', describing it as 'cheap, unfashionable but cosy'.

p. 20 'a memorandum of twenty pounds . . .'. *The Times*, 13 May 1812. According to the newspaper, Bellingham explained 'it was a bill that he expected would have been paid next day, at half-past nine o'clock'. That is, he expected it to be cashed as soon as the banks opened the following day.

Chapter Three: Riots Break Out amid Rumours of Revolution

p. 21 The resemblances between Perceval's assassination and that of President Kennedy are striking, but especially in the mysterious, deadly motives of the assassins. Because Bellingham and Lee Harvey Oswald were both killed before they could be properly interrogated, their connection to the illegal activities of, respectively, Liverpool's blockade-busting slavers and traders, and Florida's Cuban exiles, could never be adequately examined.

p. 22 '"They were whipped off . . ."'. Bath archives: *Diaries and Letters of Sir George Jackson*, vol. 1, p. 374, ed. Lady Jackson, Bentley, London, 1873.

p. 22 The disturbances in London. *The Times, Morning Chronicle*, and other London newspapers, 13 May 1812.

p. 23 '"Oh I will fire my gun . . ."'. Gillen, *Assassination*, p. 15.

p. 23 '"Perceval is down . . ."'. *An Irish Beauty of the Regency. Compiled from 'Mes Souvenirs'—The Unpublished Journals of the Hon. Mrs Calvert 1789–1822*, ed. by Mrs Warrenne Blake, London and New York: John Lane, 1911, p. 22.

p. 23 For the measures taken to restore law and order, see Gillen, *Assassination*, pp. 15–16.

p. 23 'Instead of a hired coach . . .'. Gillen, *Assassination*, pp. 15–16.

p. 24 'The keeper loaded . . .'. *The Times* and other newspapers, 13 May 1812.

p. 24 Cabinet meeting. *The Times*, 12 May 1812.

p. 24 For the activities of the Committees of Secrecy, the Aliens Office and the Home Office in gathering intelligence in general, see Porter, *Plots and Paranoia*, and McCalman, *Radical Underworld*. Aliens Office, created 1793, Porter, p. 18; Private Office in Post Office, opening letters, Porter, p. 23; Committees of Secrecy, set up ad hoc, 1794, 1801, 1812 and 1819, Porter, pp. 49–51.

p. 26   "'the speediest and most effectual measures . . .'". *The Times* and others, 12 and 13 May 1812.

p. 27   Journalism and the printing-rooms. *The Cambridge History of English literature*, 18 vols., ed. A. W. Ward, vol. 14, pp. 173–4.

p. 28   John Stoddard's tribute; reports of armed raids. *The Times*, 12 May 1812.

p. 29   "'At all events . . .'". *Irish Beauty*, p. 22.

Chapter Four: A Free and Easy Conspiracy?

p. 30   Bellingham's self-description as 'dilatory'. Sworn affidavit of Mary Stevens, BM Add Mss 48216, No. 59.

p. 30   'breakfasted with a good appetite off buttered rolls . . .'. *The Globe, Morning Chronicle* and others, 13 May 1812.

p. 31   Bellingham's appearance. Newspapers and shorthand writers in court were quite consistent in their descriptions of Bellingham's height, his long nose, long face and short hair.

p. 31   Bellingham's clothes. *Le Beau Monde or Literary and Fashionable Magazine*, April 1807 – '*A Morning Walking Dress for Gentlemen* is composed of a dark brown mixed coat, lappeled, with flat plated buttons and collar of the same cloth; or greenish mixtures lappeled, flat plated buttons and collar of cloth, and the coat must be buttoned close up. Striped toilinet, or plain kerseymere waistcoats, single breasted and bound with silk, and drab coloured kerseymere pantaloons, with Hessian boots.'

p. 31   Thanks to Newman, Bellingham's letter was reprinted in every London newspaper on 13 May 1812.

p. 32   "'a dispute which he had . . .'". *Morning Chronicle*, 13 May 1812.

p. 33   "'At first it was impossible . . .'". *The Globe*, 13 May 1812; *Liverpool Courier*, 14 May 1812.

p. 33   'His room next to the chapel . . .'. *Old Bailey Sessions Papers*. The odour of Newgate was thought to be the source of the typhus, often known as 'gaol fever', that periodically swept through the prison. Vinegar washes and nosegays of strong-smelling herbs, mint, rue and rosemary, were used to counteract it. In *Tales of Boz*, Charles Dickens described how 'the buildings in the prison, or in other words the different wards – form a square . . . The intermediate space is divided into several paved yards, in which the prisoners take such air and exercise as can be had in such a place.'

p. 34   'Bellingham indignantly rejected the suggestion . . .'. *The Times*, 13 May 1812.

p. 34   The talents of John Vickery are most apparent through his testimony in many different trials between 1800 and 1819 recorded in the *Newgate Calendar*, also known as the *Old Bailey Sessions Papers*. (For details see below.) The two Adkins brothers were solid but less brilliant.

p. 34   Hokkirk is a mystery visitor, recorded only by Newman, who duly shared his information with the newspapers.

p. 35   The 1744 Vagrancy Act allowed two Justices of the Peace to order a violent lunatic to 'be safely locked in some secure place . . . (and if necessary) to be there chained . . . for and during such time only as the lunacy or madness shall continue'. Private funds were raised to build St Luke's, Woodside, London, in 1751. At about the time that Bellingham's father was confined there, 11 staff cared for 260 inmates. Information from Resources for Mental Health Law – www.davesheppard.co.uk.

p. 35   Information about Bellingham's background. Daniel Wilson, *The Substance of a Conversation*, p. 32; Gillen, *Assassination*, pp. 43–5; based on parish registers of St Neots, Huntingdon, Bishop's

Transcripts, St Dunstan-in-the-West, and St George's, Hanover Square.

p. 35 Bellingham in Russia. BM Add Mss 48216, No. 44. Petition to House of Commons.

p. 36 Home Office information gathering. Porter, *Social History*; McCalman, *Radical Underworld*; H.O. 42/108, 115, 118–20; H.O. 102/22.

p. 37 "'that damned set of Rogues . . .'". Cole, *British Working Class Movements*, 'A letter to a Huddersfield Master', H.O. 40/41.

p. 38 Gunmakers. Durs Egg, 'Durs Egg, the Gunsmith', *Notes and Queries*, 15 July 1944; Joseph Manton, http://en.wikipedia.org/wiki/Joseph_Manton; James Purdey, http://www.purdey.com/history/history-of-purdey; William Beckwith, 'Muzzle Loaders Association of Great Britain', http://www.mlagb.com/

p. 38 "'These were the very words . . .'". 'Letter to Robert Southey', 12 May 1812, *Letters of Samuel Taylor Coleridge*, ed. E. H. Coleridge, Boston & New York: Houghton Mifflin, 1896. In *Biographia literaria* the once-revolutionary Coleridge confessed that 'I am singular enough to regard [Mr Perceval] as the best and wisest minister of this reign.'

p. 39 'free and easy' meetings. McCalman, *Radical Underworld*, p. 44. In 1811 the radical Thomas Spence wrote, 'Even under the modern tyrannies of China, France, Turkey etc, what can hinder small companies from meeting in a free and easy convivial manner and singing their rights and instructing each other in their songs?' The songs and toasts were faithfully recorded by government spies, thus preserving them for posterity.

p. 40 "'Perceval's ribs . . .'". Recorded by Frances Calvert in *Irish Beauty*, ed. Mrs Warrenne Blake, p. 22.

p. 41 'Dowling, however, had a secret . . .'. McCalman, *Radical Underworld*, p. 98. Dowling had been a Jacobin supporter, but while working for *The Observer* he was recruited as a government spy. He was to play a major role in exposing the Cato Street conspiracy in 1822. *The Cambridge History of English Literature*, vol. 14, p. 374.

p. 41   'The inadequacies of the Home Secretary . . .'. Richard Ryder's shortcomings were itemised in Gray, *Spencer Perceval, the Evangelical Prime Minister*, pp. 273–4. Ryder resigned immediately after the assassination.

p. 42   'Richard Ryder could not even speak for crying . . .'. *The Diary and Correspondence of Charles Abbott, Lord Colchester*, vol. 2, London: John Murray, 1862, p. 380.

p. 43   'Lord Eldon, was so convulsed . . .'. *Annual Register*, 1812.

p. 43   The nationwide scenes of joy at Perceval's assassination were reported in most London newspapers of 13 May 1812. The *Nottingham Journal* report, quoted in Gillen, *Assassination*, pp. 33–4.

p. 44   '"The country is no doubt . . .'". *The Love Letters of William and Mary Wordsworth*, ed. Beth Darlington, Ithaca, NY: Cornell University Press, 1981, p. 148.

p. 44   '"all the common people's heads . . ."'. 23 May 1812. *Memoirs, Journals and Correspondence of Thomas Moore*, ed. Lord John Russell, London: Longman, Brown, 1853, p. 277.

p. 44   'When the cabinet assembled . . .'. *Courier*, 13 May 1812.

p. 44   Castlereagh's opinion that the murder 'was confined to the individual . . .'. *The European Magazine*, 1812, p. 60.

p. 44   The Eldon-Ellenborough plan to hang Bellingham in front of the House of Commons was still in place on the day of the trial. Lord Ellenborough lost his temper when the plan was criticised, and Lord Grey reported, 'was in so heated a state of mind as is quite frightful in a man in his situation [Lord Chief Justice]'. Gillen, *Assassination*, p. 122.

Chapter Five: Examining the Enigma of the Assassin's Sanity

p. 46   The choice of James Harmer was probably made by the Whiggish Harvey Combe in the interests of securing as fair a trial as was possible. For Harmer's reputation and Phillips's opinion of him, see May, *The Bar and the Old Bailey, 1750–1850: The Prisoners' Counsel Act Justifying Advocacy*, p. 80.

p. 47   '"The people will now be able . . .".'. *The Times*, 13 May 1812.

p. 48   For Earl Ferrers's case, see Richard Davenport-Hines, 'Shirley, Laurence, fourth Earl Ferrers (1720–1760)', *Oxford Dictionary of National Biography*, Oxford University Press, 2004; online edn., January 2008; http://www.oxforddnb.com.ezproxy.londonlibrary.co.uk/view/article/25432, accessed 3 October 2010.

p. 48   Hadfield's case is detailed in 'Counter-Revolutionary Panic and the Treatment of the Insane: 1800' by Valerie Argent, Middlesex University, 1978; http://studymore.org.uk/1800.htm

p. 48   For the evidence of Beckwith and Taylor, see *Old Bailey Sessions Papers*, 'John Bellingham'; Beckwith specialised in very small pistols, thought to have been designed to be carried in ladies' purses and handbags.

p. 49   According to Gillen, *Assassination*, p. 84, he practised on Hampstead Heath, by Primrose Hill.

p. 50   For the story of Bellingham helping to find his landlady's child, see *The Times*, 12 May 1812. Evidently this must have come from John Vickery as a result of his questioning Mrs Robarts.

p. 50   For Bellingham's pamphlet, see BM Add Mss 48216, No. 44; other details from his petition to the Marquess of Wellesley, December 1809, No. 31.

p. 51   For the start of the Baltic Exchange, see http://www.balticexchange.com/default.asp?action=article&ID=19; for British trade see Ryan, 'The Defence of British Trade with the Baltic, 1808–1813', and 'Trade with the Enemy in the Scandinavian and Baltic Ports during the Napoleonic War: For and against'.

p. 52   Bellingham's tangled relationship with the Dutch merchants in Archangel and his fight for justice there are the subject of his pamphlet *op. cit.*, and are covered by Gillen, *Assassination*, 51–4.

p. 54   The intervention of Shairpe, the actions of Lord Leveson-Gower and Bellingham's imprisonment in St Petersburg are described in his pamphlet and in Gillen, *Assassination*, pp. 54–68; and Leveson-Gower gave his own version in a letter to Lord Castlereagh written soon after the trial and reprinted in many pamphlets, including *A Full Report of the Trial of John Bellingham*, Hull, 1812.

Chapter Six: The Victim is Seen as a Fond Father and Attentive Husband

p. 58   The financial award to Perceval's family was covered by the London newspapers, 14 May 1812; the *Courier* declaring that 'its smallness is utterly unworthy of the national character'.

p. 59   '"the most straightforward man I have ever known . . ."'. George III on his appointment of Perceval as Prime Minister on 4 October 1809.

p. 59   '"No man could be more generous . . ."'. *Memoirs of the life of Sir Samuel Romilly*, vol. III, London: John Murray, 1840, p. 37.

p. 59   For the married life of the Percevals, their irrepressible daughters and disappointing sons, see Gray, *Spencer Perceval*, pp. 10–11, 27 and 428–34.

p. 61   '"with very little reading . . ."'. Romilly quoted in Gray, *Spencer Perceval*, p. 10.

p. 62   For Lord Egmont's political views, see Hassell, *Edward Marsh*, p. 13.

p. 62   '"no information beyond what a classical education gives . . ."'. Brougham quoted in Gray, *Spencer Perceval*, p. 5.

p. 62   Perceval's early career is described in Gray, *Spencer Perceval*, pp. 12–20; '"I am sorry to say"', Gray, p. 16.

p. 63   Perceval's early political career, Gray, *Spencer Perceval*, pp. 19–34.

p. 64   '"The most striking thing I saw . . .".' Jefferson to John Page, May
        1786, *Papers of Thomas Jefferson, General Correspondence*, Library of
        Congress; http://memory.loc.gov/ammem/collections/jefferson_
        papers/mtjser1.html

p. 66   'His fourth son, John, carried into old age . . .'. Perceval, *Narrative
        of the Treatment*. In this tortured account of his descent into
        madness, John Perceval identified a tune heard on a hurdy-gurdy,
        or barrel organ, as the emblem of lost happiness. 'I fear the death
        of my poor father was at the root of all my misfortune for I can
        trace the notes of this air, to the time we were living happily in
        Hampstead.' According to *The Globe*, 13 May 1812, one of Perceval's
        sons, and John is the most likely candidate, was actually in the
        House of Commons when his father was shot.

p. 66   The political and romantic opinions of the Perceval daughters are
        from Gray, *Spencer Perceval*, pp. 431–3.

p. 68   Perceval's letters to his son. Gray, *Spencer Perceval*, pp. 429–31.

p. 69   Perceval's comments on Dudley Ryder's losses at faro. Gray,
        Spencer Perceval, p. 17.

p. 70   '"I wish that Wellesley was castrated . . .".' Wellington to his
        brother William Wellesley-Pole, October 1809.

p. 70   '"Tricking in love and tricking the public . . .".' Quoted in *The
        Gentleman's Magazine*, vol. 82, p. 590.

p. 70   '"You spend a great deal of ink . . .".' Sydney Smith, *Peter Plymley's
        Letters*. Letter 1; http://www.gutenberg.org/cache/epub/4063/
        pg4063.html.

Chapter Seven: A Prime Minister Put There by Providence

p. 73   'In his novel, *Tremaine* . . .', see Ward, *Tremaine*, vol. 3, p. 236.

p. 73   'It was a physical rather than an intellectual faith . . .'. Ch. 2,
        'Knowledge of the Lord' in *Evangelicalism in Modern Britain:
        A History from the 1730s to the 1980s* by David W. Bebbington,

London: Routledge, 1989, pp. 20–75; Venn, 'Experience is a living proof . . .', ibid., p. 56; Wilberforce, 'God has so assigned . . .', ibid., p. 61; More, 'Action is the life of virtue . . .', ibid., p. 12.

p. 75   For the illness of the Percevals' baby son, and Perceval's response, see Gray, *Spencer Perceval*, p. 12.

p. 75   Perceval's promotion to cabinet office is the subject of Ch. 5, 'Counsel for the Defence', pp. 47–57, in Gray, *Spencer Perceval*.

p. 76   '"Gentlemen, who is Mr. Cobbett? . . .'". *The Village Labourer, 1760-1832: A Study in the Government of England Before the Reform Bill* by J. L. Hammond; London: Longmans Green, 1920, p. 188.

p. 76   '"a sort of understrapper . . ."'. Gray, *Spencer Perceval*, p. 11.

p. 77   For the slave trade see Anstey, *The Atlantic Slave Trade*; Thomas, *The Slave Trade*; Turley, *The Culture of English Antislavery, 1780–1860*. Liverpool's particular contribution is documented especially in the city's outstanding International Slavery Museum and the Merseyside Maritime Museum.

p. 78   Perceval's contribution to stamping out the slave trade has been ignored by historians, and inexplicably is overlooked even in Gray's biography. Nevertheless it was considered vital by the architects of the campaign, William Wilberforce and James Stephen, and its chief agent, Judge Robert Thorpe in Sierra Leone. Pitt's refusal to move against the slave trade provoked Stephen to complain, 'Mr. Pitt, unhappily for himself, his country and mankind, is not zealous enough in the cause of the negroes, to contend for them as decisively as he ought, in the cabinet any more than in parliament', quoted in Eric Williams, *Slavery and Capitalism*, p. 149. Without Perceval's advocacy of the Guiana Order in Council, Pitt would not have had even that fig leaf to conceal his failure to match actions to words.

p. 79   The collaboration between Perceval and Stephen emerges from Stephen, 'Letters to Spencer Perceval', BL Add. MS 49177; Wilberforce, *Life of William Wilberforce*; Anstey, *The Atlantic Slave*

Trade; Wilberforce, "'Guiana slave-trade'", in *Life*, vol. 3, p. 216; "'Busy with [James] Stephen and Attorney-General'", in *Life*, vol. 3, p. 248.

p. 80 Perceval's dealings with Princess Caroline reveal a capacity for combining blackmail and moral righteousness on a par with one of Bertie Wooster's more sociopathic aunts. See, Perceval, *The Book!, passim*; and Gray, *Spencer Perceval*, pp. 75–90.

p. 82 "'My principles would govern my vote ...'". Wilberforce, *Life*, p. 307.

p. 82 "'the best regulated ambition ...'". Charles Arbuthnot, quoted in Croker, *The Croker Papers*, March 1809, vol. 3, p. 15.

p. 83 "'Mr Perceval's conduct has so fully confirmed ...'". Windsor Mss, George III to cabinet, 2 Oct. 1809, cited in Gray, *Spencer Perceval*, 254.

p. 83 "'man seems to have been abandoned by Heaven ...'". Ward, *Tremaine*, vol. 3, p. 236.

Chapter Eight: The Pervasive Power of Little P

p. 84 "'Mr. Perceval, an insignificant lawyer ...'". Hunt, *Memoirs of Henry Hunt Esq*, vol. 3, Pt. 1. http://www.fullbooks.com/Memoirs-of-Henry-Hunt-Esq-Volume-31.html

p. 84 'Little P ...'. Eldon quoted in Gray, *Spencer Perceval*, p. 15.

p. 85 'The king refused to have second thoughts ...'. Gray, *Spencer Perceval*, pp. 254–74. So fragile was the ministry in its first days that Wellesley, who had to travel back from Spain to take up office, told a friend, 'It is possible I may find the Opposition in before I can reach England.' Gray, *Spencer Perceval*, p. 257.

p. 85 The classic account of the influence of the 'country gentlemen' is Lewis Namier's *The House of Commons*, London: HMSO, 1964.

p. 86 "'in these times of imputed corruption ...'". *The Day*, January 1810, quoted in Gray, *Spencer Perceval*, p. 272.

p. 86   'In the jaundiced view of Henry Hunt . . .'. Hunt, *Memoirs*, vol. 3, Pt. 1. http://www.fullbooks.com/Memoirs-of-Henry-Hunt-Esq-Volume-31.html

p. 87   'Writing to Wellington in Spain . . .'. Liverpool quoted in Gray, *Spencer Perceval*, p. 426.

p. 88   '"the dear duke of York . . ."'. Fanny Perceval, quoted in Gray, *Spencer Perceval*, p. 423. To avoid confusion over military commanders the duke of York was the commander-in-chief, responsible for British forces throughout North America, the West Indies, India, Ireland and the UK, as well as Wellington's army in Portugal.

p. 88   Perceval's effectiveness as a cheese-paring Chancellor is explored in painstaking detail in Gray, *Spencer Perceval*, pp. 305–90; the payment to Wellington's army in silver forced the Treasury to seek dollars where they were most abundant, in Peru and Mexico where four-fifths of the world's silver was mined, and China where dollars ended up having paid for the European demand for tea, silk and china.

p. 90   '"To carry on the war . . ."'. Rose, 11 November 1809, quoted in Gray, *Spencer Perceval*, p. 344.

p. 91   'the Bullion committee'. The report of the Bullion committee is taken by economists as the most comprehensive, early analysis of inflationary pressure through an increase in the money supply. However, it is also a classic early demonstration of the capacity of economists to ignore the supreme importance of politics in creating and solving economic crises.

p. 91   '"he was aware that he was not as well informed . . ."'. Perceval to Huskisson, 28 October 1810, quoted in Gray, *Spencer Perceval*, p. 375.

p. 92   '"We think this . . ."'. *The Day* quoted in Gray, *Spencer Perceval*, p. 377.

p. 92   Perceval's financial efforts compared well with the French who could barely pay their troops, and according to Wellington in late 1811, 'thus a million of men are put into the field . . . for the pay of 4 or 500,000! . . . It is impossible that this fraudulent tyranny can last. If Great Britain continues stout we must see the destruction of it.'

p. 93   "'Of this I am certain, in a democracy . . .'". Burke, *Reflections on the Revolution in France*, 11th edn., London: Dodsley, 1791, p. 186.

p. 93   "'they [the French] have been raised up by Providence . . .'". Perceval to R. Bosanquet, Perceval Papers, quoted in Gray, *Spencer Perceval*, p. 46.

p. 94   Perceval had applied the prophecy from Daniel initially to the defeat of Napoleon by a British army at Acre in 1800, but evidently it was also applicable to the Peninsular campaign. For his biblical divination with Thomas Walpole see Gray, *Spencer Perceval*, pp. 45–6.

p. 94   Although it is difficult to defend Perceval's readiness to allow policy to be influenced by biblical divination, President Ronald Reagan showed in modern times how effective illogical decision-making could be. At the height of the Cold War, Reagan found it simpler to picture the Soviet Union as 'the evil empire', thereby cutting through the distracting complexities thrown up by Kremlinologists and other experts on Soviet politics. Like Perceval, he too relied on other-worldly guidance when complex choices had to be made, in his case, the readings of San Francisco astrologer, Joan Quigley. According to his chief of staff, Donald Regan, 'every major move and decision the Reagans made was cleared in advance with [her] to make certain the planets were in a favourable alignment'. Obviously Quigley's findings were more effective than any academic analysis in persuading an intellectually lightweight president that he was taking the right executive decision, and doubtless they contributed to the sunny sense of confidence he exuded. Spencer Perceval operated in a similar fashion. Just as

Reagan went to Reykjavik for his second summit meeting with Mikhail Gorbachev in 1985 strengthened by his astrologer's assurance that the stars were favourable for such an encounter, so Perceval drew strength for the confrontation with Napoleon from the insights of biblical prophecy.

Chapter Nine: The Beauty of Double Bookkeeping

p. 97   Ann Billett's testimony about Bellingham's state of mind was recorded in *Old Bailey Sessions Papers*, p. 271; her childhood as Ann Scarbrow was cited in Gillen, *Assassination*, p. 46.

p. 98   Burke's exposition of the sublime/beautiful polarity was exceptional in its emphasis on the sexual nature of the divide, 'its origin in gratifications and pleasures'; see Burke, *Philosophical Enquiry*, Section VIII.

p. 100 The insanity of Bellingham's father amid Scarbrow respectability, and the efforts of uncle William Daw to provide for his future, are well covered in Gillen, *Assassination*, pp. 43–7.

p. 101 One of the underpinning wonders of modern capitalism is accountancy based on double-entry bookkeeping in which each transaction is recorded twice, as an asset and liability, and balanced over an accounting period, as profit or loss. It began in fourteenth-century Venice. In *Wilhelm Meister*, Goethe categorised it, half ironically, as a science that allowed merchants to organise into a system not only the guesswork of financial trading but the endless variability of subjective thought: 'It came from the same spirit which produced the systems of Galileo and Newton and the subject matter of modern physics and chemistry. By the same means, it organizes perceptions into a system, and one can characterize it as the first Cosmos constructed purely on the basis of mechanistic thought.'

p. 103 The picture of Liverpool's recent past was vigorously drawn in

Recollections of Old Liverpool by 'a Nonagenarian' in 1836, with indications that his memory went back to the 1780s. More modern accounts are provided by Checkland in 'American Versus West Indian Traders in Liverpool, 1793–1815' and 'Economic Attitudes in Liverpool, 1793–1807'; Hyde and others in 'The Nature and Profitability of the Liverpool Slave Trade'; Hyde in *Liverpool and the Mersey: An Economic History of a Port, 1700–1970*; and Harris, *Liverpool and Merseyside*.

p. 105 Bellingham's early mercantile career is pieced together from the account given by the Reverend Daniel Wilson, *Substance of a Conversation with John Bellingham*, various pamphlets, especially *A Full Report of the Trial of John Bellingham*, and Gillen, *Assassination*, pp. 44–50.

p. 107 'Mary, "a very pleasant, affable woman" . . .'. quoted in Gillen, *Assassination*, p. 147. The strengths of Mary Bellingham's character are obvious both in her ability to maintain herself and her young child in St Petersburg for more than a year, and in her attempts to hold together her family and the unstable Bellingham.

p. 108 Specialist sources for the Russian trade are Ryan, 'The Defence of British Trade with the Baltic, 1808–1813' and 'Trade with the Enemy in the Scandinavian and Baltic Ports during the Napoleonic War: For and against'; Barty-King, *The Baltic Exchange*; and Jackson, *Hull in the Eighteenth Century*.

p. 109 Bellingham's experience in Russia is derived from his pamphlet *op. cit.*, Leveson-Gower's letter to Castlereagh, and Gillen, *Assassination*, pp. 51–4; on his inheritance from William Daw, see Gillen, *Assassination*, pp. 69–70.

p. 110 For Ann Billett's evidence, see above.

p. 112 Mary Bellingham's partnership with Mary Stevens, affidavit of Mary Stevens, see above.

p. 112 For Bellingham's fruitless search for compensation in early 1810, see Billett's evidence above; *European Magazine*, pp. 377–8. His

reconciliation with Mary, affidavit of Stevens, Gillen, *Assassination*,
p. 73.

p. 114 Despite Gillen's meticulous research, neither in her ground-break-
ing book nor in subsequent accounts of the assassination is there
any attempt to explain the strange gap between Bellingham's two
attempts to get compensation in 1810 and 1812, the impact of the
economic upheaval that occurred in Liverpool during that period,
or the sharp difference in his behaviour in the two episodes.

Chapter Ten: The Prosecution Presents its Case

p. 115 Bellingham's trial launched a thousand pamphlets, articles and
reports. The most complete are in the *Annual Register* and the *Old
Bailey Sessions Papers*. The most immediate are in *The Times*, 16
and 18 May 1812, *The Globe* and *Morning Post*, 16 May 1812.

p. 117 For Alley's character see May, *The Bar and the Old Bailey, 1750–1850:
The Prisoners' Counsel Act Justifying Advocacy*, p. 83.

p. 124 'as he confessed to Sir William Curtis MP . . .'. Bellingham's
evidence during committal proceedings, 11 May 1812.

Chapter Eleven: Bellingham and the Absence of *malice prepense*

p. 126 The sources for Bellingham's defence are as in the previous chapter.
Although more considered accounts, such as the *Annual Register*,
imply he must have been mad, newspapers assumed he was sane.
The important point was his intention – to make the jury understand his justification for killing the Prime Minister (to secure
justice), and thus to see that it was without *malice prepense*, and
consequently that it could not constitute murder. 'Had I not
possessed these imperious excitements, and had murdered him in
cold blood,' he declared, 'I should consider myself a monster.'

p. 130 '"That my arm destroyed him . . ."'. *The Authentic Account*, pp. 24–37.

p. 133   'Amazingly, Sheriff William Heygate returned to announce ...'. This extraordinary circumstance appears in the *Old Bailey Sessions Papers* for the session beginning 13 May 1812, ref no. 18120513.

Chapter Twelve: The Compelling Evidence of Miss Stevens

p. 136   'both of Liverpool's papers ...'. The *Liverpool Courier*, which was solidly Tory and pro-West India interests, and the *Liverpool Mercury*, which was solidly Whig and pro-American trade interests.

p. 136   The few indications of Mary Stevens's character, the common-sense in her affidavit, the loyalty she showed to her friend, Mary Bellingham, the stylishness of her dresses, and the love she inspired in the three Bellingham children, all point to someone who was reliable, good and interesting, a rare combination.

p. 136   For Bellingham's return to Liverpool in 1810 and business there, see Stevens's affidavit, above; Billett's testimony, above, and testimony of James Nevill, PRO 30/29/6/11.

p. 138   The decline in Liverpool's economy can be traced through reports in the *Mercury* from the summer of 1811 showing prices and sales of Irish linens, and Manchester, Birmingham and Sheffield goods all down; 'little demand for cattle', *Mercury*, 19 July 1811.

p. 138   '"It is their Traveller's mistake ...'". Mary Bellingham to John Bellingham, 18 January 1812, BM Add Mss 48216, No. 42.

p. 138   Bellingham's letter to Parton dated 11 May 1812 made it clear that buying iron was part of a larger ambition to get back into the Russian trade.

p. 139   '"I think I need not entreat you ...'". Mary Bellingham, 18 January 1812, see above.

p. 140   '"I could have wished when you had written ...'". Bellingham, 16 April 1812, BM Add Mss 48216, No. 49.

p. 141   '"If I could think that the prospects ...'". Mary Bellingham, April 1812, BM Add Mss 48216, No. 50.

p. 142 Mary Stevens's discussion with Bellingham comes from her affidavit, see above.

p. 147 According to the *Morning Chronicle*, 13 May 1812, Bellingham estimated his losses at '£7000 or £8000'.

Chapter Thirteen: The Search for the Truth behind the Murder

p. 148 "'I screamed for the gaoler . . .'". Jerdan, *Autobiography* vol. 2, p. 124. Charles Dickens also described the condemned cell in *Sketches of Boz*, 'Visit to Newgate': 'It was a stone dungeon, eight feet long by six wide, with a bench at the upper end, under which were a common rug, a bible, and prayer-book. An iron candlestick was fixed into the wall at the side; and a small high window in the back admitted as much air and light as could struggle in between a double row of heavy, crossed iron bars.'

p. 149 "'Government think to intimidate me . . .'". *Morning Chronicle*, 19 May 1812.

p. 149 "'No person can have heard . . .'". Romilly, *Memoirs*, vol. 2, p. 257.

p. 149 "'he was one of those unhappy men . . .'". Cobbett, *History of the Regency and Reign of George IV*, Ch. III, section 127. Googlebooks.

p. 150 "'And whither can the fainting eye of human misery turn . . .'". Daniel Wilson, *A Defence of the Church Missionary Society Against the Objections of the Reverend Josiah Thomas, M.A. Archdeacon of Bath*, Wilson, London, 1818, p. 37.

p. 151 The character and early life of James Stephen come from *The Memoirs of James Stephen written by himself for the use of his children*, edited by Merle M. Bevington, London: Hogarth Press, 1954. Wilberforce's comments on his character are quoted in Anstey, *The Atlantic Slave Trade*, p. 145.

p. 151 For Stephen's concern for Bellingham's soul, see Wilberforce, *Life*, vol. 4, pp. 26–7: "May 14 . . . Stephen had been this morning,

I found, praying for the wretched murderer, and thinking that his being known to be a friend of Perceval's might affect him [Bellingham], went and devoted himself to trying to bring him to repentance.'

p. 152   "'O! what will be the misery you will endure . . .'". Wilson, *The Substance of a Conversation with John Bellingham*.

p. 153   Butterworth's conversation with Bellingham, *A Full and Authentic Account*, p. 93.

p. 154   Bellingham's 'Washing book', and other receipts and accounts together with Rebecca Robarts's invoices, are all preserved at the British Museum, BM Add Mss 48216.

p. 155   "'If he had known the price would be more than eight pence . . .'". Testimony of Catherine Figgins at Bellingham's trial.

p. 156   'Vickery showed himself to be an exceptional detective . . .'. *Old Bailey Sessions Papers*, 1800–1819: his evidence regarding a theft of timber, 'we moved the timber to the office, and locked it up, (produces one of the pieces;) I put a mark on it that night, with my knife'; concerning a theft of furs, 'I saw Hamlyn the porter with a large load upon his head upon a knot in a basket, and another basket upon that; it was packed in such an awkward loose way it struck me that it was not all right'; concerning stolen bank notes, 'When I came up, I saw the two prisoners very near together, and in the hands of Joel Joseph I saw some paper . . . there was no other person near them within a dozen or twenty yards, they had taken a circular walk round the hall, and where they were there was no company . . . Joseph refused being searched by Preston [another Bow Street officer], and said, Vickery shall search me, he has known me a good while, and whatever he finds he will return me.'

p. 156   For the Bow Street Runners in general, see Cox, 'A Certain Share of Low Cunning – The Provincial Use and Activities of Bow Street "Runners" 1792–1839', School of Historical Studies: Monash University, 2003.

p. 156   Mary Clark's encounter with Bellingham, given in cross-examination at his trial, *Old Bailey Sessions Papers*.

p. 157   It is impossible to trace the source of Bellingham's money, but the quantity of his expenditure makes it clear that someone must have supplied him with funds during his time in London. Had he earned £85 from the purchase of iron, he would surely have remitted some to his distressed family in Liverpool. But his allusion to receiving 'maintenance', and the pattern of his spending, from heavy at the end of February, apparently regular in March and April, but so desperate in May that he grew upset at a charge of eight pence for laundry, indicates that the money came piecemeal, until being withheld at the end.

p. 161   The long-term significance of the Prince Regent's capitulation to Perceval in late February, following the Whigs' refusal to serve, was obvious not merely to the political classes. An intercepted letter from a group of Luddites promising to begin a rebellion explained that 'the immediate cause of us beginning when we did was that Rascally Letter of the Prince Regent to Lords Grey and Grenville which left us no hope of a change for the better'.

Chapter Fourteen: Choking to Death the Illegal Slave Trade

p. 163   '"It indeed afforded some relief . . .'". *Morning Chronicle*, 13 May 1812.

p. 165   Stephen's character. *Memoirs*, Bevington, pp. 8–20.

p. 166   Hans Sloane, *A Voyage to the Islands of Maderia, Barbados, Nieves, S. Christophers, and Jamaica, with the natural history . . . of the last of those islands; to which is prefixed an introduction wherein is an account of the inhabitants . . . trade, etc.*, 2 vols. (London, 1701–1725), vol. 1, cited in Smandych, 'To soften the extreme rigor of their bondage'.

p. 167   '"I would rather be on friendly terms . . .'". quoted in Leslie

Stephen, *Life of Sir James Fitzjames Stephen, Bart., K.C.S.I.: A Judge of the High Court of Justice*, London: Smith, Elder, and Co., 1895.

p. 168 "'Mr Wilberforce I do not think has behaved . . .'". Fanny Perceval, quoted in Gray, *Spencer Perceval*, p. 205.

p. 169 "'It has been discovered . . .'". *The Fourth Report of the Directors of the African Institution*, London: Hatchard, 1810, p. 2; Googlebooks.

p. 169 'a ship stopped in the Thames in 1810 . . .'. Christopher Lloyd, *The Navy and the Slave Trade*, London: Longmans Green, 1949, p. 31.

p. 170 Measures against the illegal slave trade initiated by Perceval in cabinet. Order in Council 16 May 1808 authorising the payment of a bounty amounting to £40 per man, £30 per woman and £10 per child released, see Tara Helfman, 'The Court of Vice Admiralty at Sierra Leone and the Abolition of the West African Slave Trade', *Yale Law Journal*, vol. 115, 2006; Perceval's instructions to officials in Trinidad and Demerara to put down illegal slaving, 1808, see Gray, *Spencer Perceval*, p. 26; Admiralty order to send two Royal Navy vessels, HMS *Solebay* and HMS *Derwent*, to patrol the west Africa coast, Perceval Papers, Perceval to Stephen, 9 August 1809; creation of West Indian commission to investigate charges of evasions of Slave Trade Act, September 1810, Wilberforce, *Life*, vol. 3, pp. 372 and 382; Order in Council requiring compulsory register of slaves in Trinidad, March 1812, Smandych, "'To Soften the Extreme Rigor of their Bondage'", p. 12.

p. 170 For the activities of Judge Robert Thorpe, see Tara Helfman, 'The Court of Vice Admiralty at Sierra Leone and the Abolition of the West African Slave Trade', *Yale Law Journal*, vol. 115, 2006; *passim*.

p. 172 Although Stephen's plan for a blockade put forward in *War In Disguise, or the Friends of the Neutral* was overtly aimed at France, Wilberforce's sons, Samuel and Robert, who were also his biographers, asserted in a footnote in their *Life of Wilberforce*, vol. 3, p. 234, seemingly based on information from their father, 'Mr Stephen aiming only at its [the slave trade's] suppression published a masterly pamphlet (*War in Disguise*) upon the rights of neutral powers. Fearing, if he mentioned the slave trade that the effect of his arguments might be diminished by a suspicion of his motives, he confined himself entirely to the general question.'

p. 174 '"and in its associated iniquity . . ."'. Stephen, *The Dangers of the Country*, p. 114.

p. 175 For the effect of Perceval's measures on Liverpool, see B. H. Tolley, 'The Liverpool Campaign Against the Order in Council and the War of 1812' in Harris, *Liverpool and Merseyside: Essays in the Economic and Social History of the Port and its Hinterland*; Checkland, 'American Versus West Indian Traders in Liverpool, 1793–1815', *The Economic History Review*, New Series, vol. 5, no. 1 (1952), pp. 58–75; Drake, 'Continuity and Flexibility in Liverpool's Trade with Africa and the Caribbean', *Business History* (1976), pp. 85–97; and Hyde, *Liverpool and the Mersey: An Economic History of a Port, 1700–1970*.

p. 177 The extent of illegal slave trading by Liverpool merchants, using foreign flags, masters and documentation, can only be inferred from discrepancies in the Registers of Merchant Ships registers. Those consulted ran from 1805 to 1812. Thus well over half the ships listed in the 1807 register changed ownership within the next two years, a huge increase over previous years. The fifty to sixty ships formerly engaged in the slave trade that left the register in the two years after 1807 represented a significant increase in the rate for former years.

p. 178 '"there was no evidence of smuggling . . ."'. Lord Liverpool, quoted in Smandych, '"To Soften The Extreme Rigor of their Bondage"', p. 12.

p. 178 "'to instruct His Majesty's cruizers . . .'". quoted in Helfman, 'The Court of Vice Admiralty at Sierra Leone and the Abolition of the West African Slave Trade'.

p. 179 Growth of the American trade. See Checkland, 'American Versus West Indian Traders in Liverpool, 1793–1815'.

Chapter Fifteen: How to Kill an Economy

p. 181 "'My Blessed Mary . . .'". quoted in Gillen, *Assassination*, p. 124.

p. 182 "'It is always a matter of dissension between me and Mrs B . . .'". quoted in Stevens, affidavit.

p. 182 "'she had decided never to raise the subject . . .'". quoted in Gillen, *Assassination*, p. 143.

p. 183 "'no person was more inclined to be domestically happy . . .'". quoted in Stevens, affidavit.

p. 183 "'uniformly cruel'". Nevill's testimony, PRO 30/29/6/11.

p. 183 For Liverpool's economic distress, see B. H. Tolley, "The Liverpool Campaign Against the Order in Council and the War of 1812' in Harris, *Liverpool and Merseyside: Essays in the Economic and Social History of the Port and its Hinterland.*

p. 184 The growth of the American trade in Liverpool is treated in Checkland, 'American Versus West Indian Traders in Liverpool, 1793–1815'; it is also apparent from 'The Minutes of the American Chamber of Commerce' Archives, Liverpool Central Library. In 1808 Alexander Baring gave evidence to the House of Commons that 'Liverpool is the principal centre of the American commerce, London houses acting almost solely as bankers for the America trade, receiving the proceeds of consignments', *An Inquiry into the Causes and Consequences of the Orders in Council*, London: Hatchard, 1808.

p. 184 For the development of American trade with Russia, see Kalevi Ahonen, 'From Sugar Triangle to Cotton Triangle: Trade and Shipping between America and Baltic Russia, 1783–1860'.

p. 186 The petition of Birmingham manufacturers is quoted in Holmberg, 'The Acts, Orders in Council, &c. of Great Britain [on Trade], 1793–1812', Napoleon Series; Government and Politics, April 2003. http://www.napoleon-series.org/research/government/british/decrees/c_britdecrees1.html

p. 187 '"Not only are the names forged . . .'". Brougham to the House of Commons, 3 March 1812.

p. 188 The tangled origins of the War of 1812, and the activities of the War Hawks, are examined in Bradford Perkins, *Prologue to War: England and the United States, 1805–1812*, Berkeley and Los Angeles: University of California Press, 1961. Google-books; 'British slavery upon the water', quoted in Perkins, p. 57.

p. 189 Pinkney's negotiations with Wellesley and Perceval, in Gray, *Spencer Perceval*, pp. 450–3; for Perceval's opposition to 'courting of negotiations', Gray, p. 451.

p. 189 Brougham's accusation that Perceval was motivated by 'scorn of the Americans' was cited by Reginald Horsman in *The Causes of the War of 1812*, Philadelphia: University of Pennsylvania Press, 1962, p. 58.

p. 190 '"The Americans swarm on the Coast . . .'". Helfman, 'The Court of Vice Admiralty at Sierra Leone and the Abolition of the West African Slave Trade'.

p. 190 'From a peak of about eighty thousand slaves . . .'. Eltis, 'Slave Departures from Africa, 1811–1867'.

p. 191 The impact of the American embargo on Liverpool trade. Checkland, 'American Versus West Indian Traders in Liverpool, 1793–1815'.

p. 191 '"the distress in this town'". *Liverpool Mercury*, 12 June 1812.

p. 192 '"the temerity in a moment of premature triumph'". *Mercury*, 18 October 1811.

p. 192 '"Rely on one thing . . .'". Grundy to Jackson, 28 November 1812, quoted in Perkins, *Prologue to War*, p. 356.

p. 193 '"Now, after this . . .".'. *New York Evening Post*, 26 January 1812.

p. 193 'The *Mercury* columnist who described Perceval . . .'. *Liverpool Mercury*, 19 August 1811.

p. 193 Breed's application for credit. 'A Letter to Messrs Hughes & Duncan' by Richard F. Breed, Liverpool 1812.

p. 194 That Liverpool's most respectable citizens were ready to use violence to attain their ends was attested by William Roscoe. A polymathic poet and banker, and courageous campaigner against the slave trade, he became a Liverpool MP in the election of 1806, but his supporters were beaten up so badly by gangs of dockers that he withdrew from the 1807 contest. The violence, he told the *Mercury*, was organised by the West India merchants who controlled the city.

Chapter Sixteen: The Russian Connection Returns

p. 196 Lord Holland's meeting with a Birmingham manufacturer. Holland, *Further Memoirs of the Whig Party*, London: John Murray, 1905, pp. 131–2.

p. 197 '"Aye," Castlereagh admitted, "but one does not like to own . . .".'. Wilberforce, *Life*, vol. 4, p. 35.

p. 197 The *Mercury* on rejoicing over the assassination. *Liverpool Mercury*, 25 May 1812.

p. 198 '"about a million in money". . . .'. Richardson, evidence to 1812 House of Commons committee on Order in Council, quoted in Checkland, 'American Versus West Indian Traders in Liverpool, 1793–1815', p. 157.

p. 199 For evidence of Richard Statham's business character, see 'Papers of Richard Statham', *passim*, Acc 55, Secure Room, Liverpool Central Library.

p. 200 William Gee affidavit, 'Papers of Richard Statham'.

p. 200 'E. Peck's cramped handwriting . . .'. The evidence that Peck &

Phelps existed in 1801 dates the beginning of their partnership earlier than any of the dates, usually 1818 or 1821, assigned by company histories of their successor company, Phelps Dodge & Co.

p. 200 Letter of Bellingham to Parton. *Liverpool Mercury*, 25 May 1812.

p. 203 British bankers in the American-Russian trade. See Ahonen, 'From Sugar Triangle to Cotton Triangle: Trade and Shipping between America and Baltic Russia, 1783–1860'; Ryan, 'Trade with the Enemy in the Scandinavian and Baltic Ports during the Napoleonic War: For and against'; Dorfman, 'A Note on the Interpenetration of Anglo-American Finance'; Stanley Chapman, 'British Marketing Enterprise: The Changing Roles of Merchants, Manufacturers, and Financiers, 1700–1860', *The Business History Review*, vol. 53, no. 2, Early Commercial Aviation, Summer 1979, pp. 205–34.

p. 205 For the activities of Peck & Phelps, and Phelps & Peck, see Ahonen, 'From Sugar Triangle to Cotton Triangle'; Dorfman, 'Interpenetration of Anglo-American Finance' (especially for the Wilson-Phelps connection); Diary of Anson G. Phelps, Documents Room, New York Public Library. A history of Phelps, Dodge & Co. in 1950 quotes Phelps writing in his diary that while he had not attained 'what my ambitious heart would call worldly prosperity', he had at least been able, 'by the goodness of God', to pay his debts.

Chapter Seventeen: Where the Money Came From

p. 209 Elisha Peck's character was inevitably subsumed by his American-based partner, Anson Phelps, who morphed the business into the beginning of today's multibillion-dollar metals conglomerate. But the thirty years of their partnership testifies to a harmony of views, and to their common tendency to cut business and financial corners, and adhere to fundamentalist tenets of religious belief.

p. 210 "'Nothing could more surprise him . . .'". Baring, quoted in *Annual Register*, 1813, p. 111.

p. 210 "'As England is contending for the defence . . .'". Perceval to the House of Commons, 3 March 1812.

p. 211 "'If any thing was wanting . . .'". Russell to Secretary of State James Monroe, 4 March 1812.

p. 211 Bellingham's final claims for justice. See Gillen, *Assassination*, pp. 74–80.

p. 214 "'The measure is perfect madness . . .'". *New York Evening Post*, 21 April 1812.

p. 214 "'Ye who live by farming . . .'". Handbill issued in Boston, Massachusetts, April 1812, 'Let every Federalist do his duty and Massachusetts will yet be saved!'

p. 217 Sidney's Alley used to run from Piccadilly Circus to Leicester Square. According to *The Survey of London*, it was redeveloped in the 1840s. But it was evidently a fairly fashionable shopping arcade. Thomas Challenier occupied No. 7, according to *Kent's London Directory*, 1810–11.

p. 218 I have spent more time than I can justify trying to work out how General Isaac Gascoyne could have known that it was Perceval who had been killed.

p. 220 'the prisoner "received a small box . . .'". *The Times*, 18 May 1812.

p. 223 The poignancy of the final sentence of this last letter, published in almost every London newspaper on 19 May 1812, emphasises how completely Bellingham was caught up in his plan. Nothing existed outside it.

Chapter Eighteen: An Execution Ends all Cares

p. 224 The scene of Bellingham's execution is a composite of several descriptions, mostly relying on the *Edinburgh Annual Register*, *The Complete Newgate Calendar*, vol. V, and *The Full and Authentic Account*.

p. 224 "'called too soon . . .'". Cobbett, *Political Register*, 23 May 1812, vol. 21, column 669.

p. 228 "'I saw the anxious looks . . .'". Cobbett, *Political Register*, ibid., section 133.

p. 230 "'You'd be astonished to find how shy . . .'". Liverpool letter to J. J. Cossart, of Lombard Street, London, quoted in Gillen, *Assassination*, p. 147.

p. 230 The history of Phelps, Dodge & Co. comes from a company history written in 1950, online 'A history of Phelps, Dodge, 1834–1950'; Phelps's dubious role in the Wilson Bank scam comes from Dorfman, 'A Note on the Interpenetration of Anglo-American Finance, 1837–1841'.

p. 230 Elisha Peck's movements have been deduced from his appearance in New York trade directories from 1812, and his reappearance in *Gore's Liverpool Directory* from 1815. The West Haverstraw Village History, online, records his arrival on the ship *Samson* in 1830 in the United States with a rolling steel mill from England, and his foundation of the company town of Samsondale, named after the ship, on the River Hudson.

p. 231 Leveson-Gower's letter and donation to Mary Bellingham are contained in 'Letters of George Canning to John Drinkwater', 920 CAN, Liverpool Central Library, Archives; quoted in Gillen, *Assassination*, pp. 142–3.

p. 232 Mary Stevens's 'new and elegant assortment of Millinery' was advertised in the *Liverpool Mercury*, 5 June 1812.

p. 233 Advertisement of Mary Bellingham's bankruptcy. *Liverpool Mercury*, 13 November 1812.

Chapter Nineteen: Understanding Why it Happened

p. 234 "'the sepulchral Perceval . . .'". Smith, *Peter Plymley Letters*, p. 35.

p. 234 "'Nothing could be more calm . . .'". Quoted in Gray, *Spencer*

Perceval, pp. 458–9. Jane Perceval's reaction, Gray, p. 458. Perceval's funeral, Gray, p. 461.

p. 235 "'Perceval was never more easy . . .'". Ward, quoted in Gray, p. 456.

p. 236 Williams's dream. Gillen, *Assassination*, pp. 153–4.

p. 236 The term 'murder money' was used by Edward Marsh, great-grandson of Spencer Perceval and later Winston Churchill's secretary, according to his biographer Christopher Hassell.

p. 237 Henry Hunt's attack on Jane Perceval. Hunt, *Memoirs of Henry Hunt*, vol. 3, online http://www.gutenberg.org/cache/epub/8463/pg8463.txt

p. 237 The lives of Spencer Perceval's children attracted the attention of diarists like Charles Greville, see *The Greville Memoirs*, and John Croker, see *The Croker Papers*. The adherence to Edward Irving's charismatic Church attracted particular attention to Spencer Perceval junior, from both Greville and Hassell, in *Edward Marsh*. John Perceval's descent into and recovery from lunacy were agonisingly described in his *Narrative of the Treatment*, and by its twentieth-century editor, the noted anthropologist Gregory Bateson.

p. 241 Hunt's analysis of Perceval's fate, *Memoirs* vol. 3, online http://www.gutenberg.org/cache/epub/8463/pg8463.txt

Bibliography

British Museum Collections

49189. SPENCER PERCEVAL PAPERS. Vol. XVII (ff. 97). 'Memoirs' of Perceval; 1812. Partly (ff. 1–12b) *printed*. An anonymous biography, amplifying the life published in the *National Advertiser*, 20 May 1812, and reprinted in the *Gentleman's Magazine*, May–June 1812. Includes (ff. 95–96) a receipted bill for publication work, 1812. Apparently suppressed (see f. 97) by Lord Arden.

49173–49195. Correspondence and papers of the Hon. Spencer Perceval (b. 1762, d. 1812), Prime Minister, and of his family; 1782–1922, n.d.

Add. MSS. 46920–47213, 48216

Add. Ch. 75439–75450

PRO 30/29/6/11 T 29/116 (747) T 29/117(5215)

HO 42/121, which includes a petition and letter from Bellingham, and HO 42/123

Stephen, James, 'Coup d'oeil on an American War', Perceval Papers, 33/98–105

Liverpool Central Library Archives

Letters of George Canning to John Drinkwater jun. 1812–14, 1822 transcript 920 CAN

Minutes of the American Chamber of Commerce

Papers of Richard Statham Acc 55; Secure Room

Gore's Directory for Liverpool 1800, 1802, 1807, 1810

Liverpool Register of Merchant Ships 1802–8 Reel 25 Abolition and Emancipation Pt. 2 Slavery Collection from the Merseyside Maritime Museum; published by Adam Matthews publications, 1998

New York Public Library

Documents Room, *Diary of Anson G. Phelps*

Printed Works by Rt. Hon. Spencer Perceval

Anon., but really Spencer Perceval, *The Duties and Powers of Public Officers with respect to Violations of the Public Peace*, [London, 1792]

—*A Review of the Arguments in favor of the Continuance of Impeachments, notwithstanding a dissolution*, p. 123. W. Clarke, London: J. Stockdale, 1791

—*"The Book!" or, the Proceedings and correspondence upon the subject of the inquiry into the conduct of Her Royal Highness the Princess of Wales . . . To which is prefixed a Narrative of the recent events that have led to the publication of the original documents. With a statement of facts relative to the child, now under the protection of Her Royal Highness.* [Superintended through the press by the Rt. Hon. Spencer Perceval] [With an appendix of documents, depositions, etc.], pp. 246, 108, London: M. Jones, 1813

—*The Church Question in Ireland. Speech as prepared by . . . Spencer Perceval, for the Debate on the first Roman Catholic Petition to the United Parliament*, May 1805. Now first published, . . . with an introduction, . . . notes and comments by D[udley]. Perceval, Edinburgh, 1844.

Pamphlets reporting on John Bellingham's trial, etc.

A full and authentic report of the trial of John Bellingham Esq, at the sessions; house in the Old Bailey on Friday May 15 1812 for the Murder

of the Rt Hon Spencer Perceval, Chancellor of the Exchequer, &c in the
Lobby of the House of Commons on Monday May 11 1812 . . . taken in
short hand by Thomas Hodgson esq. printed by Charles Squire,
Furnival's Inn Ct., Holborn, for Sheerwood, Neely and Jones 20
Paternoster Row, 1812

The Trial of John Bellingham for the Assassination of the Right Honourable
Spencer Perceval . . . Taken in short hand, by Mr. Fraser. To this is
added, an account of Bellingham's execution, etc. p. 103, London: R.
Mercer, 1812

A Full Report of the Trial of John Bellingham for the Murder of the Right Hon.
Spencer Perceval . . . in the lobby of the House of Commons . . . Including
the arguments of Counsel and his own defence at length. Accompanied with
a faithful narrative of every circumstance connected with the atrocious deed,
and of Bellingham's conduct from his committal to the time of his execution.
Together with a copy of Bellingham's memorial, and of Lord Gower's statement. To which is added a sketch of the life of Bellingham. [With a
portrait.] p. 55, Hull: J. Craggs & J. Simmons, 1812

An Authentic Account of the Trial and Execution of John Bellingham, for
the assassination of the Right Hon. Spencer Perceval; with a vindication
of the character of Sir Francis Burdett from the aspersions of some of the
London prints.

An Account of the Trial of John Bellingham, for the wilful murder of the
Right Hon. Spencer Perceval in the lobby of the House of Commons,
Brighton: John Forbes, [1812]

The Trial of J. Bellingham, a Liverpool merchant, at the Old Bailey, on
Friday, May 15, 1812, for the assassination of the Right Hon. Spencer
Perceval . . . With every particular attending the sad catastrophe, and
other important information. Taken in short-hand (Second edition), p.
26, London: W. Lewis, [1812]

An authentic account of the horrid assassination of the Right Honorable
Spencer Perceval, (Prime Minister of the United Kingdom,) who was shot
in the lobby of the House of Commons, by James [sic] Bellingham, a

Liverpool merchant; also, the trial of the murderer, which took place at the Old Bailey, before Lord Chief Justice Mansfield; with a particular account of the execution. Printed by T. Evans; London, 1812

Old Bailey Sessions Papers, John Bellingham, killing: murder, 13th May, 1812

Annual Register 1812, 'Assassination of Mr Perceval. Appendix to Chronicle: The Right Hon. Spencer Perceval; Trial of John Bellingham for the murder of the Rt Honourable Spencer Perceval. Assassination of Mr Perceval, and Parliamentary Proceedings thereupon.'

Newspapers

The Atlas
The Day
The Globe
The Liverpool Courier
The Liverpool Mercury
The Morning Chronicle
The Nottingham Journal
The Times

Contemporary Publications

Adams, John Quincy, *The Writings of John Quincy Adams*, vol. 9 (ed. Worthington C. Ford), New York: Macmillan, 1904; www.ebooksread. com/authors-eng/john-quincy-adams

Anon, *Recollections of Old Liverpool by A Nonagenarian*, Liverpool: J. F. Hughes. 1836

Burke, Edmund, *Philosophical Enquiry into the Origin of our Ideas of the Sublime and the Beautiful*, New York: Collier & Son, 1909–14; www. bartleby.com; 2001

Croker, John W., *The Croker Papers* [Correspondence and Writing, ed. Louis Jennings], London: John Murray, 1885

Cruchley, G. F., *Cruchley's London in 1865: a handbook for strangers, showing where to go, how to get there, and what to look at*, London: Cruchley, 1865

Goethe, Wolfgang von, *Wilhelm Meister's Apprenticeship*, New York: Collier & Son, 1917; www.bartleby.com, 2000

Greville, Charles F., *The Greville Memoirs: a journal of the reigns of King George IV and King William IV*, vols. I and II, London: Longmans Green, 1874

Holland, Lord Henry, *Further Memoirs of the Whig Party: 1807–1821 with some miscellaneous reminiscences*, London: John Murray, 1905

Hunt, Henry, *Memoirs of Henry Hunt Esq*, 3 vols., London: Dolby, 1820. www.wattpad.com/12477-memoirs-of-henry-hunt-esq-volume-1

Jerdan, William, *The Autobiography of W. J.*, 4 vols., London: 1852–53.

Paine, Tom, *The Rights of Man being an Answer to Mr Burke's Attack on the French Revolution*, Boston: Thomas & Andrews, 1791

Parliamentary History, vol. XXVIII

Perceval, John T., *Narrative of the Treatment experienced by a Gentleman, during a state of mental derangement; designed to explain the causes and the nature of insanity, and to expose the injudicious conduct pursued towards many . . . sufferers under that calamity* [By John Thomas Perceval], p. 278, London: Effingham Wilson, 1838

Smith, Sydney, *Peter Plymley's Letters* [Published from 1804 in *The Edinburgh Review*] http://www.archive.org/details/peterplymleyslet04063gut

Stephen, James, *The Dangers of the Country* [First published 1807, US edition Bradford; Philadelphia, 1897] http://www.archive.org/details/dangerscountry00stepgoog

Stephen, James, *War In Disguise, or the Friends of the Neutral*, London: Hatchard, 1805

Stephen, James, *The Memoirs of James Stephen*, ed. Merle Bevington, Hogarth Press, London, 1954

Walpole, Sir Spencer K.C.B., *The Life of the Rt. Hon. Spencer Perceval*, 2 vols., London: Hurst and Blackett, 1874

Ward, Robert Plumer, *Tremaine: or The Man of Refinement*, London: Henry Colburn, 1825

Wedderburn, Robert, *The Horrors of Slavery; exemplified in the Life and History of the Rev. Robert Wedderburn* [First published 1824], ed. Iain McCalman, New York and Princeton: Wiener Publishing, 1991

Wilberforce R. and I., *The Life of William Wilberforce*, London: John Murray, 1838

Wilson, Daniel, *Sermons and Tracts*, vol. 2, London: George Wilson, 1825

Wilson, Daniel, *The Substance of a Conversation with John Bellingham, the assassin of the late Right Hon. Spencer Perceval, on Sunday, May 17, 1812, the day previous to his execution: together with some general remarks*, London: J. Hatchard, 1812

Professional Journals

Ahonen, Kalevi, 'From Sugar Triangle to Cotton Triangle: Trade and Shipping between America and Baltic Russia, 1783–1860', *Jyväskyla Studies in Humanities*, no. 38 (2005), University of Jyväskyla, Jyväskyla

Argent, Valerie, 'Counter-Revolutionary Panic and the Treatment of the Insane: 1800', Middlesex University (1978)

Barnhart, William C., 'Evangelicalism, Masculinity and the Making of Imperial Missionaries in Late Georgian Britain, 1795–1820', *The Historian*, vol. 67, issue 4 (2005)

Binfield, Kevin, ed., *Writings of the Luddites*, Baltimore, Maryland: The Johns Hopkins University Press, 2004

Chapman, Stanley D., 'British Marketing Enterprise: The Changing Roles of Merchants, Manufacturers, and Financiers, 1700–1860', *The Business History Review*, vol. 53, no. 2

Checkland, S. G., 'American Versus West Indian Traders in Liverpool, 1793–1815', *The Journal of Economic History*, vol. 18, no. 2 (June 1958), pp. 141–60

Checkland, S. G., 'Economic Attitudes in Liverpool, 1793–1807', *The Economic History Review*, New Series, vol. 5, no. 1 (1952), pp. 58–75

Dorfman, Joseph, 'A Note on the Interpenetration of Anglo-American Finance, 1837–1841', *The Journal of Economic History*, vol. II, no. 2 (Spring 1951), pp. 140–47

Drake, K., 'Continuity and Flexibility in Liverpool's Trade with Africa and the Caribbean', *Business History* (1976), pp. 85–97

Dreschler, Seymour, 'Whose Abolition? Popular Pressure and the Ending of the British Slave Trade', *Past & Present*, May 1994

Eltis, David, 'Slave Departures from Africa, 1811–1867: An Annual Time Series', *African Economic History*, no. 15 (1986), pp. 143–71

Helfman, Tara, 'The Court of Vice Admiralty at Sierra Leone and the Abolition of the West African Slave Trade', *Yale Law Journal*, vol. 115, no. 5 (2006), pp. 11–22

Holmberg, Tom, 'The Acts, Orders in Council, &c. of Great Britain [on Trade], 1793–1812', The Napoleon Series; http://www.napoleon-series. org/research/government

Hyde, F. E., *Liverpool and the Mersey: An Economic History of a Port, 1700–1970*, Newton Abbot: David & Charles, 1971

Hyde, Francis E., Parkinson, Bradbury B. and Marriner, Sheila, 'The Nature and Profitability of the Liverpool Slave Trade', *Economic History Review*, 2nd series, vol. V (1953)

Jackson, Gordon, *Hull in the Eighteenth Century: A Study in Economic and Social History*, London: Oxford University Press, 1972

Kenwood, A. G., 'Fixed Capital Formation on Merseyside, 1800–1913', *Economic History Review*, vol. 31 (1978), pp. 214–37

Moran, Richard, 'The Modern Foundation for the Insanity Defense: The Cases of James Hadfield (1800) and Daniel McNaughtan (1843)', *Annals of the American Academy of Political and Social Science*, vol. 477, The Insanity Defense (January 1985), pp. 31–42

Ryan, A. N., 'The Defence of British Trade with the Baltic, 1808–1813', *English Historical Review*, vol. 74, no. 292 (July 1959), pp. 443–66

Ryan, A. N., 'Trade with the Enemy in the Scandinavian and Baltic Ports during the Napoleonic War: For and against', *Transactions of the Royal Historical Society*, Fifth Series, vol. 12 (1962), pp. 123–40

Smandych, Russell, '"To Soften the Extreme Rigour of Their Bondage": James Stephen's Attempt to Reform the Criminal Slave Laws of the West Indies, 1813–1833', *Law and History Review*, 23.3 (2005), 28 September 2011; www.historycooperative.org/journals/lhr/23.3/smandych.html

Wood, Marcus, 'William Cobbett, John Thelwall, Radicalism, Racism and Slavery: A Study in Burkean Parodics', *Romanticism on the Net*, no. 15 (August 1999), University of Montreal

Worral, David, 'Kinship, Generation and Community: The Transmission of Political Ideology in Radical Plebeian Print Culture', *Studies in Romanticism*, vol. 43 (2004)

Publications

Anstey, Roger, *The Atlantic Slave Trade and British Abolition*, London: Macmillan, 1975

Barty-King, H., *The Baltic Exchange: The History of a Unique Market*, London: Hutchinson Benham, 1977

Blake, Mrs Warrenne, ed., *An Irish Beauty of the Regency. Compiled from 'Mes Souvenirs' – The Unpublished Journals of the Hon. Mrs Calvert 1789–1822*, London and New York: John Lane, 1911, p. 22

Burton, Elizabeth, *The Georgians at Home*, London: Longmans Green, 1967

Cole, G. D. H., *British Working Movements: Select Documents 1789–1875*, London: Macmillan, 1951

Cox, David J., *'A Certain Share of Low Cunning' – The Provincial Use and Activities of Bow Street 'Runners' 1792–1839*, Cullompton: Willan Publishing, 2010

Crosby, Alfred W. jr, *America, Russia, Hemp and Napoleon: American Trade with Russia and the Baltic, 1783–1812*, Columbus, Ohio: Ohio State University Press, 1965

Gillen, Mollie, *Assassination of the Prime Minister: The Shocking Death of Spencer Perceval*, London: Sidgwick & Jackson, 1972

Gray, D., *Spencer Perceval: The Evangelical Prime Minister, 1762–1812*, Manchester: Manchester University Press, 1963

Greene, Lorenzo Johnston, *The Negro in Colonial New England, 1620–1776*, New York: Columbia University Press, 1942

Harris, J. R., ed., *Liverpool and Merseyside: Essays in the Economic and Social History of the Port and its Hinterland*, London: Frank Cass, 1969

Hassell, C., *Edward Marsh, Patron of the Arts*, London: Longmans, 1959

Hill, Peter P., *Napoleon's Troublesome Americans: Franco-American Relations, 1804–1815*, Washington, DC: Potomac Books, 2005

Longford, Elizabeth, *Wellington: The Years of the Sword*, London: Weidenfeld & Nicolson, 1969

May, Allyson Nancy, *The Bar and the Old Bailey, 1750–1850: The Prisoners' Counsel Act Justifying Advocacy*, Chapel Hill, North Carolina: UNC Press, 2003

McCalman, Iain, *Radical Underworld: Prophets, Revolutionaries and Pornographers in London 1795–1840*, Cambridge: Cambridge University Press, 1988

Parry-Jones, William, *The Trade in Lunacy: A Study of Private Madhouses in England in the 18th and 19th Centuries*, London: Routledge & Kegan Paul, 1972

Pollard, Arthur, ed., *The Penguin History of Literature*, vol. 6, 'Faith and Doubt in the Victorian Age' by A. O. J. Cockshut

Porter, Roy, *A Social History of Madness*, London: Weidenfeld & Nicolson, 1987

Porter, Roy, *Mind-Forg'd Manacles: A History of Madness in England from the Restoration to the Regency*, London: Penguin, 1987

Porter, Roy, *Plots and Paranoia*, London: Unwin Hyman, 1989

Sherwood, Marika, *'Oh, What A Tangled Web We Weave': Britain, the Slave Trade and Slavery, 1808–43*; http://www.shunpiking.com/bhs2007/200-BHS-MS-britishStrade.htm

Thomas, Hugh, *The Slave Trade: The History of the Atlantic Slave Trade,
    1440–1870*, London: Picador, 1997, p. 589

Turley, David, *The Culture of English Antislavery, 1780–1860*, New York:
    Routledge, 1991

Ward, William, *The Royal Navy and the Slavers: The Suppression of the
    Atlantic Slave Trade*, London: Allen and Unwin, 1969

Williams, Eric, *Capitalisation and Slavery*, Richmond, Va; University of
    North Carolina Press, 1944

Acknowledgements

Like Blanche Dubois, historians are always beholden to the kindness of strangers. In my case, I am indebted first to the late Mollie Gillen who discovered John Bellingham's laundry book in the Public Records Office. Everything about it was neat: the linen backing, the writing, the lists, the accounts. Nothing could have conveyed more immediately Bellingham's fastidious, organised character. Set against the appalling destruction he was planning, it was impossible not to wonder how the contradiction could have been resolved. My next debt is therefore owed to the staff at the archives of Liverpool City's Central Library and at the International Museum of Slavery who guided, suggested and helped me to sources for the angry decade in the city when it was tipped over like a beehive, its trade in slaves stamped out, more or less, and its American business scattered. The murder was Liverpool's revenge.

For me, the key to the bigoted, but evidently attractive character of the victim, Spencer Perceval, was provided by the extraordinary memoir of madness written by his son, John, and his baffled desire to find a meaning in life. I am grateful to the archivists at the Fitzwilliam Museum, Cambridge, who suggested this source, and at the Wellcome Institute for their expertise on the period's shifting approach to insanity. More generally I owe much to the knowledge of librarians at the London Library, the British Library, and the New York Public Library.

I would also like to record my thanks to my agent, Peter Robinson, to Anna Simpson, senior editor, and to Michael Fishwick, publishing director, at Bloomsbury, for making such a beautiful book out of this idea.

Closer to home, I must express how much it means in the solitude of writing to have the love and support of friends and family, especially of Paul Houlton and Charlotte Desorgher to whom this book is dedicated, of Clico and Gerald Kingsbury, of Lyn Cole, and of my darling wife, Marielou.

Finally, I want to acknowledge with boundless gratitude the unpayable debt I owe to George Gibson, publishing director of Bloomsbury USA, who is the best of editors and the staunchest of friends.

Index